JANE HAMMOND | PAPER WORK

Mount Holyoke College Art Museum
South Hadley, Massachusetts

in association with

The Pennsylvania State University Press
University Park, Pennsylvania

JANE HAMMOND | PAPER WORK

EDITED BY MARIANNE DOEZEMA

Library of Congress Cataloging-in-Publication Data

Designed by Diane Jaroch Design,
Rockford, Illinois
Printed in China by Everbest Printing Co.
through Four Colour Imports, Louisville, KY
Published by The Pennsylvania State University
Press, University Park, PA 16802-1003

The Pennsylvania State University Press is a member of the Association of American University Presses.

It is the policy of The Pennsylvania State University Press to use acid-free paper. Publications on uncoated stock satisfy the minimum requirements of American National Standard for Information Sciences—Permanence of Paper for Printed Library Material, ANSI Z39.48–1992.

All photographs are by Peter Muscato, except the following:
PAGE 6: (Marcel Duchamp), courtesy of Yale University Art Gallery; (Jasper Johns), Paula Goldman
PAGE 19: Photography © 2004 The Metropolitan Museum of Art. © 2006 Man Ray Trust/Artists Rights Society (ARS), New York/ADAGP, Paris
PAGE 92: R. H. Hensleigh

MOUNT HOLYOKE COLLEGE ART MUSEUM
5 September–17 December 2006

TUCSON MUSEUM OF ART
16 February–29 April 2007

CHAZEN MUSEUM OF ART
University of Wisconsin
24 June–12 August, 2007

ARKANSAS ART CENTER, LITTLE ROCK
7 September–11 November 2007

HERBERT F. JOHNSON MUSEUM OF ART
Cornell University
19 January–30 March 2008

FINE ARTS MUSEUMS OF SAN FRANCISCO, DE YOUNG
3 May–31 August 2008

DETROIT INSTITUTE OF ARTS
1 October 2008–10 January 2009

CONTENTS

FOREWORD

Jane Hammond established a formidable reputation as a painter during the 1990s, a decade that was dominated by film, video, photography, performance art, and installation. When linked with other artists, however, she is seldom compared primarily with painters. Often it is her interest in the relation between pictures and language that fascinates. In 1999, Hammond's work appeared alongside that of Sue Coe, Glenn Ligon, Kiki Smith, and Felix Gonzales-Torres in an exhibition of visual works concerned with narrative. Writing on the show, *New York Times* critic William Zimmer described Hammond's *The Wonderfulness of Downtown*, a color lithograph, screenprint, and collage, as "the most visually arresting."

By focusing specifically on her stunning works on paper, this exhibition adds an important dimension to our understanding of the artist's oeuvre. The objects gathered together here demonstrate compellingly that Hammond is the quintessential paper artist. As Nancy Princenthal articulates in her essay, Hammond began her career with printed material, and the duplication of imagery continues to be fundamental to what she does. She has worked with virtually all print media and has pushed their limits. Her captivating drawings and prints collage together myriad techniques and materials, as well as ideas and feelings, creating a stream of mental associations and visual stimuli.

It has been a true pleasure to work with Jane on every aspect of this project. We established contact not long after I arrived at the Mount Holyoke College Art Museum. I already had a keen interest in her work and would like to have brought to the museum her one-person exhibition, *Jane Hammond: The John Ashbery Collaboration*. Initially unaware that she was an alumna, I cannot now recall when I became cognizant of that fact. In any case, I am gratified to have been the facilitator of this project at the institution where Jane feels her professional life was launched.

As Jane explained at the exhibition's opening in September 2006, she came to the college with an interest in science. Leonard DeLonga, a professor in the art department, had a transforming effect on her. Not only was he a charismatic personality and caring instructor, but he provided a role model as a working artist as well. Jane graduated in 1972 as a studio art major.

Starting the MFA program at the University of Wisconsin, Jane realized how much she had really learned from Professor DeLonga. Concerned at first by being unprepared for discussions of conceptual art, she wished her favorite professor had been more diligent in exposing his students to theory. But soon she realized that what DeLonga had engendered in her—a profound love of art making—was much more significant. That passion sustained her as she set out to establish a career as an artist. In 1989, only eight years after moving to New York City, she received her first one-person show at Exit Art. Since then, she has exhibited her work in galleries and museums nationally and internationally.

This exhibition, its accompanying publications, and the national tour not only afford the first opportunity to explore the centrality of the artist's paper-based media, but also—and more important—they enhance our appreciation of her artistic accomplishment, her technical virtuosity, and her intellectual ambition.

From the start, Jane wanted Nancy Princenthal and Faye Hirsch, both prominent contemporary art scholars, to write for this book. Nancy's essay considers the artist's creative process and its relationship to narrative. Faye focuses on printmaking, examining several projects in succession. Doug Dreishpoon, senior curator at the Albright-Knox Art Gallery, has been a welcome addition to the project team. He crafted a substantial interview on the basis of two intensive conversations with Jane in the spring and summer of 2005. The text contains revealing insights about Jane's artistic and personal interests and concerns. Judith Brodie, curator of modern prints and drawings at the National Gallery of Art, served as outside reader of the essays, which have benefited from her astute observations and suggestions. The book side of this project was also served well by the keen eye and critical oversight provided by Cherene Holland and Jennifer Norton at Penn State Press. Diane Jaroch designed the publication with great skill.

Charles Lovell, director of the Harwood Museum of Art at the University of New Mexico, conceived the idea of an exhibition of Jane's work on paper. He was a supportive partner during early stages of the project but ultimately handed the reins over to me. I am grateful for his congeniality and his collegiality. Mary Sabbatino, director of the Gallery Lelong, also supported the project from its inception. Thanks also to Craig McNeer, Jane's partner, who made this project a priority at a number of key moments.

Jane and I both want to thank another Mount Holyoke alumna, Elizabeth Dee, who joined the staff at the Luhring Augustine Gallery in New York when Jane was showing her work there. In conversation over one of their first business lunches, they discovered their mutual affiliation with the college. It was Elizabeth who encouraged me to be in touch directly with Jane, and then made sure the connection was made. Since then, Jane has moved on to the Galerie Lelong and Elizabeth moved on to establish her own gallery, but the two have remained friends and colleagues.

My capable colleagues here at the Mount Holyoke College Art Museum skillfully executed countless tasks associated with bringing the exhibition to fruition. At several critical junctures they assured me that our small "dream team" did indeed have everything under control. I am especially grateful to Linda Best, collections manager, who orchestrated the process of bringing large and fragile objects from all over the country while also planning the complexities of sending them on a national tour. Kate Dalton, the museum's Art Advisory Board Fellow, provided invaluable administrative support, as well as a much-appreciated sense of humor.

Our profound thanks go to all of the lenders, without whose generosity this exhibition would not have been possible. On behalf of the artist and the museum staff, I would like to extend heartfelt thanks to Betsy and Frank Babb, Guy and Nora Barron, Viretta Brady, Byron and Eileen Cohen, Beth Rudin DeWoody, Kimberly and Robert Fischer, Susan and Arthur Fleischer Jr., Sunny and Brad Goldberg, Jim and Beth Kempner, Sally and Wynn Kramarsky, Ruth Lingen, Brooke and Daniel Neidich, Bud and Barbara Shark, Mr. and Mrs. Judson P. Reis, Paul and Mary Delle Stelzer, Jo Ann and Peter Wood, and those who wish to remain anonymous, as well as Dieu Donné Papermill, The Metropolitan Museum of Art, Pace Prints, and Universal Limited Art Editions. We extend our thanks also to our colleagues at the institutions participating in the exhibition's national tour, especially Julie Sasse, chief curator and curator of modern and contemporary art at the Tucson Museum of Art and Historic Block; Mary Ann Fitzgerald, exhibitions coordinator at the Chazen Museum of Art, University of Wisconsin–Madison; Ellen A. Plummer, executive director of the Arkansas Arts Center; Andrea Inselmann, curator of modern and contemporary art at the Herbert F. Johnson Museum of Art, Cornell University; Karin Breuer, curator of contemporary graphic art at the Fine Arts Museums of San Francisco, de Young; and Nancy Soijka, curator of prints at The Detroit Institute of Arts.

The exhibition was made possible in part by the Lucy P. Eisenhart Fund, the Susan B. Weatherbie (class of 1972) Exhibition Development Fund, the Mount Holyoke College Art Museum Friends of Art, and a generous grant from the Andy Warhol Foundation.

Marianne Doezema
Florence Finch Abbott Director
Mount Holyoke College Art Museum

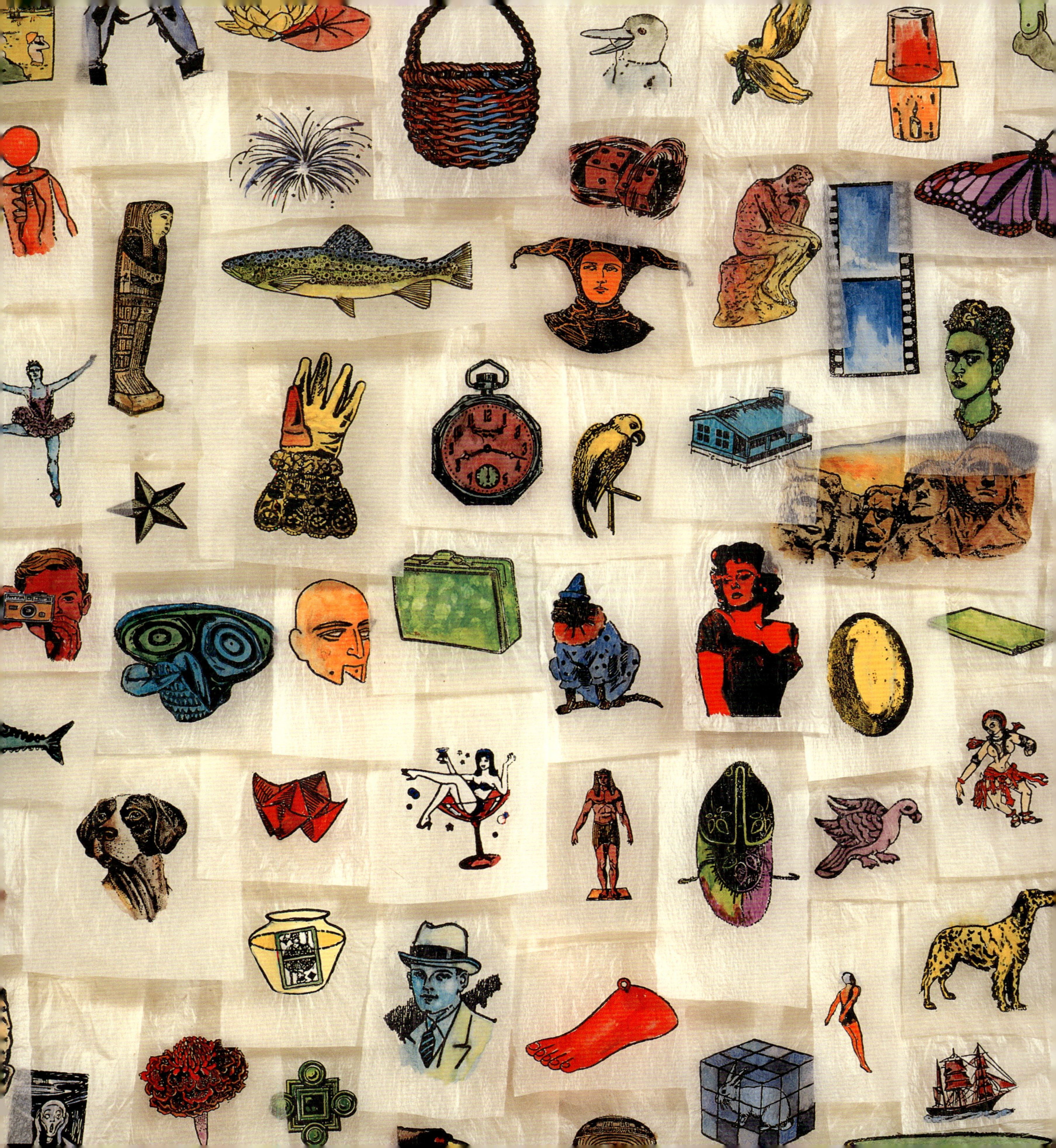

Reading Between the Lines: Works on Paper by Jane Hammond

Nancy Princenthal

Hammond's Uncertainty Principle

To the uninitiated eye, Jane Hammond's drawings are unruly gardens of delight, bountifully fertile but altogether ungoverned by law or logic. For anyone familiar with her work, they are also the very model of tidy husbandry. Since 1988, Hammond has constructed her compositions around a family of images—276 of them—assembled from a tremendous variety of print sources. (Her lexicon was put together during nearly a decade spent mostly in Baltimore, where she taught from 1980 until 1990 at the Maryland Art Institute.) "At the beginning," Hammond said in an interview with David Lehman, "I was looking for a surrogate for style"—in other words, for a kind of procedure that would inhibit recourse to purely subjective visual choices. But she was also, from the beginning, looking for expressive license. As she puts it, "I was trying to figure out how to make a kind of work that was decentered and variable, wandering and unpredictable even to me."[1]

The evidence is that she succeeded. "To this day, I don't know why I chose some things and not others. As to the number, at a certain point it seemed like enough.... If I had twenty images it would have been too gamey and pat. If I had 5,000 you would never apprehend any structure. It would feel like chaos." Moreover, the built-in flexibility of her system has allowed for a kind of internal randomness-generator, and surprises have proliferated. "Over time," she says, "entropy seeps in and the rules break down and things get more complex."[2]

One aspect of the program that Hammond has relaxed is her identification system. At first, she titled her paintings with strings of numbers, corresponding to the numbering of the image bank, but by 1990 she had begun to name her work with words, embracing the kind of semantic cross talk that has proliferated since. Notable in this respect is her collaboration with poets. In 1993, John Ashbery provided, at Hammond's invitation, forty-four titles for new work, to which she applied herself for eight years. In 2002 she collaborated with Raphael Rubinstein on a book project. Both collaborations speak to the enduring importance to Hammond of poetry and also of written language more broadly—as source material, as organizing structure, and as a kind of overarching metaphor. In fact, all of Hammond's work can be considered an exploration of words as things—not (or not only) in the sense that typography has visual interest, but because semantic units have many sides, and can be turned around and looked at from the back and from underneath. Visual correspondences can be found that plug in like different atoms in the creation of a molecule, the variability of the attachments creating structures with wholly unrelated shapes and functions. The very logic of the system breeds unpredictability.

As its susceptibility to sub-molecular analogy suggests, Hammond's work can be understood to proceed from the most physically precise understanding of language and, simultaneously, from one that is completely disembodied. That second approach is the one Hammond herself generally takes. "For fifteen years I've been using this term 'recombinant structure,'" she told Douglas Dreishpoon in an interview for this catalogue. "For fifteen years, I've been using this term 'the bodilessness of information.'" At the beginning of those fifteen years, in the later 1980s, digital imagery was a novelty, and the Internet—as a source of information and, more important, as a model of connectivity—barely existed. By now, the fluid relationships it facilitates between distant bodies of thought, and also between their disparate representations, have become commonplace in both visual and textual culture. That technology-based fluidity was anticipated in Hammond's work, and now runs alongside it, illuminating (and from time to time contributing to) its progress. In an interview for the *New York Times*, she told Amei Wallach, "I think my work deals very directly with the time that we live in. There's a surfeit of information, increasingly bodiless because of the computer, and I bring to this an interest in how meaning is constructed."[3] Just as logic provides a fertile ground for chaos in Hammond's work, its materiality—that is, the mostly old-fashioned, hand-drawn, and mechanically reproduced illustrations that form the core of her vocabulary—becomes the basis for radical ethereality.

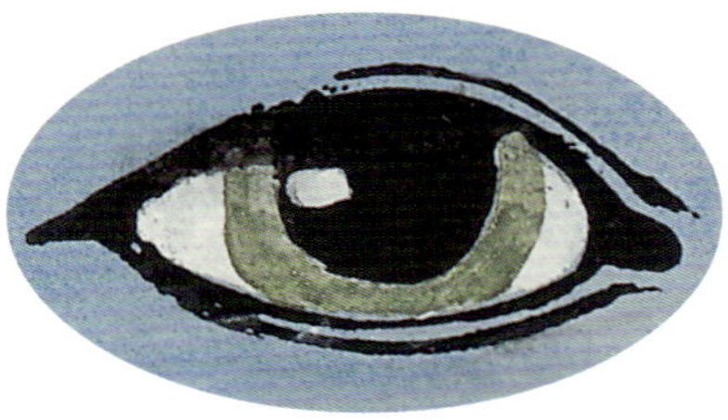

This paradoxical immaterial physicality in Hammond's work, like its ordered chaos, sets up a motivating dynamic. "Because painting is less body than sculpture, it seemed to me that it held more information," Hammond told Dreishpoon. "If you were to extend that analogy, you would say that words are even less body than painting, and they can hold even more information ... and there is something about paper as opposed to painting that feels to me now like it holds more information." Her pursuit of ever richer and less physically substantial forms of communication has, it seems, led Hammond inexorably toward working on paper, which is maximally thin and flexible. The pursuit, she acknowledges, is—fruitfully—endless. To writer Faye Hirsch, Hammond observed that "nothing physical is ever as nimble as the mind."[4]

And yet, Hammond makes objects that are in some respects surprisingly conventional—and even, in many examples, increasingly sculptural. Hammond's work is always handmade, usually laboriously, in a way that draws attention to details —of draftsmanship, of texture and weight, of visual expression and its nuanced dialects, and of composition. Although by generation and inclination she is a kind of Conceptualist, Hammond violates that movement's prohibitions against visual delight in everything she makes. Of all the paradoxes her work embraces, this may be the most engaging, not for its confounding duality of order and its opposite, or matter and spirit, but for its tenaciously held pleasure principle, which insists on finding sensual satisfaction even where the intellect is determined to hold dominion.

CHICKENS AND EGGS, HARLEQUINS AND HUSSIES

Her paintings, Hammond says, arrive in her mind ready-made and never require preparatory drawings. With drawings, however, she proceeds from a *tabula rasa*. As she told Hirsch, "I begin a painting with an almost complete idea in my mind of what it is going to look like. With rare exceptions, I start the drawing with nothing."[5] Fittingly, the earliest drawing in this exhibition is *Premonition* (1990). Its subjects include a blood-red chicken, its body dripping paint, and, suspended above, two pale, perfectly shaped eggs. Contemplating the grisly question of which came first is another fowl, this one of cartoon lineage, its plumage laughably sparse, body polka-dotted, and eyes agog. One bird is drawn; the other is a rubbing from a carved linoleum block, both executed, as is Hammond's habit, with skill and grace, but no flourish of subjectivity. Their origin in print media is clear. But the problem of priority they raise is far from resolved, and easily transferred from chicken and egg to artist and image. It finds Hammond occupying a position both fraught and comic. To use the drawing's own idiom, she has put herself in a place that is a little like Wile E. Coyote charging off the cliff, only to be suspended for an instant in midair. In fact, it is altogether characteristic of Hammond's work then and now that she approaches the big questions of late Modernism, including especially those that concern originality and authenticity, with as much goofy humor as erudite intelligence.

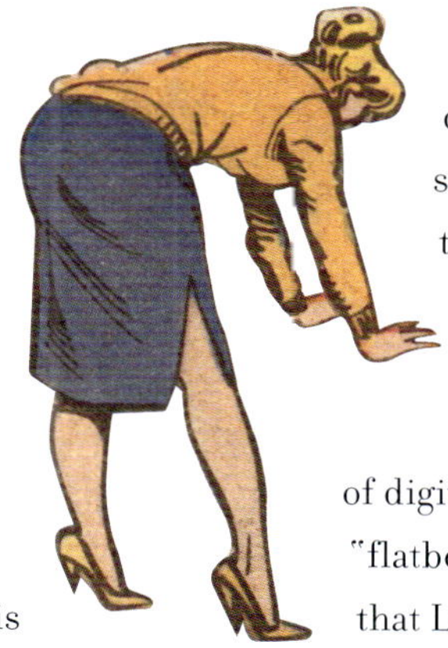

Both intelligence and humor are apparent in the relationship of figure to ground in this drawing, which—again like Road Runner—finds the two birds perilously suspended in space. Without the benefit of a horizon line or evident gravity (notice especially those fragile hanging eggs), the figures can only cleave tentatively to the transparent surface of the Japanese paper that is their support. The spatial condition that prevails in *Premonition*, as throughout Hammond's drawings, can be compared to the infinitely mutable space of digital imaging. It also conforms to the "flatbed" space of mechanical reproduction that Leo Steinberg identified as Robert Rauschenberg's most radical invention and associated (in 1972) with the dawning information age in Conceptual art and beyond. This Rauschenbergian (or Steinbergian) flatbed, on which orientation matters not at all because the imagery it holds—all borrowed from elsewhere—comes to rest only provisionally, accords well with Hammond's work.

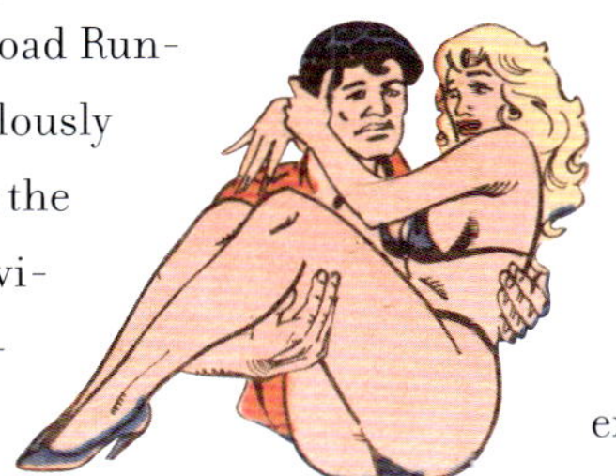

All of this may seem like a lot to deduce from one relatively simple and small drawing, even if it is considered representative, in embryo as it were, of themes that recur in Hammond's work. But then all of Hammond's drawings teasingly, and irresistibly, invite continuous interpretation. In so doing, they follow the trajectory of early Conceptualism less closely than that of Surrealism, with which Hammond is as often associated, a connection evident, for instance, in the postcard series of 1993. Using vintage postcards, Hammond combines stock characters of exoticism—Mexican fishermen hauling in their nets, a spear-bearing American Indian—with damsels in distress, or simply on display, breasts and buttocks much in evidence. In one case, a brawny hero comes to the rescue, though his baleful expression suggests he has more on his hands than he bargained for. These are modest works, close in spirit to the ephemera on which they are based, but again it is characteristic of Hammond to squeeze outsized expressive issues into arrogance-puncturing objects.

Nothing is more effective at deflating vanity than a good clown—or at expressing the sorrows that lurk in every pleasure garden. For both reasons, clowns and their kin have been favored by artists (and writers) for centuries, from the elegant jesters in Watteau's baroque comédiens and fêtes to Picasso's mournful harlequins to Paul McCarthy's notoriously malevolent, blood-and-viscera-spewing clown. Hammond's own many representations of professional charmers owe something to each (though considerably more are indebted to the tradition of gentle amusement than to violent disruption). Her three-dimensional paper *Clown Suits* (1994–95) are brightly colored and boldly patterned, with simple diamonds or dots on one half and on the other a rich selection of her image-bank icons—a seesaw, a steak, and a trained monkey are among those on one suit; a walnut, a pair of scissors, and a single staring eye on another—which here mischievously hint at designer logos run amok. Gathered at ankles and wrists but otherwise shapeless, with double-ruffed collars and conical hats topped with pompons, these clown costumes have a kinship with baby outfits: they are shaped not only for comfort but also for their patron's amusement. Their silliness, as with most clowning, is a little humiliating and a little melancholy.

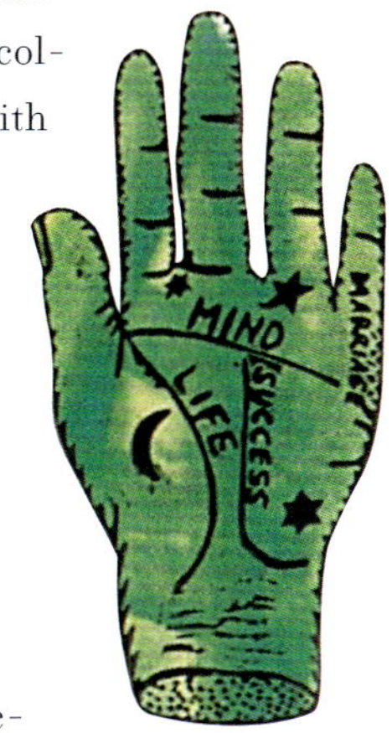

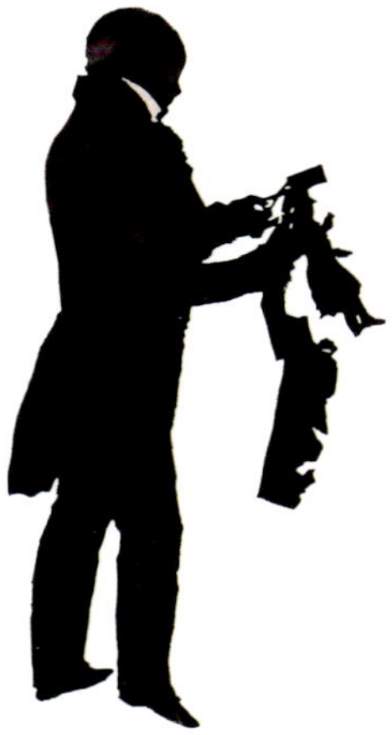

Among the same family of entertainers are magicians and other artists of deception, who also figure prominently in Hammond's work. In *Electric Kachina* (1997), a group of roughly three-foot-high mixed-media drawings on Japanese paper, Harry Houdini struggles out of leg-irons and manacles, and also out of confinement in a corner of the bustling composition. Above him, a palmist's chart looms, its lines measuring life, success, marriage, and, as an inscription more mysteriously indicates, "mind." The release this chart promises from the perils of uncertainty is, of course, just as deceptive as Houdini's. *The Crush of Circumstance* (1999) features what appears to be a snake charmer holding court at center stage, a slender reptile dangling from one of his outstretched hands. Just below, a man cutting his own likeness from black paper appears in the form of a black-paper silhouette: self-invention as the mirror image of deception, positioned to reflect each other in endless regress. Elsewhere, a Hollywood beauty springs from a wishing well, and a white rabbit appears from nowhere at all, with not even a top hat in sight. By causing the unlikeliest beings to appear out of thin air, Hammond rather explicitly casts herself as a magician (and what artist does not, to some degree?). But her drawings are, distinctively, conjuring acts in form as well as content, their densely layered and concatenated images floating and colliding with more grace than spatial credibility. Drifting up from variably transparent depths, as in dreams, or reflections on moving water, the drawn, printed, stamped, collaged, transferred, and rubbed fragments together suggest the intimacy—acknowledged, and deplored, by so many religions—between benign representation and the apostate's black arts.

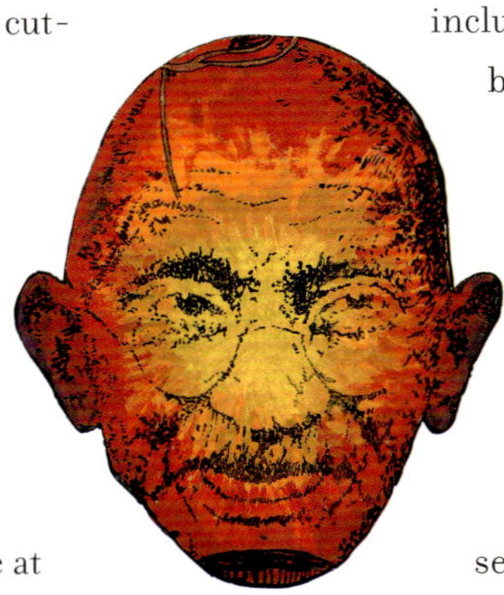

Drawing's founding deceptions are nowhere more apparent than in Hammond's many images of rope and string. Knotted, coiled, spooled, and spinning—and sometimes self-transforming as we watch—her rope tricks play on the analogy (irresistible to an artist so clearly fond of puns) between the linear armatures of narrative (the story line) and pictorial description. The drawing *Past Time* (1998) contains lines of nearly every variety, from electrical cord to the knottiest tangle of nautical twine. It also includes a Möbius strip-like ribbon, a bent playing card, an origami frog, and two delicate photos of an egg-filled bird nest. At the center of the drawing is a portrait of Mahatma Gandhi, his disembodied head aflame in yellow, orange, and red, burning like a sun in the drawing's otherwise serenely blue visual field. Again, it is possible to construct a narrative linking its disparate elements. Gandhi's spiritual and intellectual strength might be interpreted as the energy source for the (metaphorical) battery (electrical wires connect to his head) that powers the nascent life all around him, offering a solution to life's knottiest problems, a safeguard against eggshell-thin fragility, and moral courage as a substitute for luck (viz. the playing card). It must be conceded that this reading relies on grasping at threads as treacherous as they are sumptuous. But it is in the nature of Hammond's method that the risk is part of the pleasure and altogether to the point.

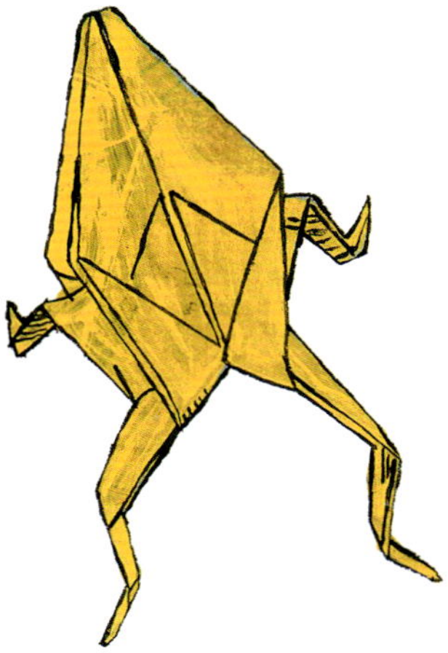

Among the many associations to linear form, none is more potent perhaps than a lifeline, referred to not only in the many representations of sturdy ropes but also, more explicitly, in the palmist's chart. In the first case, it alludes to a line that saves and protects lives, and in the second to a line that measures the limits of our mortal term, forming the kind of symmetrically opposed dyad that appears repeatedly in Hammond's work. Indeed, a great many of the pictorial elements in her glossary flip back and forth not between two meanings, but between two spatial readings. Examples in *Past Time* include several geometric figures whose leading faces can seem to advance and recede, and also the spatially ambiguous playing card. Optical puzzles like these are a hinge between magic and science, illustrating weak spots in the human visual system that invite the imagination to intercede. Such puzzles were crucial to nineteenth-century physiologists in developing an understanding of vision as a phenomenon that is as much constructed within the body (or mind) as it is constrained by external phenomena. This understanding, in turn, played an important part in the emergence of Modernist subjectivity in a process that was deeply reciprocal. For all these reasons, optical puzzles are a hinge in Hammond's world, too.

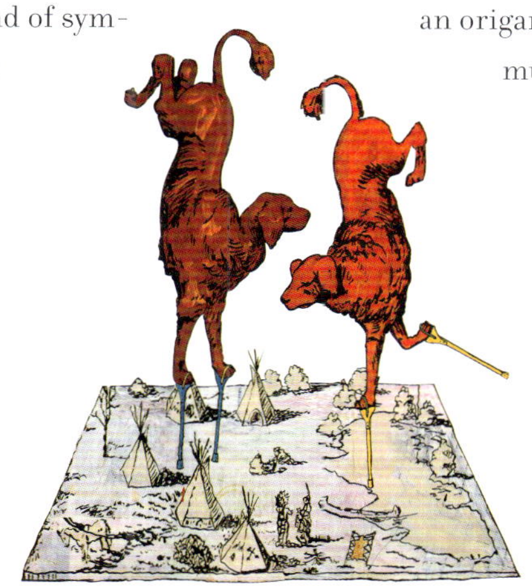

This pivot parallels another that appears throughout Hammond's pictorial lexicon. Hammond chooses many of her images because of the links they establish between objects that are animate and those that are inert, sentient and the obtuse. Thus the prevalence of trained animals, dolls, fetishes, and ritual objects of all kinds, including the silent, faithful friends that psychoanalysts call "transition" objects. In the enchanted world of childhood—or in the universe as rippled by magical thinking at any age—an origami frog can jump with at least as much vigor as the specimen in a glass of water beside it, to return to the imagery of *Past Time*. Spiritual practice is often a guarantor for such vivified objects, as in *Electric Kachina*, which features the eponymous "doll" in the form of a grinning red head with cowrie-shell eyes and feathers for ears. The cutaway rendition of a cozy single-family house that tumbles through the center of *Electric Doll House* (1998) shows a different foreign object menacing every room, including a goggle-eyed wolf (surely Little Red Riding Hood cannot be far) leering from an upstairs bedroom. More benign is the cymbal-clapping marine mammal that performs his role in *Still Life with Seal* (1999); friendly, too, is the tiny dancing monkey in *Crush of Circumstance*, who is joined by a costumed pig as well as the charmed snake and leaping white rabbit that have already been noted. The canine stars of *Dog Dance* (1993) balance on stilts as they stride across a gameboard-like rendition of a Native American encampment complete with half a dozen little tepees, two conversing figures in feathered headdresses, and a single drying hide.

In fact, games are another recurring motif in Hammond's work, which can be compared in its entirety to a board game or, perhaps, a faux-Victorian *Sim City*: Hammond creates the characters, establishes a minimal set of constraints, and sets them in motion in an endless match in which both she and her viewers participate. It is significant in this regard that Hammond herself often appears among the other characters. In *Martin House Me* (1999), two identically drawn representations of her head are shown separately mounted on wooden stands placed on a gridded board—Jane as her own chess piece, jumping with naughty glee from art to life and back again. Also in this drawing is a toy box and a clown-headed rattle (along with much else, including a cup holding a bird, a hexagonal, bright red Baroque building, and a clutch of men in funny hats). The high incidence of children's playthings and anthropomorphized animals contributes to a geography that seems to lie somewhere on the other side of the looking glass. Indeed Lewis Carroll's learned and playful literary intelligence, his fascination with puzzles of logic and mathematics, and, not least, the John Tenniel drawings that accompanied his best-known books, all seem close in spirit to Hammond's work.

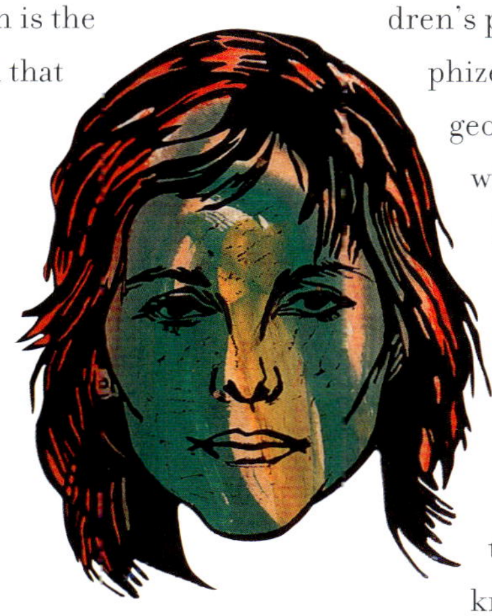

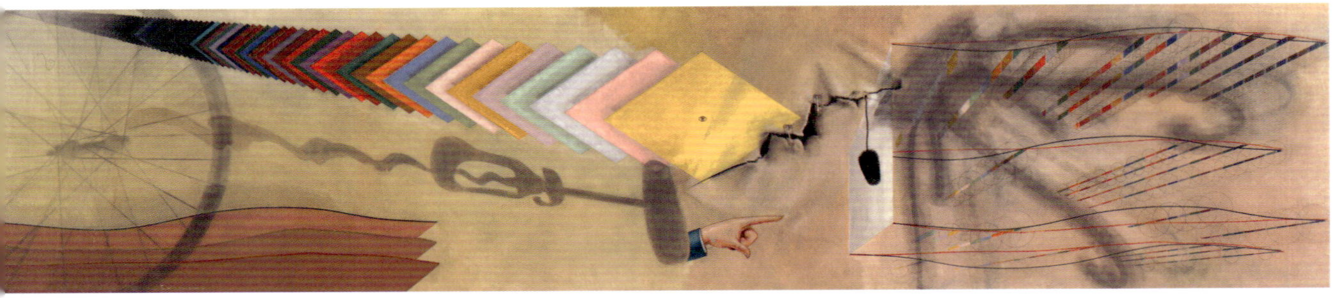

Marcel Duchamp (French, 1887–1968)
Tu m', 1918
Oil on canvas, with bottle brush, three safety pins, and one bolt
$27^{1}/2$ x $119^{5}/16$ inches
Yale University Art Gallery
Gift from the Estate of Katherine S. Dreier

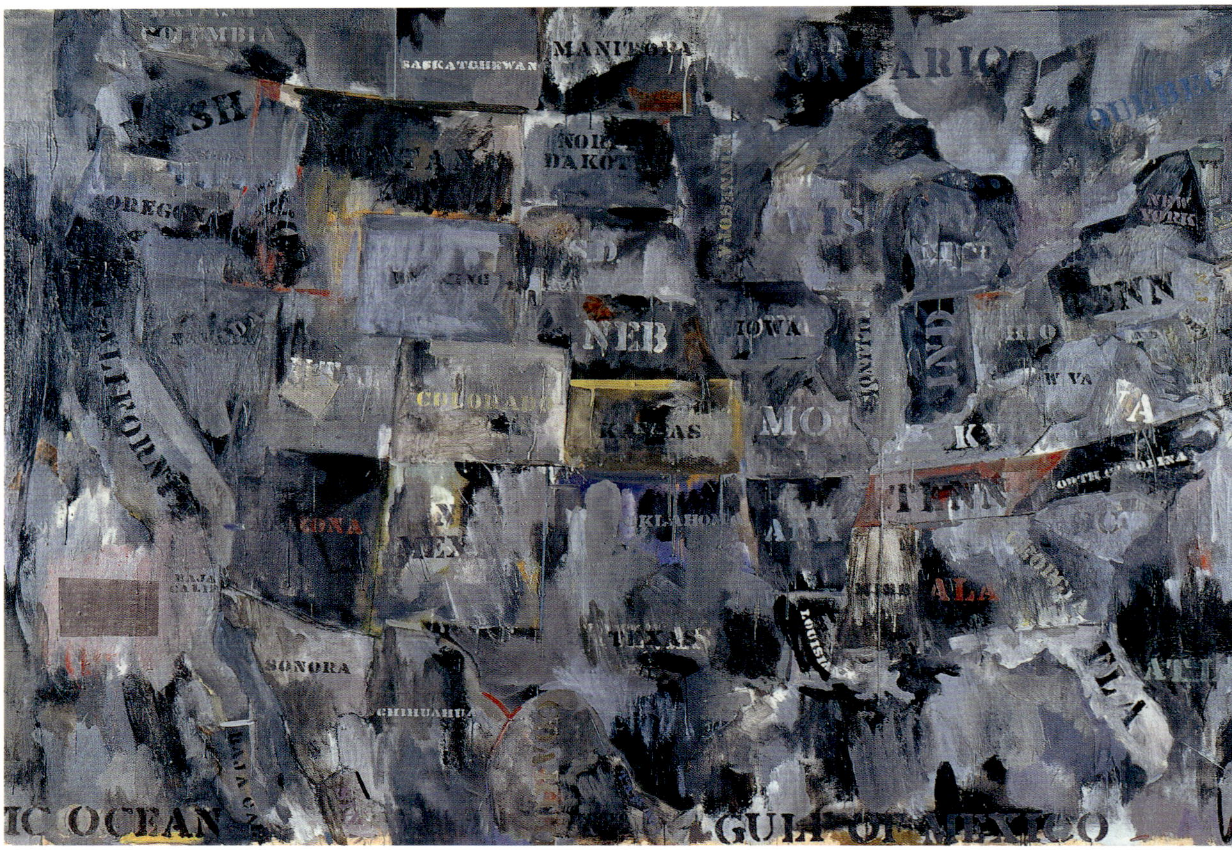

Jasper Johns (American, b. 1930)
Map, 1962
Encaustic and collage on canvas
60 x 93 inches
Museum of Contemporary Art, Los Angeles
Gift of Marcia Simon Weisman

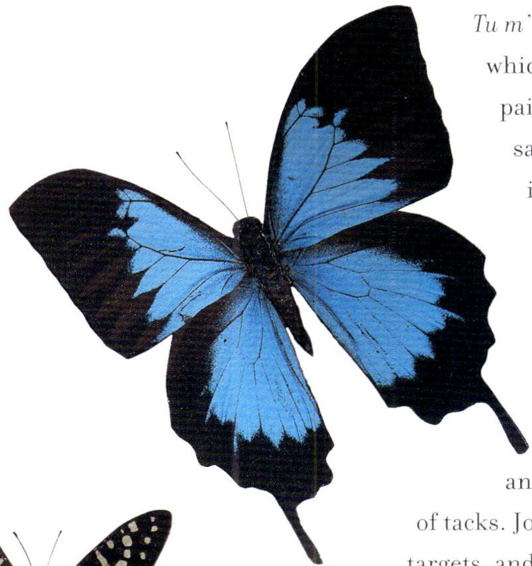

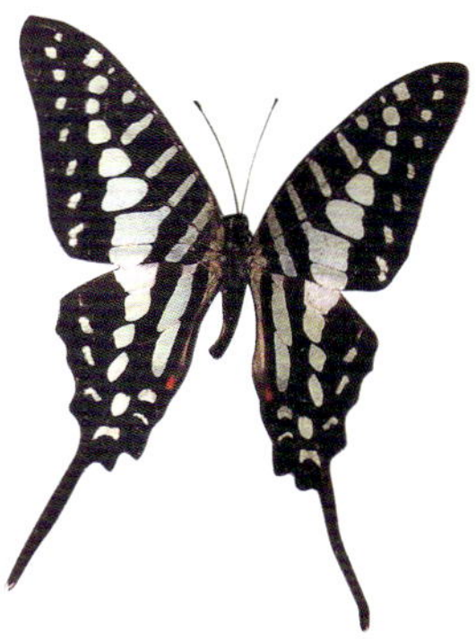

In making the leap from art to life and back again, Hammond acknowledges the figures that loom largest on the same course, including Marcel Duchamp and Jasper Johns. Duchamp's *Tu m'* (1918), the glossary-like painting in which Duchamp brings together a sign-painter's handiwork, house-painters' samples, traced shadows, *trompe l'oeil* illusionism, and real objects, including actual safety pins spanning a painted tear in the canvas, seems to be one reference point for Hammond's *Still Life with Seal*, with its assortment of manually and mechanically reproduced images and, particularly, its scattered handful of tacks. Johns's landmark paintings of flags, targets, and, especially, maps, with their double-exposed presentation of an object and its likeness, lurk behind Hammond's images, too. Such deliberate confusion is particularly prevalent in Hammond's most recent work, which often tips into three dimensions, as did some earlier work as well (the *Clown Suits*, for instance). A series of collages made in 2004 and 2005 combine hand-drawn maps with assorted paper butterflies, digitally scanned from actual specimens and then painstakingly cut and collaged to handmade bodies and antennae, which gives them three-dimensionality. The materials Hammond used for these works include handmade papers, gouache, acrylic paint, graphite, colored pencil, archival digital prints, and horsehair. Each collage bears the title *All Souls* and is subtitled with a place name (Hefei, Cordoba, Babel).

The maps are wondrous in the way of lavish Victorian book illustrations—the lettering elegant but often obscured by successive layers of information, the mapped lands alluring and distinct. *Cordoba*, for instance, has the blue-black gleam of the lining of a mussel shell, while *Hefei* and *Babel* are sunstruck and pale, their cartographic markings as fine as capillaries. The individual butterflies are realized with similar attention to detail in their lapidary markings and gemstone colors.

In these maps Hammond emphasizes natural features (bodies of water, broad details of topography) and ancient cities rather than national boundaries, favoring those landmarks that are most enduring. The fragility of the butterflies, their epic migratory patterns, and the brevity of their lives are, by contrast, all the more pronounced. At the same time, they can also be identified with an especially powerful figure for the mechanism of chaos, the so-called "butterfly effect," by which the flutter of a gossamer wing on one side of the world can cause a typhoon on the other. As it happens, their presence in Hammond's work is tied to both the habits of heroic travel and to a single, cataclysmic event. On the afternoon of September 11, 2001, a great number of Monarch butterflies alit on the flowers in her window box in lower Manhattan, not far from the World Trade Center towers. Perhaps, she says, they were migrating to a place west of Mexico City for the end of October—for the Day of the Dead, or All Souls day (hence the titles of the works), and Halloween, associated with the colors orange and black, which

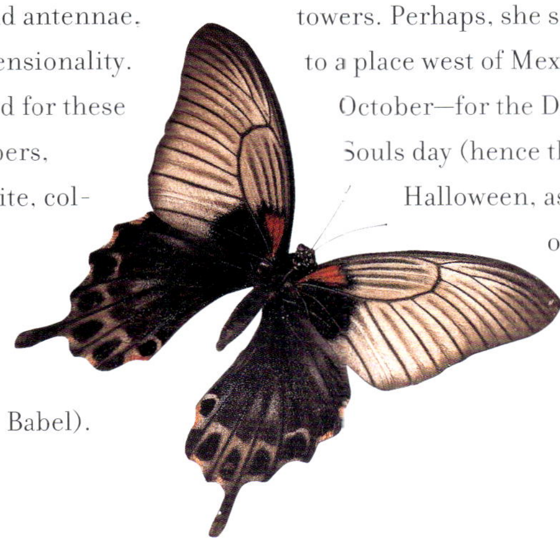

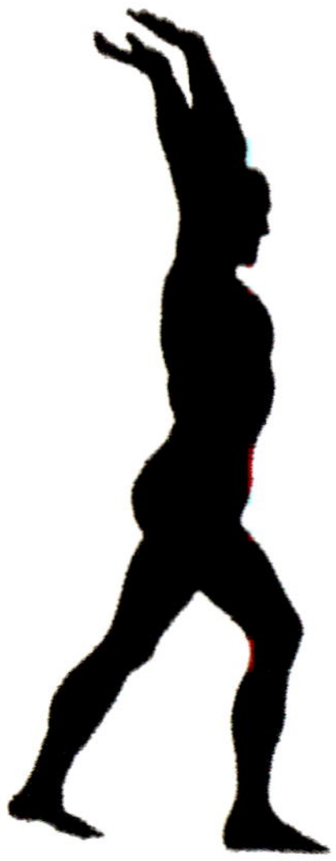

are also the colors of the Monarch butterfly. Although Hammond does not elaborate on that fateful day in interviews or, more to the point, in her work, the viewer can sense the pressure of the event behind the delicate workings of these intricate collages, complicating the far-flung geographies they trace, and agitating the insects that hover above them. At the same time, a host of purely personal associations animates the butterflies and their backgrounds, from Hammond's grandmother's brief but vividly recollected stay in Luxor (the first map, *Babel*, is of the Mideast) to her father's descriptions of winged insects by way of analogy to planes, based on his experience as a naval pilot.

Hammond's inclination to work in three dimensions, and in a guardedly personal domain, can also be seen as a motivation for her involvement with books in which her images are restored, much altered in the transit, to the format from which many of them derived. All artists' books ask readers to reorder their viewing practices, enjoining them to look when they are more accustomed to reading and sometimes, as is especially important with Hammond's work, to employ the habits of reading while looking. Moreover, their fundamental invitation to imaginary departure from the material world makes artists' books—all books objects of sorcery, one of the many reasons why they appeal to Hammond. Indeed the renowned magician and historian Ricky Jay calls the book in all its forms the "oldest manufactured conjuring prop." Jay and Hammond were brought together in 1995, along with Vija Celmins, Glenn Ligon, Philip Taaffe, and William Wegman, for a project called *The Magic Magic Book*, published in an edition of one hundred by the Whitney Museum of American Art as part of a series edited by May Castleberry. Following the venerable magic-show format, *The Magic Magic Book* is tabbed with thumb cuts (like some dictionaries and Bibles). These allow practiced readers or performers to make it seem as though they are progressing one page at a time, while actually they are skipping past whole groups of pages (and the illustrations they contain). On subsequent presentations, the concealed images can be made—as if magically—to appear. Each artist participating in *The Magic Magic Book* was allotted a tabbed section. Hammond, whose previous involvement with the imagery of magic made the book a welcome opportunity, contributed images silhouetted in black, including harlequins and rabbits, a trained bear, and a ballerina, some of which came from historical blow books.

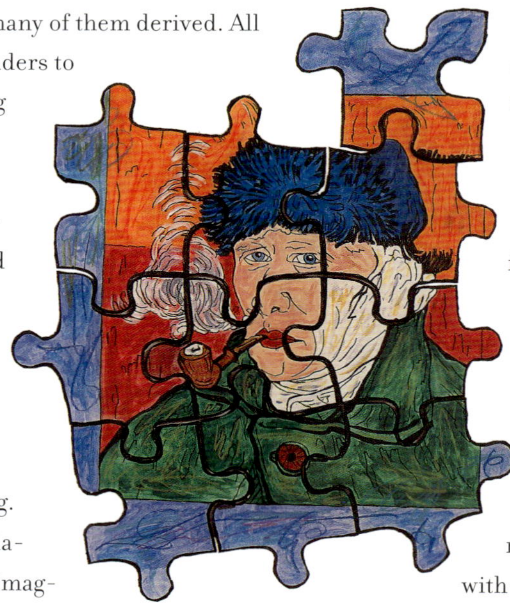

Hammond's sensibility makes her an equally good match for Raphael Rubinstein, with whom she collaborated on the book *Be Zany, Poised Harpists / Be Blue, Little Sparrows* (2002). Published by Dieu Donné in an edition of thirty, this lavish publication combines images by Hammond with a quartet of poems by Rubinstein, whose predilection for rule-driven poetry, in which he follows the practices of the Oulipo poetry group, is in close harmony with Hammond's. Just as important to both artist and poet are the moments of absurd humor and pure delight that they can produce within such constraints. In *Be Zany*, Rubinstein used a formula in which his poems progressed from a rule of two (two-letter words, two to a line, two lines to each of a pair of stanzas) to lollapaloozas of eight-letter words written eight to a line, and so on. Hammond's illustrations include photo-based images of paired soap bubbles, a small album of vintage postcards, mischievously altered on the back, and an epic foldout collage.

While artists' books are themselves outliers among the fine-art media, Hammond has also explored the genre's own marginal territories, as in the scrapbooks she assembled in 2002 and 2003. Hammond takes the illustrations in these assemblages mostly from books and other print media and returns them to their original format, only now reborn as autographic images—that is, as handmade items tidily simulating opened handmade books. Composed with an unusual degree of economy and clarity, the scrapbooks present themselves as code-breakers, atlases for Hammond's universe, a puzzling place occupied by a burning cigarette in a tin ashtray, a few dominoes, tiny heads of Picasso and Elvis, and handmade novelty boxes (*Scrapbook [Ship in Bottle]*, 2002–2003), or a van Gogh self-portrait in the form of a jigsaw puzzle, a few dried pansies, and

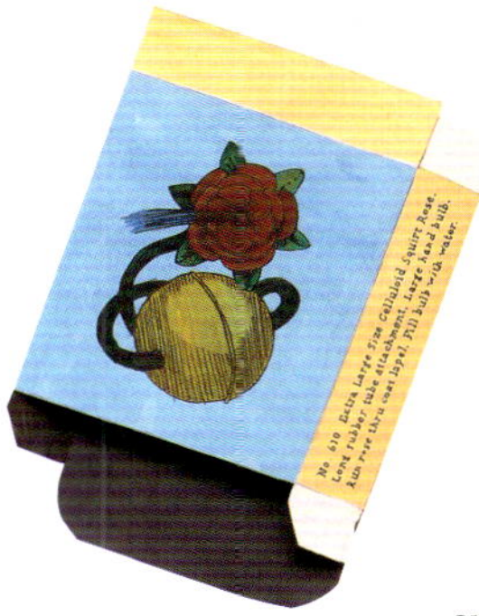

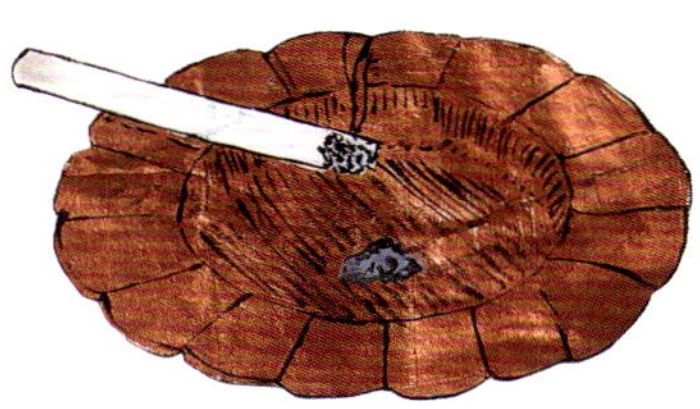

an assortment of celebrity-portrait commemorative stamps, including those of Frida Kahlo, Andy Warhol, and Lucille Ball (*Scrapbook [van Gogh]*, 2003).

Other bibliophilic and pedagogic excursions have taken Hammond to Asian exercise books and Western lecture halls. In *Twelve Wishes* (2000), she introduced elements from her image bank to sheets taken from the pages of an antique Chinese notebook already illustrated with reproductions of ink drawings, creating cryptic but graceful unions between disparate notation systems. *Chalk Talk* (2000) consists of sixteen simulated individual slate boards (the drawing surfaces are gessoed paper covered with blackboard paint), each used to diagram in chalk, as if for a scientific presentation, a molecular element from Hammond's own periodic table. On several of these faux slates, a pentimento of one image appears, as if drawn and erased on a real blackboard, beneath the finished drawing of another. The dialogue between these several generations of images creates a ghostly colloquy. There is a choral resonance too among the images assembled in several drawings that were executed on small sheets of gampi paper hung in irregular grids—like stamp collections, or laundry on the clothesline. Here the Hammond lexicon can again be reviewed in a presentation format that toys with the conventions of collecting and connoisseurship.

In the same family of works are the recent *Matchbooks* (2003) and *Stamp Book* (2005), both of which condense Hammond's imagery into discrete objects that are, not coincidentally, variants on books. The first bears single images on each cover; the second, published by the artist in 2005 in an edition of six, is a compilation of stamps based on every painting created in response to a John Ashbery title. Each one (there are sixty-four in all) has been scanned, reduced, and augmented with an elaborate border that includes the designation of an invented price, the monetary unit of which implies a country of origin. Extravagant in size and detail, these jewel-like, digitally output stamps are housed one to a page in a sumptuously produced book (the binding was done by Damara Kaminecki). The dialogues preserved in this book, between painter and poet, unique and multiple objects, and single and multiple cultures become positively orchestral, without losing their essential modesty. Apropos *Stamp Book*, Hammond says, "I like the idea of live cultures, as in yogurt," which, like sourdough starter or embers from a fire, can be passed along from one context to another in a continuous cycle of

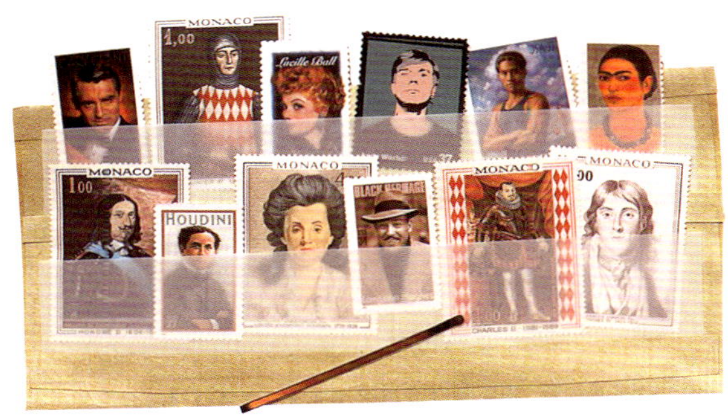

use and self-replenishment, its powers of sustenance growing exponentially.

Lately Hammond has been experimenting with objects, generally made of paper, that have other functional associations. Several works relate to the theater, for example, *Paper Model for Backstage: Secrets of Scene Painting* and the backdrop-like *Trail of Tears* (2003). Dramatic too is *Extravagant Reflex* (2003–4), in which the constituent squares of paired grids are filled in with tufts of brightly dyed feather boas. A chart between the two grids names each color, in a form of found poetry: "Stendhal, Checkers, Linoleum" for red mixed with black, or, more simply, "Snow" for white. Extravagant, as the title promises, in hue and texture, and divorced in content and imagery from Hammond's previous work, this collage nonetheless sustains with a deliciously light touch Hammond's ongoing involvement with weighty questions: How is meaning assigned and understood? How is information coded and regulated? What difference does repetition make to sensual experience?

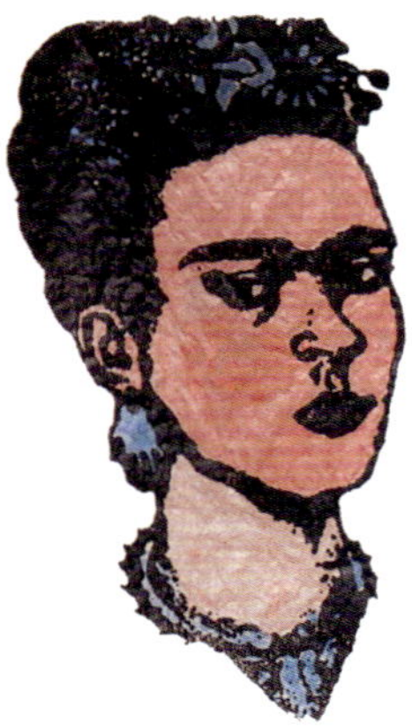

With the heartbreaking *Fallen* (2004–5), which is not included in this exhibition, Hammond departs quite radically from established practice. This three-dimensional work is an ankle-high pile of sumptuously colored and varied autumn leaves, digitally printed in stunning detail from real specimens. Each leaf is named in honor of a soldier killed in Iraq. These, then, are real objects, captured, identified, and again set adrift in the world, their meaning doubled. At the same time, Hammond has recently turned to photographs, digitally altering black-and-white prints in which she allows the real world to insinuate itself, while at the same time manipulating its ostensibly documentary representations with increasing freedom, and often decidedly audacious humor.

SPEAKING TRUTH TO CHAOS

Dedicated though she is to the physical world, Hammond's relation to objectivity is complicated. "My work is a fiction that's woven of facts," she has said.[6] Of course, the same is often said of all kinds of narratives, including those that claim historical accuracy. But Hammond's emphasis is distinctively on a kind of infinite present. As we watch, stories are created by the assembly of communicating images, rather than deriving from any fixed, anterior set of references. "Building meaning from the outside in as well as the inside out" is how she accounts for her methods.[7] The chanciness, and interpretive tolerance, of this process would make most artists deeply uncomfortable—and may well do the same for some viewers. That is not to say, however, that Hammond's work is easy in any sense. In fact, such leniency is most often associated with considerable difficulty—as is true of the famously recondite poetry of John Ashbery, which is particularly susceptible to conflicting interpretation. The difficulty of Ashbery's work is said by David Lehman to reflect the poet's belief that "misunderstanding is a creative process, another word for metaphor."[8] It is a belief just as readily associated with Hammond. That is, the reader's or viewer's effort at making sense re-creates the artist's own and reaches for the same insight, the same unnamed but pungent precipitate of known quantities mixed together in unfamiliar ways.

To be sure, there is by now a self-explanatory element to Hammond's growing body of work. A devoted viewer can achieve a kind of fluency, which can be supported by exploring the external connections it implies, including those to other artists. As she told Douglas Dreishpoon, "I'm a cross between Sol LeWitt and Frida Kahlo," Hammond herself has said, naming a particularly unlikely connection between a founding father of hands-off Conceptualism and the patron saint of homemade, self-exposing figurative painting (a self-portrait by Kahlo is in fact an element in Hammond's lexicon). The art historian David Carrier has compared Hammond's work to the memory-box assemblages of Joseph Cornell, the disjunctive landscapes of de Chirico, and (with Ashbery) to Raymond Roussel's proto-Surrealist poetry. Carrier also cites Duchamp and Johns.[9] Critic and curator Ingrid Schaffner also links Hammond's work to Cornell's boxes and to James Joyce's *Ulysses*,[10] along with Mayakovsky's found-sound poetry, Max Ernst's landmark collage-novel, *La Femme 100 Têtes* (1929), and, closer to the present, the echt-1960s Terry Gilliam animations for Monty Python. In this connection, Robert Smithson's early collages seem relevant as well. To connect all these dots (and others that have been noted) is to trace a labyrinth—or a thicket of images that looks a great deal like a composition by Jane Hammond.

If one thing unites Hammond's interests, it is a strong literary tilt. She has a preference for borrowing images and objects from beyond the boundaries of fine art. It can even be said that a common ingredient results from an unexpected distillate: call it an extract of realism. Here Hammond's core vocabulary, of late nineteenth- and early twentieth-century illustrations, links her not only to the Surrealists but also to such American realist painters as William Harnett and John Peto, among whose favored subjects were still lifes assembled on wooden doors, the backs of frames, and other flat vertical surfaces—like printers' flatbeds, or scrapbooks. Just as the Surrealists would do in the twentieth century, Harnett and Peto pressed the most ordinary scraps of everyday life for the surplus impression, the extra measure of perceptual and emotional stimulus that held meanings not quite reducible to names. Between them (or Tenniel) and Ernst—and between both and Hammond—is a circle connecting waking and dreaming, where logic travels freely between the regimes of physical and psychic law.

Within this wide orbit, other circuits can be traced. Certain forms of mysticism (the numerology of the Kabbalah, for instance) similarly squeeze ordinary signs for extra (and particularly for extraworldly) meaning. It is a tradition to which Conceptualism has always had a strong affinity, acknowledged from the outset, sometimes with irony but never without some truth, by several first-generation Conceptualists. Notably, Sol LeWitt in the first of the thirty-five "Sentences on Conceptual Art" wrote in 1969: "Conceptual artists are mystics rather than rationalists. They leap to conclusions that logic cannot reach."[11] A certain hardheaded mysticism is present in Frida Kahlo's most acutely personal paintings. And it is in Jane Hammond's work too, which constitutes a magisterial primer for reading between the lines.

NOTES

1. Interview with David Lehman, *Bomb*, fall 2002, 33.
2. Ibid., 34, 33.
3. In Amei Wallach, "To a Painter, Words Are Worth a Thousand Pictures," *New York Times*, October 13, 2002, Arts & Leisure, 35.
4. Faye Hirsch, "Paper Pulse: A Conversation with Jane Hammond," *Art on Paper*, March–April 2002, 67.
5. Ibid., 67.
6. Lehman interview, *Bomb*, 30.
7. Ibid.
8. Ibid., 31.
9. David Carrier, "Jane Hammond, Cleveland Center for Contemporary Art" (review), *Artforum*, March 2002, 144.
10. Ingrid Schaffner, "Dear Reader, On Jane Hammond's Collaboration with John Ashbery," in *Jane Hammond* (Cleveland: Cleveland Center for Contemporary Art, 2001), 14–15.
11. Sol LeWitt, "Sentences on Conceptual Art," first published in *0-9* (New York), 1969, and *Art-Language* (England), May 1969, reprinted in Alicia Legg et al., *Sol LeWitt* (New York: The Museum of Modern Art, 1978), 168.

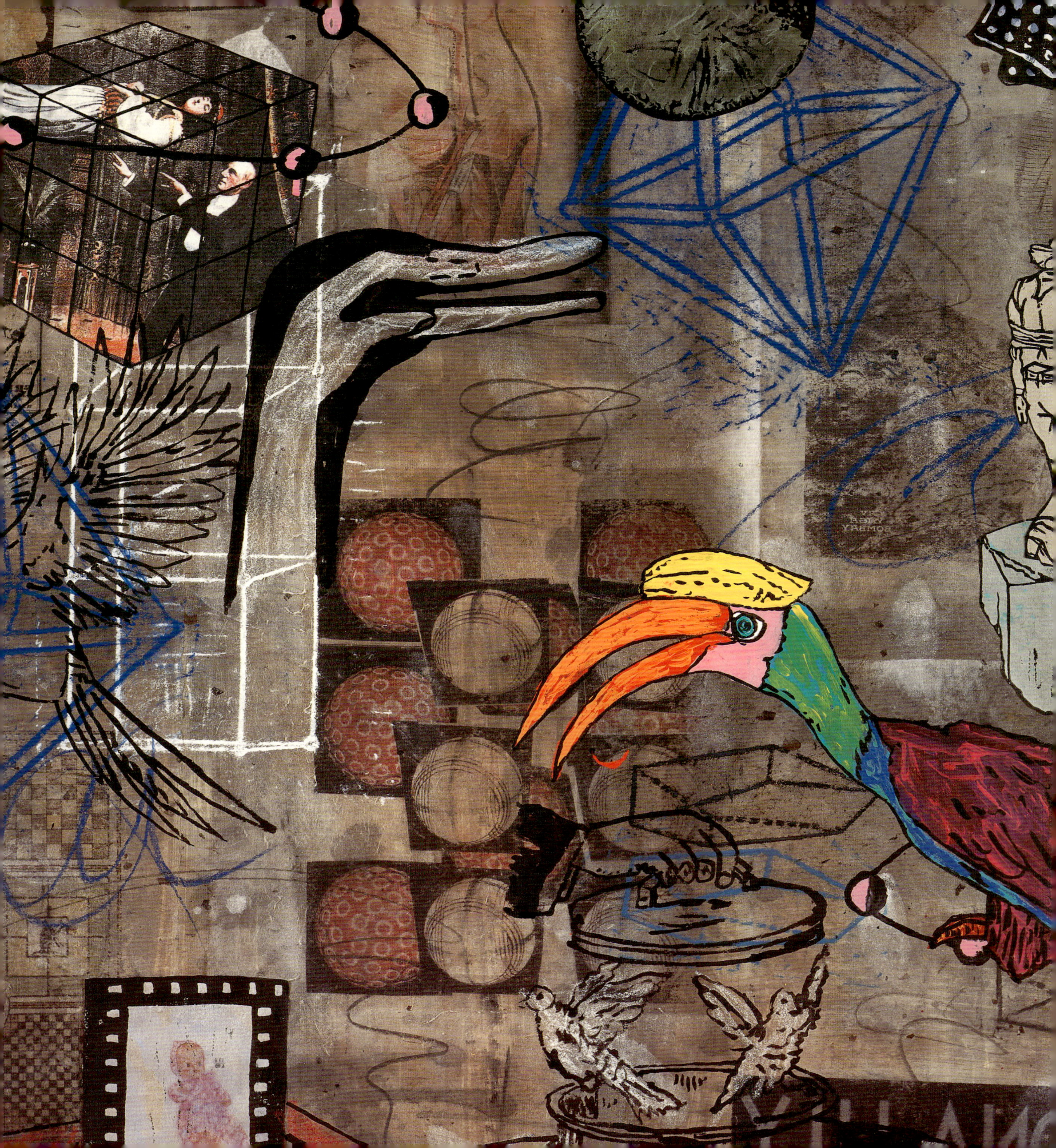

I

In 2001, Jane Hammond completed *Tabula Rosa*, a vertical inkjet print that presents her full-scale self-portrait, nude, seen from behind, covered in a welter of "tattoos." These represent a generous selection from her image bank, a repository for the hundreds of pictures, mainly illustrations from printed matter, that she has extracted over the years from a wide variety of sources and used and reused in her paintings, drawings, and prints. Because she is constantly recycling them in different combinations, many of the archaic-looking representations she chose for the tattoos are familiar to those who know her work: an acrobat, a wishbone, a clown, a ringed snake, a Buddha, various types of flowers—a peony, a chrysanthemum, a rose—in full bloom. Behind her knee is a Japanese courtier from the floating world; her ankle is bound in green ribbon. A pair of parakeets perches on her right shoulder blade, and a domino box explodes its contents on her left buttock in an off-color pun. A feather tickles her wrist and two bathers swim across her thigh in opposite directions.

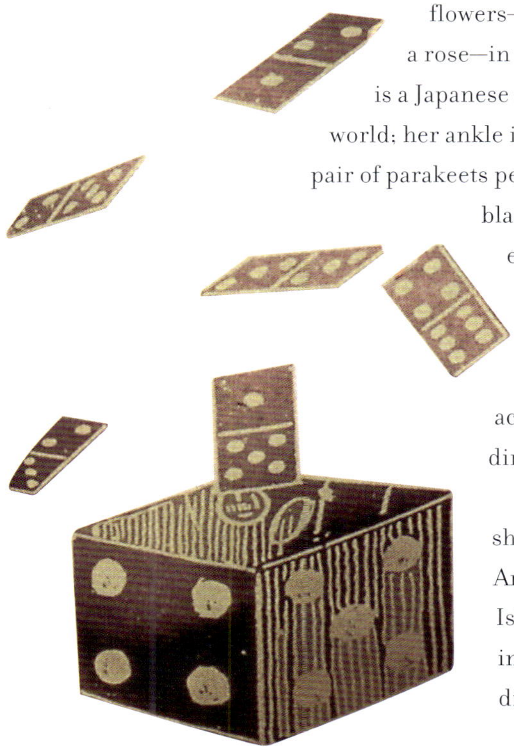

To create the print, which she did at Universal Limited Art Editions (ULAE) on Long Island, Hammond scanned the images into the computer and digitally collaged them over the photograph of herself. Each digitized tattoo had to be carefully tweaked so that it fell in a natural way over her skin and the curvature of her body (notice, for example, the snowflakes that look as though they are disappearing around her calf and hip), and the final image was printed out on a single large (75 x 30 inch) sheet of custom-made Japanese paper of a kind not generally used in inkjet printing. Sensuously textured, the print was the first Hammond made using exclusively digital processes.

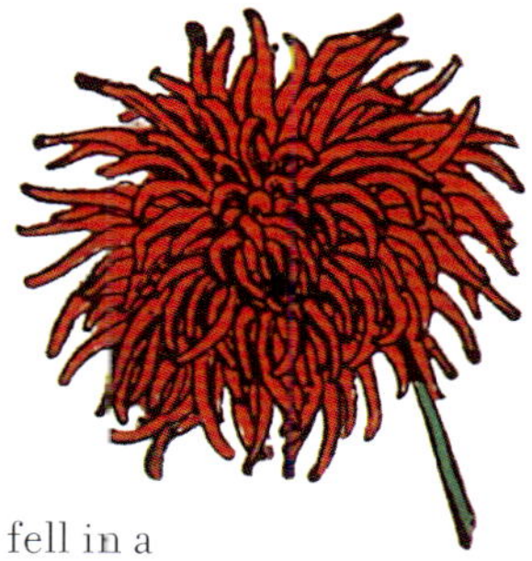

Hammond's portrait appears often in her work, but nowhere else as a monumental, photographic nude. Adopting a classic pose in the history of art (one thinks, for example, of Matisse's series of five bronze relief "backs," which he made over a period of twenty years), Hammond's *nu de dos* is perhaps unique in the history of artistic self-portrayal. The fact that she is turned away from the viewer, concealing her identity even as she is vividly exposed, indicates an ambivalence about self-revelation that may be seen to carry throughout her self-portraiture. As she has often said, identity is not one thing. In *Wonderful You*, a painting from 1995, Hammond paints herself as Superman, a toreador, the martyred Saint Sebastian, a Buddha, a snowman, placing her head on the bodies of each of these figures. Masquerade is

Hammond's customary mode of self-portrayal as she adopts the various personas of her lexical subjects.

Tabula Rosa represents a departure and an anomaly. For one, the tattoo images—as surely bearing Hammond's signature as any style she might have devised from scratch—have taken up residence on her body, colonizing its surfaces. She may be masquerading as a tattooed lady, but the images have a greater integrity than in *Wonderful You*, where they are rather comically transformed by her donning them as personas. The inversion of Hammond's relationship to her images in *Tabula Rosa* seems to me a profound statement about the fusion of an artist and her work, about the manner in which, in the end, the person of an artist is overtaken by the work that lives on, and into which she disappears as time passes. Moreover, unlike the paintings, this work is essentially a photograph, and as such, whether rightly or wrongly (since it is so assiduously manipulated), we take it as an index to reality. Hammond has generously and even bravely exposed herself in her middle-aged woman's body, a mark of time passing as much as of full-blooded life; it is perhaps no accident that the tattoo-flowers are wholly in bloom, for, like them, Hammond has been arrested at the moment of her own maturity. In both these respects—in the use of photography, by definition a record of the past, and in the disappearance of the artist into her work—*Tabula Rosa* seems to me to be a meditation on mortality and the afterlife of the work of art, and as a result has a particular poignancy.

Hammond revels in the chance encounters provoked by her incessant combining and recombining of imagery and materials. Her identity as an artist—and as a character in her own work—is very much bound up with the practice of collage, one of fracturing and reconstructing, of multiplicity and open-endedness. Hammond is no expressionist, plumbing the depths of her psyche for some singular font of inspiration. Her approach is extensive and wide-ranging. Throughout her work, the self-portrait is just another collage element, as "recombinant" as any other of her images. Hammond's lexicon itself reveals and conceals her person; the images are appropriated, to be sure, which usually implies the renunciation of style. But in the types of choices she makes—of images with an archaically literary look reused over a period of years, with repetition breeding familiarity—they unerringly bear her signature and in the end constitute a style of sorts.

II

Printmaking has been important to Hammond from the start of her career, and whether she is making a print or a unique paper piece, printing techniques often figure in the process. Nearly all the material she has found over the years, all the little scraps of paper that constitute her 276-part lexicon,[12] are taken from printed sources—and Hammond is an inveterate bibliophile when it comes to a certain type of illustration. She rummages through antiquarian bookshops, libraries, and flea markets in search of her printed paraphernalia; lately the Internet has provided her with new sources. Printed matter figures heavily in her taste and is the genesis of nearly everything she makes. When I asked her about whether her method of working on paper came out of prints, she replied, somewhat elliptically, "Out of how you can live in this world, a forest of signs, and still be yourself, and your many selves."[13] The multiplicity of prints—the possibility of creating many versions rather than just one—facilitates the expression of her particular construction of an unfixed and metamorphic identity.

While teaching at the Maryland Institute in the 1980s, Hammond was given a grant to make a print; her assistant proceeded by preparing one plate for an etching. This procedure ran counter to Hammond's preference, which, at least in regard to works on paper, tends toward mixed media. So Hammond carved an additional twenty-three linoleum-block plates that she printed in variations over the single-plate etching. It was the start of a method she would follow for years. She now has several hundred carved, reusable linoleum blocks, in addition to custom-made rubber stamps and lithographic cutouts, all containing images from the lexicon that she deploys in her unique works as well as her prints. The rubber stamps, for one, were used to produce works like *Untitled (Red Frog #2)* (2000), consisting of small pieces of gampi paper stamped in ink, then retouched in watercolor, and tipped onto a backing sheet in a delicate, mosaic-like grid. In addition, Hammond often transfers, through solvent, her many Xeroxed images to canvas or paper. Even apart from the elaborate editioned pieces she makes in workshop collaborations, Hammond is immersed in prints, which for her are as much a means to an end as a finished product.

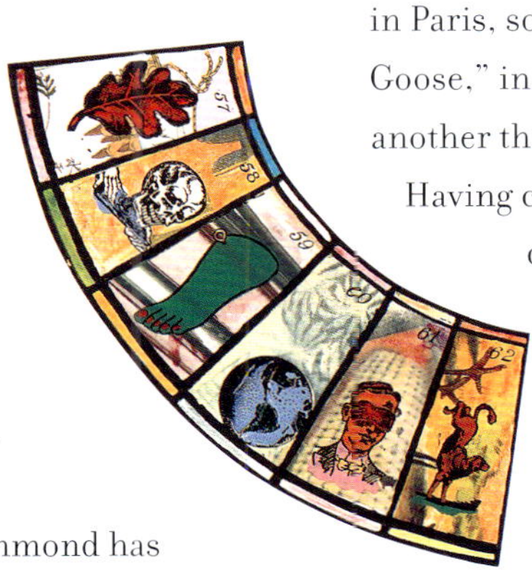

Over the past decade, Hammond has come to rely increasingly on digital tools, with printouts forming the backgrounds for many of her drawings as well as, in the exceptional *Tabula Rosa*, and more significantly perhaps in her recent photomontages, constituting a medium complete in itself. "I like a print that's supposed to be a print," she says, meaning that for her the print she finishes must feel as if this is the only way it could have been made. None of Hammond's prints is an image made "after" a painting, though it might be related to one; a print for her is a primary object. When working in paper, whether it is a unique work or an editioned print, Hammond likes to engage in a complicated process—for her, that is part of the interest of making art.[14] Generally she prefers to mix the computer-generated printout with other techniques such as relief printing and hand-coloring to give the work a richer texture.

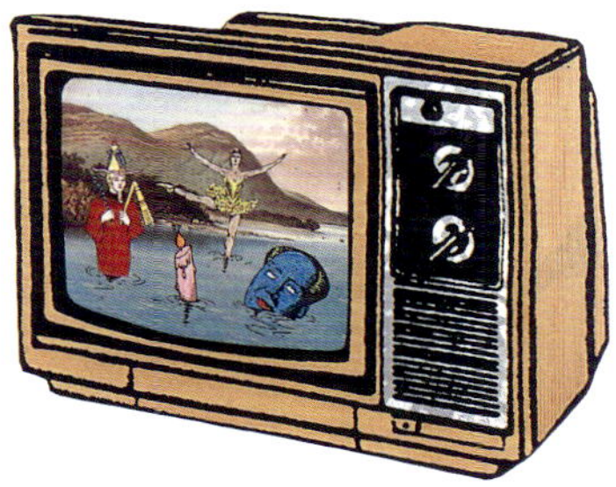

For her 1999 print *From the Goose to the Girl*, for example, which she made at Pace Editions in New York, Hammond was displeased with what she saw as a flatness in the Iris printing alone. The print is based on a real gameboard that she found in a bin at the Marais in Paris, something called "The Game of the Goose," in which players race against one another through sixty-three illustrated squares. Having created a collage of sanded postcards, can labels, wood-grain paper, wax, various papers, and crayon, Hammond had the work reproduced digitally and used this digital print solely as a ground. Over this translucent ground, much like that of her drawings, Hammond printed colors in pochoir and the black lines in relief; she then made some additions by hand. The legend at the center reads, "Jeu de l'Elga," followed by the rules of the game in French

For a later Pace project, Hammond again used digital printing in combination with other techniques. She says she has observed that Iris printing by itself can look something like a frozen video image. Wishing to explore that quality, she made *Six Sets* in 2001. This is a series of six prints, each presenting an antiquated television console made of wood veneer relief-printed in black over silver foil. Each console displays on its TV screen a landscape with mountains in the background and a lake or river in the foreground. Six different scenes take place in the water, most containing a sinking or bobbing figure, a reference to the culmination of the Hindu festival Ganesh Chaturthi, in which celebrants toss or immerse statues of the god Ganesh in the river Ganges. Among Hammond's players are a zebra with a blue monkey on its back, with a nearly submerged Buddha nearby; a bright yellow horse, knee-deep in water and mounted by a kachina mask; and a bust of Einstein in a boat, traveling with a pair of burning candles and a die. For the digital landscape, Hammond scanned an old Irish postcard that she tweaked in Photoshop, changing it to the television's format and adding a subtle scrim of lines to make it look even more evanescent. For each of the prints in the edition

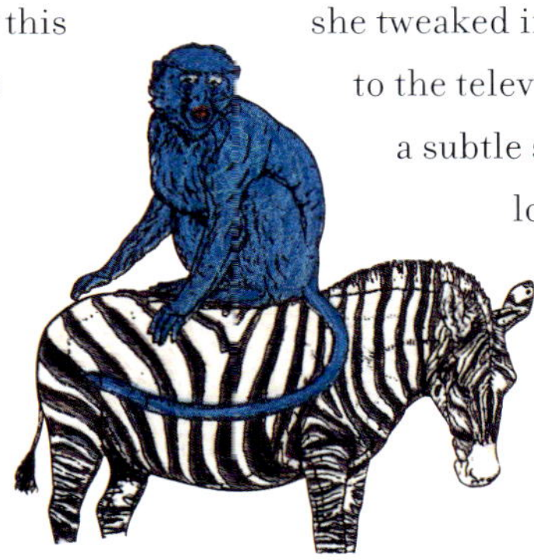

of fifteen, she hand-touched (as identically as possible) the various figures in brilliant shades with the result that her characters pop out, creating tableaux more like those of a shadow box than a TV show.

Preworkshop planning and the challenge of execution, as well as the opportunity to collaborate with others, tapping the skills and creativity of a variety of experts—all are features of printmaking with which Hammond feels at home. "You're getting outside of yourself and you're giving up a certain degree of control, but in a way, you are freer for it," she has said about her collaborations with poets.[15] The same might be said of her collaborations with printers. The complexity of printmaking that some find daunting is precisely what draws her to the medium. What begins as a multiplicity of steps and options—the separate printing stages, the various matrices and techniques, the multifarious source material—dissolves to form a seamless whole. A print can be a force of illusion, and the trickster sensibility of Hammond embraces it partly for that reason.

"I like art with a high degree of internal contradiction," Hammond says, "where order is wrenched out of a huge amount of chaos."[16] When Hammond goes to a workshop to make a print, she has a fairly clear idea of what she wants to do and arrives with "tons," as she has said, of materials. Sorting through these as she works on the project, she often winds up transferring them to various types of matrices and combining them in various media, itself a kind of collage process. Hammond's first published print was made at ULAE, the workshop founded by Tatyana Grosman in 1957, which has always been known for its willingness to accommodate an artist's most ambitious and esoteric needs. Since 1991, when she made *Presto*, a ten-color screenprint and lithograph, Hammond has completed eight ULAE projects, each of them technically demanding. The most recent is *Scrapbook* (2003), which displays hand-assembled Iris-printed cutouts on pages, much like a real scrapbook. (Among the relics included is a tiny version of *Tabula Rosa*.)[17] In the manner of Jasper Johns, who has made numerous prints at ULAE since the early 1960s, Hammond uses the medium to expand the contexts in which to create her open-ended tableaux, like Johns recycling the elements of a personal lexicon.

Clowns of various sorts appear frequently in Hammond's work, but perhaps nowhere as oddly as in *Clown Suit*, a three-dimensional print made in 1995 at ULAE, using lithography, screenprinting, and collage. It is a clown costume complete with its pointed cap; the body is meant to be stuffed and the hat suspended so that it hovers above. *Clown Suit* is, like *Tabula Rosa*, a self-sufficient personage, at once palpably present and decidedly absent, and is likewise covered with images. Divided vertically down the middle, the suit displays, on one half, a harlequin pattern of red and white diamonds filled with Ham-

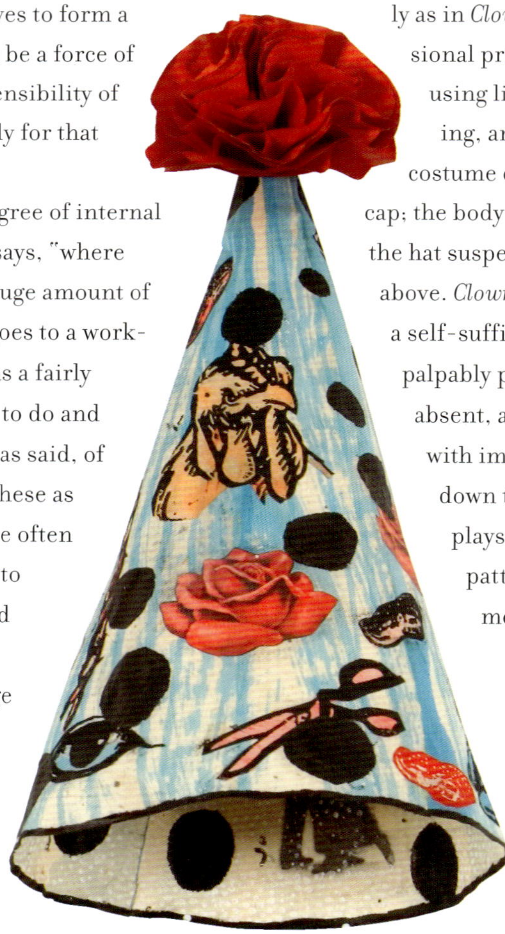

mond's rubber-stamp imagery, which she applied directly from the stamps to a plate and then lithographed. The other half, dominated by a tall, blooming chrysanthemum, contains mainly screenprinted emblems on a green ground covered with photolithographic images. The whole was printed onto sheets of strong, malleable Japanese paper that were sewn together on a prototype model devised by Hammond with a friend. The print has detachable rice-paper pompon buttons that can be transferred to either side of the costume, depending on which side is displayed.

When I asked her if she considers the clown an alter ego, Hammond replied that creating a work of art is like putting on a costume, something she has loved to do since she was a child.[18] In the painting *Dumb Show*, executed around the same time (1994–95) she was making the print, Hammond placed her own head on the body of a dancing Pierrot. In one sense, then, *Clown Suit* might be considered a surrogate of the artist, at once present and absent, and the piece related thematically to the later *Tabula Rosa*. Such an interpretation does not close off other readings, of course; nor does it take away from the essential mystery of the piece, which, in being uninhabited, feels like a relic, with the contingent quality that attends all of Hammond's iconography. It is as if, for each image, there is a missing narrative, never to be retrieved.[19] This quality of being unmoored from singular origins sets her imagery free to be placed in any and all different contexts—a semiotic freefall that is the mark of a postmodernist practice.

Still more replete is the great print *The Wonderfulness of Downtown* (1997), another ULAE feat. This time Hammond appears in the costume of a sixteenth-century conquistador standing on the waves beneath a map of lower Manhattan, surrounded by three square-rigged ships from the Age of Exploration. The print, pieced together from several separate sheets, imitates the look of early printed maps, which might present a cartouche with the portrait of a patron or explorer, and sometimes vignettes of ships plying the waters off the mapped terrain. The staggered outline of this very large print (59 1/2 x 62 inches) is also reminiscent of some early maps.

The terrain is Manhattan, a freehand rendition gridded into an approximation of the streets and blocks below 14th Street, in predominantly yellow screenprint. Interspersed are more than forty photographs, printed offset and "stuck" to the surface by pretend screenprinted refrigerator magnets. "The photographs, taken roughly where they are located on the map," wrote Hammond, "depict incidental, particular, everyday things: three Dominican men outside a funeral home; a colorful, hand-painted dragon boat that was moored in the Hudson for a while; a cat sitting on my front steps. The things the world is really made up of."[20] In real life, as in the representation, Hammond took on the persona of an explorer, roaming the blocks of downtown neighborhoods and claiming for her print the kind of random incident that pleases her (in one photo, the artist Deb Kass was home to wave from her apartment in TriBeCa).

The title, *The Wonderfulness of Downtown*, is taken from a list of forty-four titles that the poet John Ashbery invented at Hammond's request in 1993. She worked with the list for eight years, producing, altogether, sixty-two paintings based on them.[21] This is her only print, however, with an Ashbery title. In her 1994 painting *The Wonderfulness of Downtown*, Hammond shows herself rowing a canoe in the spot where, in the print, a large compass is located; the vignettes are painted, and there are no "magnets." The water in the painting is a loosely rendered field of brushstrokes, mainly in shades of blue, while in the print sky and water are combined in a photolithograph of the actual surface of water overlaid by eddies of blue-printed tusche. Borrowed in the print are some ideas from another of the Ashbery paintings—*A Parliament of Refrigerator Magnets* (1994)—in which painted refrigerator magnets illusionistically "stick" color solvent-transfer images, photographic in their sources, to a canvas shaped like an open book. It depicts a spread from an imaginary atlas, with orange and red continents, souvenirs and emblems, and, at the center, the half-submerged head of Hammond herself balancing a lit candle (shades of Einstein in *Six Sets*). A comparison of the print with the paintings vividly demonstrates the manner in which Hammond recycles ideas and motifs in a spirit of protean free association.

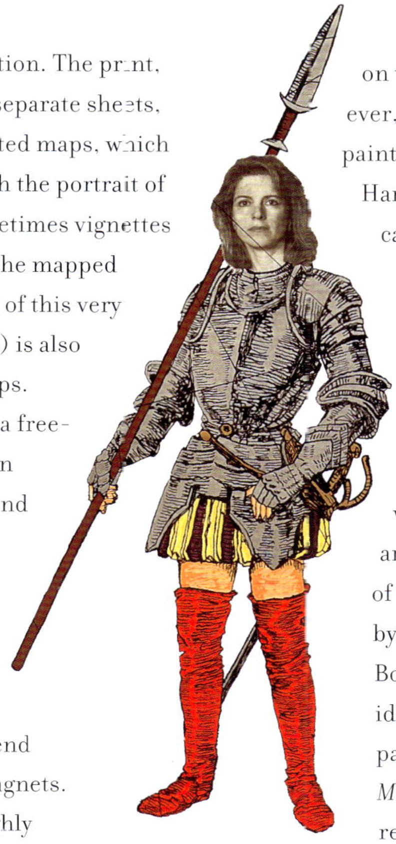

III

In what direction is the volcano? The Cape? The Lake? The Strait? The Mountains? The Isthmus? What is in the East? In the West? In the South? In the North? In the Northwest? In the Southeast? In the Northeast? In the Southwest?

—ELIZABETH BISHOP, epigraph to *Geography III* (1970)

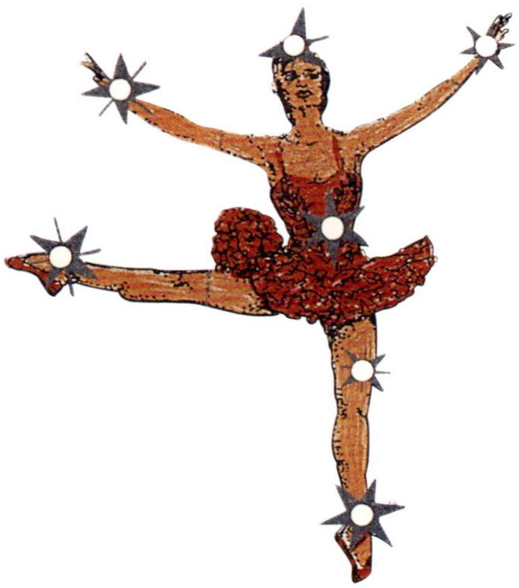

Aside from the individual motifs, broader tropes provide the settings in Hammond's work: rooms and theaters, for example, in which her figures solipsistically engage in their various activities,[22] or games, or, as in *The Wonderfulness of Downtown*, maps. Much like her forebear Joseph Cornell, Hammond avidly collects images of all kinds of maps—which, of course, are always prints. In the fifteenth and sixteenth centuries and beyond, cartographers published and disseminated the engravings and woodcuts they made of maps of new lands and of constellations and topographies. Hammond follows in this tradition. For her most recent print, *My Heavens!* (2004), made at Shark's Ink in Lyons, Colorado (a new venue for the artist), Hammond turned to star maps, referring to a subset of cartography and navigation she has always found interesting.

My Heavens! consists of a double-lobed sheet of Thai mulberry paper chine-colléed over two larger sheets of Amate paper, which in turn sandwich a sheet of silver Mylar. Each of the 280 stars in Hammond's fantasy constellations was cut out by hand to allow the silver to show through. Hammond transferred her star maps to plates that she then lithographed in sepia tones in a number of different directions. She deliberately added smudges and scratches to convey a feeling of antiquity. Her intent was to create an allover effect much like that of the heavens as one looks directly upward. The multicolored constellations at the center are, of course, entirely invented. There are no Sumo wrestlers in the real heavens, no rampant horses, no monkey swinging from a vine. (Nor, for that matter, are there really dippers, a water-bearer, the belt of Orion.) Hammond says she thought about the way humans have imagined real constellations, the way that linkages were devised to make sense of what is, after all, a grand chaos. In thinking of this history of invented correspondences—to gods, to common objects—Hammond discerned that they share a formal quality of being physically stretched out. They are images that as connect-the-dot constructions are far-ranging rather than compact. Consequently, when she searched her lexicon, she chose figures in stretched-out poses or with parts that jut out—a ballerina in arabesque, an oarsman rowing, a water-bearer shouldering his buckets, an antlered reindeer, a long-legged, long-billed heron. The twelve-color lithograph has the quality of a child's coloring book, with the figures executed in bright, unnatural hues against an indigo firmament, a vivid contrast to the atmospherics of the sepia-toned border.

Maps are a way of ordering information. They are a natural lure for an artist who is immersed in overabundance. From the time she was a child, Hammond invented classificatory systems; even then she was a collector, a naturalist gathering specimens. "When I was a kid," she says, "I made grids on our property with stakes and string, the way a surveyor would mark off land, and I'd identify everything inside the grid, like rocks and trees, and grubs and birds, and list them in notebooks."[23] As much as Hammond has engaged in a process of amassing a vast world of images, she has also been challenged to organize them and arbitrarily limit herself—to invent ways of mapping her way

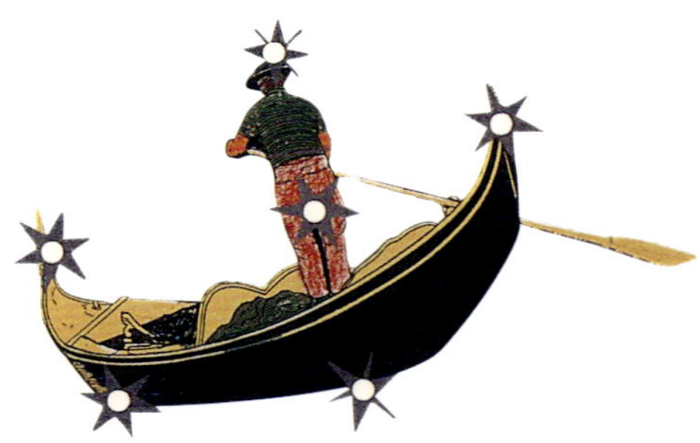

through them. There were the forty-four Ashbery titles, of course; and, in her early career, Hammond challenged herself to use just six colors and two sizes for her paintings. Her collaborations impose limits of sorts, and she finds working partners with whom she shares an affinity: the poet Raphael Rubinstein, for example, who, for their book *Be Zany, Poised Harpists / Be Blue, Little Sparrow* (2002), used an arbitrary, numerically constricted formula for his four poems.[24] Poets who write in prescribed forms, like the sonnet or the sestina, find that the rules can provide a certain creative liberation. So it has been for Hammond, with her 276 "pieces of information," a number not too great and not too small, which has helped her to filter the barrage of visual stimuli that is also her inspiration. In the beginning, she used the numbers under which she categorized her images as titles for her works. She abandoned that system with the advent of the Ashbery titles, and indeed many of her former systematizations have fallen, one by one, by the wayside. Lately, however, it seems as if even her lexicon, which has served Hammond for so long, has begun to show some wear, eroded somewhat by her turn to photography.

Habitué of junk shops and flea markets, Hammond has discovered on the Internet an endless marketplace to hunt for images fitting her lexicon, which, being mainly answered by photographs when its elements are Googled, is undergoing a shift. Hammond's process began literally, as she perused the Web for books and other objects of the sort she previously sought out exclusively on foot. From there she began to search her categories, coming up with results that surprised her. The most unexpected images would turn up, all photographic in nature, and she began to purchase them online, in addition to acquiring miscellaneous photographs at her usual haunts. (In this, she shares a general rise of interest on the part of artists and art historians, curators and collectors, in found vernacular photography, a popular topic for books and exhibitions.)[25]

Hammond assembled a group of scrapbooks, organized into her categories, in which she placed her newly found material. The imagery looks different now, sometimes unrecognizable as a term in her lexicon. Her tastes have broadened. The accessibility of photography, its pervasive use by ordinary people, has undermined the somewhat esoteric, literary nature of Hammond's choices, and also it has personalized her work in curious ways. The decontextualizing impulse that has always marked her appropriations is even more apparent in photography, which we expect to be tied to a real-life situation that, once explained, will be familiar to us: family gatherings, tourist spots, baby pictures. The loss of an original context can be especially jarring in photography, an effect long exploited by artists who have realized that even the successful identification of a photographic source matters little when the picture is reconstituted as something else. The suspension of disbelief is a constant lure. One need only think of Man Ray's photograph of *Dust Breeding* (1920), resembling an extraterrestrial landscape. Even when the image is explained as a close-up of dust gathering on Duchamp's *Large Glass*, it retains its inscrutability.

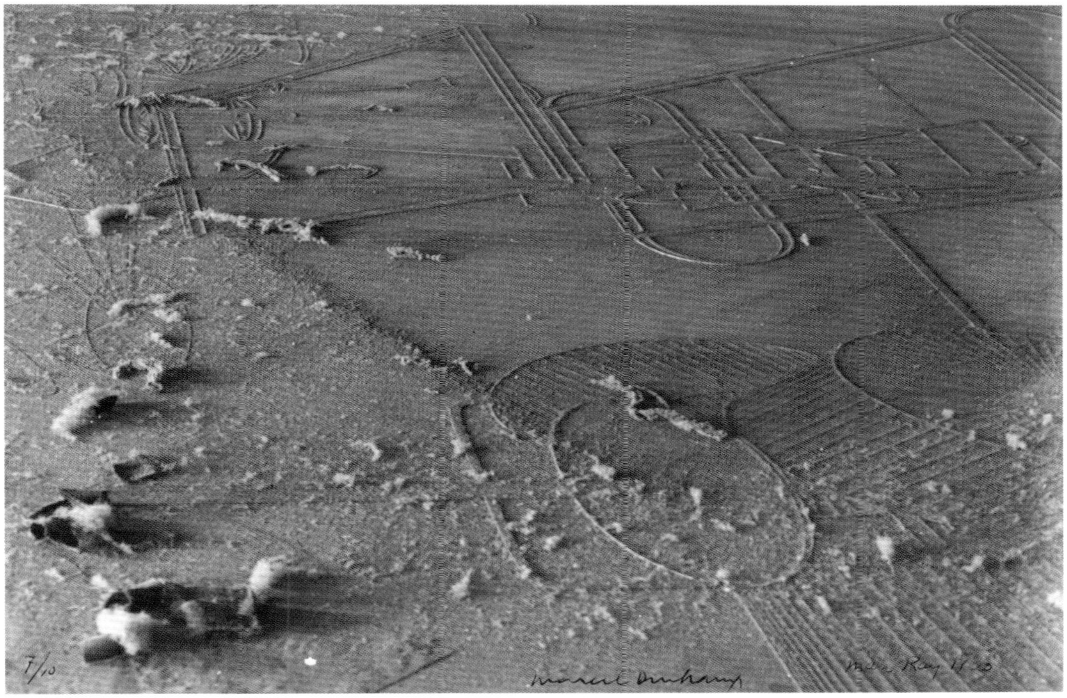

Man Ray (American, 1890–1976)
Dust Breeding, [Duchamp's Large Glass with Dust Motes], 1920, printed ca. 1967
Gelatin silver print
9 7/16 x 12 inches
The Metropolitan Museum of Art, Purchase, Photography in the Fine Arts Gift, 1969. (69.521)

Hammond has, in a sense, arrived late to the nearly century-old technique of photomontage, spearheaded by the Russian Constructivists, Dadaists, and Surrealists. She has approached it not out of an interest in the medium for its own sake nor out of a desire to attach herself to this particular genealogy of modernist practice—running from Alexander Rodchenko through Jerry Uelsmann and any number of contemporary photographic pasticheurs. Instead, her turn to photography has evolved as something of a natural choice, almost accidental, as she has pressed against the limits of her own system that, for all its elasticity, has repeatedly expanded in unforeseen ways.

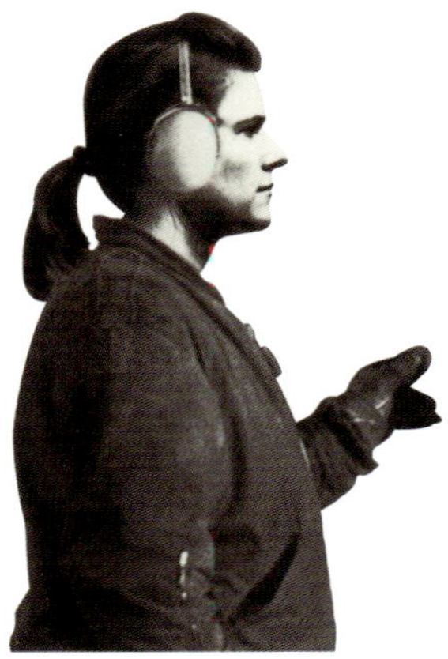

As with her prints, Hammond makes the process of creating a finished photograph labor-intensive, spending hours with a technician, tweaking the smallest details of the scanned image—deepening a shadow, slightly enlarging a hand—in a manner akin to how she might work, in turn, on a painting. Not content, again, with a purely digital output, Hammond has insisted in her black-and-white photographs on printing the digitally conceived images in silver gelatin, giving them the fine, glossy, seamless quality that she feels is best achieved in that medium, and the look and general scale (14 x 17 inches) of a traditional photograph.

Hammond has begun combining family photographs with found images, deepening the personal dimension of her artistic project while at the same time alienating it from a discernible history. Her use of the family photographs is anything but transparently autobiographical. Hammond clearly has no interest in engaging the confessional mode so pervasive in contemporary art, where the inclusion of personal history usually means the exposure of some sort of trauma. This is despite her abandonment of the relative chasteness that characterizes her work in other media. The new eroticism in her photographs is due in part to the connection of photography to pornography and the fact that so many Internet searches wind up in erotic cul-de-sacs. The presence of sexually explicit vignettes in Hammond's photographs makes one realize the degree to which that quality is missing in her earlier work.

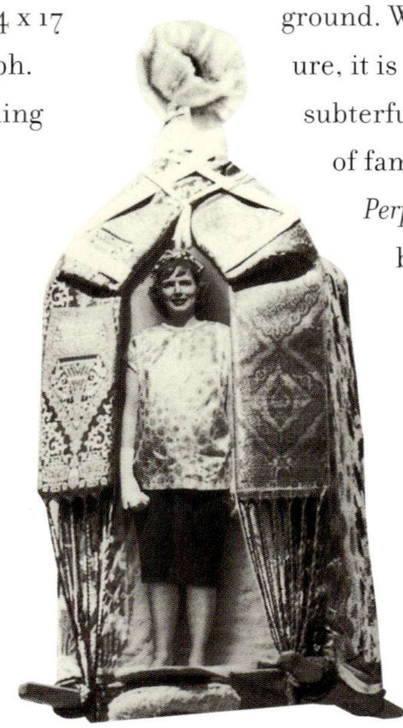

And the erotic motifs can come as something of a shock, particularly when combined with images of children or with her own family pictures—for example, in works like *October First (Mom's Birthday)*, where a woman in an obscene pose, graphically revealing her genitalia, poses in the foreground of a picture of the child Jane and her family celebrating a birthday party. The remnants of the party are represented by a group of balloons strangely clinging to the ceiling (they were really like that in the original snapshot), which feel like they could pertain either to the family or the woman in the foreground. With the intrusion of this obscene figure, it is as if something of the psycho-sexual subterfuge that is the constant undercurrent of family relations has been exposed. In *Perpetual Love*, a shadowy window in the background reveals a paddling scene as, in the foreground, two young girls from a bygone era play Ping-Pong. Perhaps disturbing to an age in which childhood sexuality is a hot point for social hysteria, the children turn their glances toward the pornographic scene, as if startled.

Playfully, Hammond makes it part of the game. In *Friendly Beast*, the twin turbines of a jet are the repositories of two close-up shots of female gentialia; in a droll touch, Hammond is the headphoned mechanic servicing the craft.

There are other disjunctions, some involving family members, that are not quite as unsettling as these. Jane's pregnant mother is paraded like a saint in a Tunisian procession, the tall headdresses of the men capped by the poppies she grew in her garden (*Mahdia: Tunisian Men Honor My Mother and Her Poppies*). In *My Birth*, a clay figurine of Jane as a child is being fashioned by a scientist/artist as her Lilliputian parents lounge nearby under what looks like an electrical tower; the backdrop is a giant map of the United States. Seamless, neat, and more directly dreamlike, even surreal, than any of her previous work, the photographs place Hammond and her relatives in fantastical yet strangely believable realms.

Even in the erotic scenes, there is something very Hammondesque that survives—something of her signature sensibility. The archaism she loves, for example, is still present in period details: in the console television in *October First*, reminiscent of the televisions in *Six Sets*, the pre–World War II acrobats of *Tour Royale*, or the post–World War II Ping-Pong players. Also, the obliviousness of the Hammond family in *October First* to the massive foreground distraction is similar in tone to the narcissistic disengagement of characters in the scenes she constructs in theaters and rooms. In *Chai Wan*, high-rise balconies in a Chinese tenement are filled with players very similar to

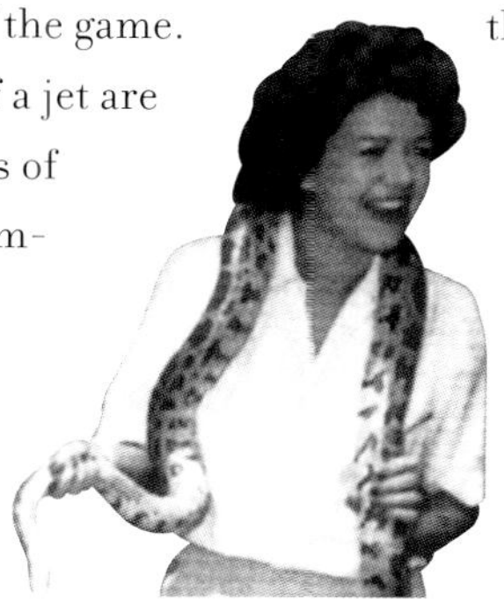

those seen in so many of Hammond's character-crowded works, with similar anachronisms and anomalies. It too becomes a kind of theater, with separate, semiprivate scenes enacted by women appearing in doorways along its tiers: one with a pumpkin-head, another performing an Asian dance, still another (Hammond's mother?) with a python around her neck. The photograph allows fantasy to enter the quotidian lives of women, transformed from laundry maids into exotic beings from far-flung lands and eras.

With photography, Hammond has opened an entirely new terrain to be mapped, or perhaps merely to be traversed. For the area is vast, our lives so permeated with photographs that it is difficult to see where one leaves off and the other begins. Much has been written about the mirage of contemporary consciousness, where authenticity and rootedness surrender to the endless flux of images. In a sense, the trope of Hammond tattooed with her own lexicon is even more fully realized in her photographs, which, in their seamless fusion of worlds, speak to the absence of boundaries between people and the forest of signs in which they dwell.

NOTES

12. Within each "piece of information," as Hammond calls them, there can be as many as forty "things." So there can be many types of snowmen, for instance, or many manifestations of a certain type of knot or arithmetical pattern. Any firsthand quotes not otherwise cited come from my conversations with Hammond in August 2005.
13. Faye Hirsch, "Paper Pulse: A Conversation with Jane Hammond," *Art on Paper*, March–April 2002, 67.
14. See "Working Proof," in *Art on Paper*, March–April 200[illegible], 64.
15. From an interview with David Lehman about her Ashbery collaborations, in *Bomb*, fall 2002, [illegible]3.
16. Hirsch, "Paper Pulse," 66.
17. It should be noted that one of the prints Hammond produced at ULAE was a 2001 Iris print for the benefit "Doctors of the World Portfolio," which included prints by seven artists. The print is similar to *Tabula Rosa*; at half the size, it shows the naked backside of a child, also tattooed.
18. In Hirsch, "Paper Pulse," Hammond relates how she used to dress up the family dogs, and even dead pheasants that her father brought home from hunting, which she would wheel around in baby carriages (69).
19. When Sue Scott, in 1995, asked Hammond if the clown symbolized her, she responded, "I rarely use the word 'symbol' in my work.... Sometimes I use the clown for questionable gender and sometimes it's simply that I'm playing with the shapes of the hat and the nose. I do think that people who become artists do so because they feel apart in a way. And I think this clown with its elaborate costume is foolish and beautiful and artificial. This is something about being an artist." Sue Scott, "Selective Visions," *Art & Antiques*, November 1995, 94.
20. Jane Hammond, "The Wonderfulness of Downtown," in Naomi Miller and Karen E. Haas, *Mapping Cities*, exh. cat. (Boston: Boston University Art Gallery; Seattle: University of Washington Press), 84.
21. The collaboration was the subject of a traveling exhibition, *Jane Hammond: The John Ashbery Collaboration, 1993–2001*, which originated at the Cleveland Center for Contemporary Art and traveled to the Contemporary Museum, Honolulu, and the Blaffer Gallery, the Art Museum of the University of Houston, in 2001–2. It was accompanied by a catalogue with essays by Ashbery, Ingrid Schaffner (who is especially perceptive about Hammond's literariness), and the curator, Jill Snyder. See also Judith E. Stein, "The Word Made Image," *Art in America*, May 1995, 98–101.
22. For a discussion of Hammond's interest in theatrical tropes, see Raphael Rubinstein, "Backstage at the Memory Theater," in the brochure published for Hammond's installation *Back Stage: Secrets of Scene Painting*, at the Whitney Museum of American Art at Philip Morris, New York, 2002.
23. From a statement dating to 1993, in Judith Oleh Richards, ed., *Inside the Studio: Two Decades of Talks with Artists in New York* (New York: Independent Curators International), 116.
24. For an analysis of the book and its number-driven poems, see Nancy Princenthal, *Be Zany, Poised Harpists, Be Blue, Little Sparrows: An Artist's Book with Poems by Raphael Rubinstein*, Dieu Donné Lab Grant Program Publication Series No. 3 (New York: Dieu Donné Papermill, 2002).
25. Although there has been interest in the topic of found photographs from at least the late 1970s, these objects were being collected by the late 1990s, as evidenced in such exhibitions as *Snapshots: The Photography of Everyday Life, 1888 to the Present* (San Francisco: San Francisco Museum of Modern Art, 1998), *Other Pictures: Anonymous Photographs from the Thomas Walther Collection* (New York: Metropolitan Museum of Art, 2000), and, in the winter of 2005, *In the Vernacular: Everyday Photographs from the Rodger Kingston Collection*, which was accompanied by a two-day conference (Boston: Boston University Art Gallery, 2004–5). See also the writings of Geoffrey Batchen: for example, *Each Wild Idea: Writing, Photography, History* (Cambridge, Mass., The MIT Press, 2002), and, more recently, *Forget Me Not: Photography and Remembrance* (Princeton: Princeton Architectural Press, 2004).

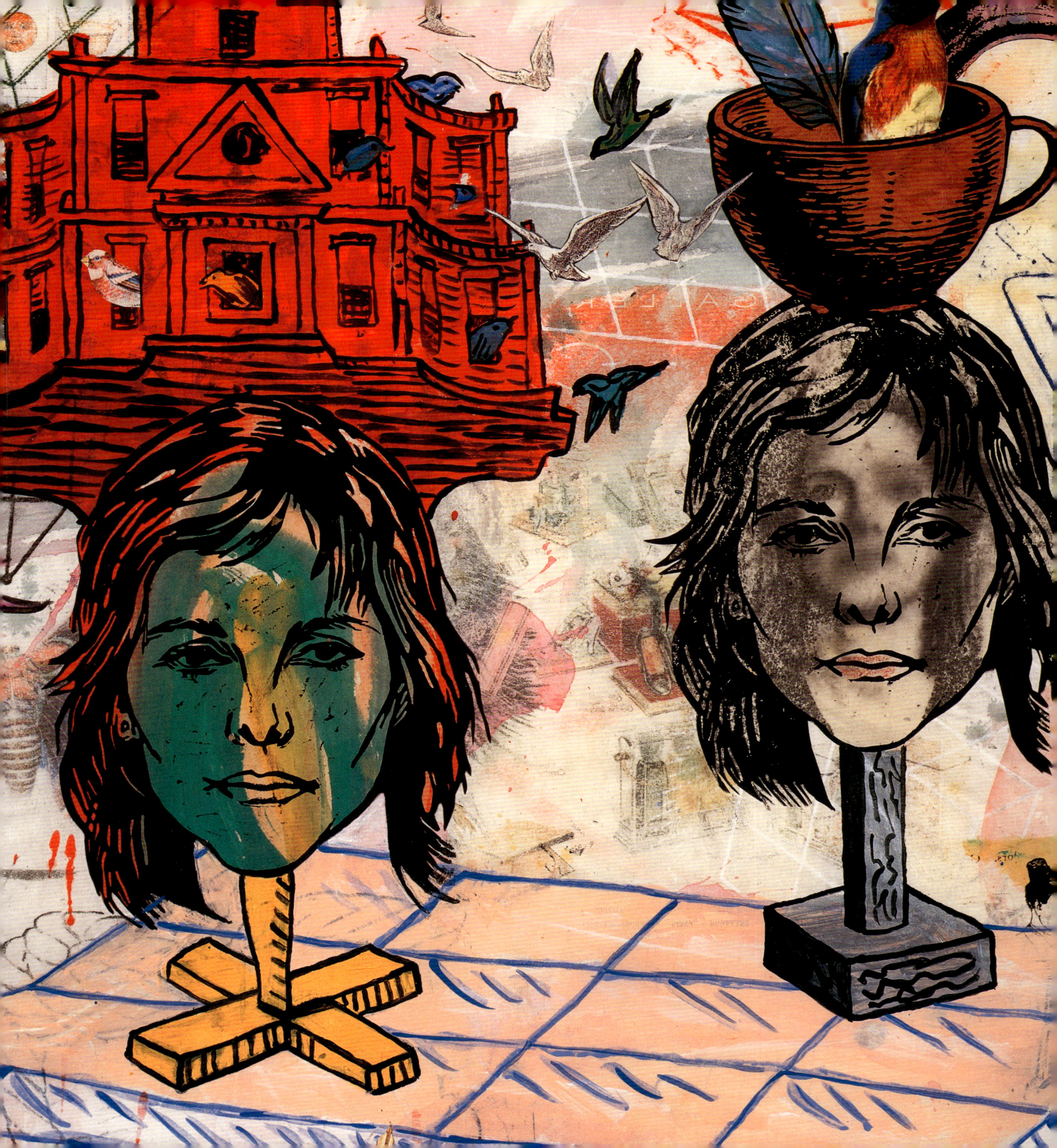

Interview with Jane Hammond

DOUGLAS DREISHPOON

The following conversation combines two recorded sessions, the first of which took place on May 3, 2005, the last day of Jane's exhibition at Galerie Lelong. We focused mainly on the paper works and paintings there, and especially on Jane's recent foray into photography. The second session took place about two months later at Jane's Grand Street studio on a beautiful day in July. After reviewing both transcripts and realizing that many of the same topics were discussed more cogently in the second session, we opted for this interview as the primary text and gleaned from the first when appropriate. The final text was revised and edited by both of us in several e-mail exchanges. —D.D.

DOUGLAS DREISHPOON:

The exhibition being organized by the Mount Holyoke College Art Museum concentrates on paper, a most ephemeral material, ancient even, and something you've consistently gravitated to for your work.

JANE HAMMOND:

I make many different kinds of works *on paper.* Some of them are photographs, some prints, many unique objects, but paper ends up being a huge part of my practice. I think it's becoming even bigger, and I'm starting to brew up a theory about this that revolves around the fact that my work is fundamentally about information. You know the context has really changed around my work. And I would have to say that it has "come up" underneath me. For example, when I first started giving slide lectures, I would make the comment that my work was like recombinant DNA, in its polyglot nature its lexicon, and combination of elements in different ways to make figurative paintings, nonfigurative paintings, paintings with flat space, or deep space, or whatever. People would always double-take on that word, "recombinant," because it was a relatively rarely used word fifteen years ago. Now, it's an everyday word. The huge explosion of information on the Internet has made it easy to combine and recombine. The culture of rap music also has really grown up around this idea and practice. Rap is recombinant.

It's no accident that I mention the Internet and music together because the thing they have in common is bodilessness—the bodilessness of information is the recombiner's pleasure. And I think that this marries with paper. Paper is less corporeal than stretchers, than wood; it's almost like ether. And when I'm in the mood for something closer to pure information, closer to music, closer to language—because language is the most bodiless—I'm in the mood for paper. It's less freighted with a lot of corpus.

DD

Talk to me about bodilessness. Does it privilege the mind?

JH

I think of myself as both a conceptual artist involved with a lot of very "mental" ideas and as someone who loves making things by hand. I started out as a sculptor. I made large objects and videos. When I moved to New York, I started making some things on paper because I had five jobs, no money. I was afraid to stop working, the way you're afraid to stop jogging, because it's too hard to get started again. I had all the biases against painting that many who came of age in the late 1970s had. Barry Le Va was my favorite artist in graduate school. So, out of those drawings I sort of backed into making paintings. And then I liked paintings; I am sort of a "more-is-more" person and I felt like you could get more information into a painting because it was less *bodied* than a sculpture. Those early drawings led me to painting and painting led me to printmaking and other types of drawing. But it is something about this increased bodilessness and this ability to hold more different kinds of information that attracts me. Recently, I have even made some Mylar pieces, which have almost no color and are quite transparent. And then the photos, they're very unbodied. As I pull information from radically different contexts and combine and recontextualize things, well, I think it's more elastic the more bodiless the information is. This is different from how painting feels. Paper has no smell, you know.

I am reading this book right now, which is a leftie-critique of copyright law. And it's very smart. The author makes the point that this entity, which in our culture now is referred to as "intellectual property," was something Thomas Jefferson thought of as intellectual policy. It's interesting and perhaps strange that we think of ideas as things. And you can see that this dovetails with Marxism, because if you weren't so hung up about property, you wouldn't be so upset about sharing. And the author traces this idea of intellectual property in contradistinction to certain African American traditions such as the blues, where ideas of authorship were different. At the heart of it were ideas of touching communal signs, of sharing, and of your "version." It's completely different from what we were brought up to believe about Pollock or Picasso as these lone geniuses. But you realize that part of this whole thing has to do with the fact that before *records* (commodities), there is just singing. One of these musicians, not Muddy Waters, but someone of his era, refers to the blues as "air" music, that the songs are in the air, which likens the singer to a kind of early radio, a receiver, a downloader. It feels to me like the Internet is kind of air in this sense of "air music." This is really exciting, because I feel that the way I've been working, I've been riding a wave for twenty years and the water just got thinner, swooshier, and slipperier. It's more like air, like air music.

DD

If ideas are as ephemeral as air, then the capitalist notion of private property and the modernist myth of originality seem like moot constructs.

JH

Yes, and, importantly, they're constructs that braid together.

DD

Right, but you're talking about bypassing a system, perhaps not even a system but an anti-system, where things are naturally present and available. The notion of oral tradition brings us back to language, questions of who owns it, and whether it's a unique formulation or something that accommodates every human being who internalizes it.

JH

And every specific time they use it. I see this lexicon of mine—the language it makes and the way it creates meaning—as a living thing capable of infinite variation. But I am also still a big collector of its elements. I go to flea markets and fairs and dealers now. I collect photographs madly. I can't wait to get up in the morning and go. Prowling through book fairs is another thing I love. I don't know, I guess I am like a collector, or like a trapper.

DD

I'm reminded of Breton's anointed circle of surrealists and their outings to flea markets in search of sundry objects, associative triggers for visual and lingual images.

JH

Yes, but I have a slightly different idea about this than the Surrealists. The Surrealists had too much respect for their own subconscious. They also had a privileged hierarchy of signs—you know, shit, fire, etc. I'm really interested in seeing these new things out in the world, as collaboration. I've always worked with found information, with elements originating in the world, in the voice of an "other." I don't know if that's as obvious to other people as it is to me. Because I've largely translated it into paint, and because I have an active hand in the process of painting, it may seem so "mine." And of course a great deal of my being is in there. But when I talk to myself about my paintings, I always use this word "jammed." It's a reference to how each constituent element in the painting is coming from a disparate source, from another culture, from another time. Each one is freighted with the way they drew in England in the 1890s, or an Art Deco sensibility, or the way woodcuts looked in Germany in 1500, or Chinese ink drawings. And I've always valued these inconsistencies. You know, there is a rabbit on a branch; the branch is much more detailed than the rabbit is; the branch is seen from the left; the rabbit is seen from the right. That's what I call jamming. I like the collision of the otherness, of the voices behind my voice. So, when I'm at the flea market, I'm not seeing this thing as something that is going to trigger my powerful, authorial, supreme unconscious, which is very Andre Breton to me. I see it as a bit of collaboration, where I have left some space for the voice of the other person. And I actually believe that leaving that space is what ends up allowing the viewer to enter when the piece is done. It's not only about me.

DD

What you've just described reflects the difference between Freud and Jung: solipsistic politics and ego yielding to mythic archetypes with multiple identities. What I'm hearing is that you're the medium for your own story's voice, as well as for other voices, as embodied in other images.

JH

Yes, I agree with that, but I am also willing to go to a place where I am a kind of mixologist, and after I made this mix, you and I together, and this guy down the street will figure out what it means. That is interesting to me, too.

DD

Let's get back to paper. Paper equates with drawing and drawing equates with the germination of ideas. Ideas sketched on paper easily bypass expectations because they generate spontaneously.

JH

Well, that's the traditional idea about drawing, that it is generative.

DD

Is that true given the way you work?

JH

I certainly don't see drawing as a preparatory medium. I sometimes get an idea first as a paper piece, but I've also made paper pieces that came out of paintings that came before.

I also don't see myself as someone who "draws" as much as I see myself as someone who makes things with paper. I think I'm privileging paper over the pencil. I certainly am a great lover of paper. I have almost a collection of paper in my drawers and then when you add in all the books I have, and the paper ephemera, and now hundreds and hundreds of photographs. Well, I'm really in love with paper, in many forms, and printing, too.

One thing I do believe about paintings is that when you make a painting, you make a decision, sort of an armchair decision in a way, beforehand, about its size and shape. And that decision is pretty incontrovertible. With works on paper you can change that all along. That's a pretty fundamental difference.

I really don't think too much about essential differences between media. I would rather ponder a discovered particularity than construct a generalization. It's not an accident that my show is called *Paper Work* because "paper work" is a very open phrase that doesn't really imply a medium. It could be painting or photography or printmaking or any combination thereof. I make lots of things that are all printed, but you wouldn't call them prints because they are unique—like the "gampis" or the matchbooks. And they are also hand-painted. My drawings like *Past Time* have lots of solvent transfers, and crayon and graphite frottage, and each sheet of paper is really a collage of several sheets of different papers glued together. Before I ever took a drawing instrument to them, they were probably more *painted on* than *drawn.* I don't actually have an answer to "what do I think drawing is." Because I don't have a practice that is just drawing, or that is classically drawing, or that is capital-D drawing. I feel like I do all these paper things and they kind of leak and bleed into each other.

DD

Constructive and empirical.

JH

Here's a good example. When I went to make *My Heavens* with Bud Shark, he has a way of doing lithography, where you make the different layers of the lithograph—of which there were twelve in that print—on sheets of Mylar. I had used Mylar before, but not much. His studio is in a very remote place and there is also a Xerox machine there. So you're sort of on a desert island with Mylar and a Xerox machine, at least to a New Yorker. It's funny, because I fell in love with printmaking in a very out-of-the-way place, and when you are in an out-of-the-way place and you have certain things with you, then you really tend to explore what are the seven things I can do with spaghetti, anchovies, and garlic—because the store is too far away. So I started playing around with Mylar. And I started dripping different viscosities of paint on the Mylar. And then I let the drips dry. And they are very cool because you can see that they are drips, but you can see right through them, too. And then I Xeroxed the drips. Which was like some kind of funny trope between reproduction, semiotics, and psychic automatism. But it just happened. And then I was changing the size of the drips with the Xerox machine. That led to those two Mylar collages that I had in my recent Galerie Lelong show. It's a drawing idea that came out of a printmaking technique. Those drawings with their fractured, glassy look are now suggesting to me the subject, not the technique, for another print.

DD

Any given idea is packed with possibilities.

JH

I'm not thinking I ought to pack them; it is just that this is who I am.

DD

You mentioned systems earlier. There are systems to the way you work, archival systems, not necessarily thematic in the way that someone like Leon Golub preferred to archive his visual fodder, but systematic nonetheless.

JH

But I am changing the criteria for what systematizes it, frequently.

DD

Right. So any viable system is as in flux as the way you deploy it.

JH

Yes. That's smart of you. And that is the "it" of what I am interested in, the sort of feedback loop between what's being said, how the saying affects the "what," and the whole cybernetics of the creation and decoding of meaning.

DD

Given your peripatetic history, you seem primed for the moment.

JH

My boyfriend, Craig, remarked to me recently that the whole idea of a "search," a word that we hear all the time now, is something that has been an essential part of my practice all along.

Half of the time I get ideas in my head and translate them, so to speak, into the language of my lexicon. But the other half of the time I'm searching through this lexicon of information and ideas come from that search. This is why I've made the point that I work both from the inside out and from the outside in—it's a reference to these mirrored processes. Anyhow, a significant part of the time I've been involved in this searching, this surfing, if you will. And links. A great example here is my Ping-Pong photograph, *Perpetual Love.* I had an idea in my head about wanting to make a very polyglot still-life photograph. So I thought I would look for a picture of a Ping-Pong table. I was imagining a broad horizontal surface on which I could park a multitude of objects. So I searched for Ping-Pong and in doing so found a photograph, which is freighted with the Second World War. I was drawn to it because I'm friendly with Judy Pfaff and Trevor Winkfield, both of whom spent their early childhood in postwar England and fondly recall playing in the rubble. But from there I discovered Ping-Pong bondage. I didn't know about Ping-Pong bondage. I'm no bondage expert. A link took me there.

DD

Sounds like the cyber equivalent to the Tower of Babel, with a vast associative matrix.

JH

And the associations aren't always yours. You see, that is what's interesting about the link. It's not the free association of André Breton. It's someone else's idea of a connection. It wasn't anywhere in my brain. I found it. I mean, first there is the Surrealist idea of free association, and then there are fifty years of brain research that basically question the idea of "free." And now, there's another brain in the room.

DD

Maybe "random" would be a better word.

JH

But it isn't completely random. "Random" would be, for example, you throw all these photos into the hopper and a blindfolded person pulls one out. There's a link in that computer's mind, so to speak, between Ping-Pong and bondage that doesn't tie into any childhood experience Jane Hammond had, any articles she ever read, any nerve impulse that ever jumped over her synapses. It's in *that* brain. I think that is so cool. Temporally, it's the opposite of the Surrealist in the flea market because the association is preceding the found object, not emanating from it.

DD

Your early years on the move appear as patterns of flux. Had the context been a more stable one, the outcome, artistically speaking, might have been different.

JH

There's probably some real truth to that. I certainly have often noted that so many artists are from these shifting, improvised, broken and reformed backgrounds. You know, I joked to Judy Pfaff once, a woman who was moved around so much in her childhood, passed from relative to relative, that she was basically making these temporary houses, these places for herself, the little nomad.

DD

Identity mirrors circumstance, to survive maybe.

JH

Yes. I think that's mostly true, but I also think identity isn't necessarily an essentialist thing. I've done two paintings that are self-portraits as a group, in which they are all Jane, but there are nine or ten different people. There's a Jesus and Santa Claus, Mickey Mouse and Superman, and a shaman and a knight. I think that one of the more interesting things about people is how we are all so different. As a child I always found it was interesting to go home with someone. You would often discover that they were very different with their parents than they were in school. Or you can have a girlfriend that you know really well, but you have no idea how she acts around men. And I really like that about people. I saw a man I know well the other day with his grandchild, and I realized that I have never before seen him with a little kid. We all have these different sides.

DD

You're receptive to multiple sources, situations, and identities that morph continually depending on time, place, and disposition. Let's get back to the photographs. What progression, what mental stops, brought you to the medium?

JH

The progression was that about a year ago I started making the three-dimensional paper scrapbooks, like *1000 Yen* or *Ship in a Bottle.* They are open books with all manner of images and media affixed to their pages. To backtrack a step, those unique scrapbooks came out of the print I made at ULAE in 2001, which is titled *Scrapbook.* For that print I made a rayogram of a frog skeleton, and for the subsequent unique scrapbooks I decided to try and incorporate some glossy photos, so there would be a real heterogeneity of media as well as images. To backtrack even further, for my ULAE print *The Wonderfulness of Downtown,* I took a series of photographs all over lower Manhattan, which I collaged onto the map. So anyhow, a year ago

I started buying photography on the Internet for the scrapbooks. I was searching for items in my lexicon: snowmen, ventriloquists, and bears. Right away it became very interesting. For example, in searching for bears I found four photos, all of them from Germany in the 1930s. Each photo shows a couple at the beach; the woman is in bathing attire and the man is in a full-body polar bear costume.

DD

Where did these images come from?

JH

One came from New Zealand and one from England and one from a dealer in Buffalo. You know, it's some kind of German trope I stumbled on. So then I started searching for more things and making artist books to hold my photo lexicon. I made books of acrobat photos and books of rabbit photos. I'm sure I've bought thousands of photos by now at yard sales and flea markets. Some of them only become interesting en masse. For example, there are lots of snow and snowman photos—because it's ephemeral. But many of the snowman photos are very small, and I'm thinking why would anyone photograph such a small snowman? But, you know, I'm from Connecticut. After I'd seen about twenty-five of these little snowmen, it dawns on me that this is Georgia. This is a freak snow in Alabama and this is the only snowman this kid is ever going to make.

Then I called my mother and begged her to let me borrow all our family photographs. I have to plead with her, but eventually I get three giant bags stuffed with loose photos. I spend four days looking at them and I spread them and my bought photographs all over the house in little constantly changing piles.

So what happened after that is, as I'm thinking about the photographs, I'm misremembering them.

DD

How so?

JH

I was cooking dinner one evening when it occurred to me that I was misremembering them and that *that* was the photography I wanted to make: the pictures in my head.

DD

Going through three bags of family photographs must have been an eye-opening and sobering experience.

JH

I told my mother that if you were an anthropologist you would think we spent all our time fishing, making snowmen, and observing magnolias.

DD

Who took the pictures?

JH

The women. So, out of the misremembering came this idea of trying to figure out how to make fictional photography. You know when I lecture about my painting I say that I make fictions out of facts. I start with found information, but it's not about appropriation or the death of originality, or a critique of the author. It's about making something out of something else. I make things out of other things. And as I've said before, there is an element of collaboration to this, or relishing other people's hands and voices and eyes. So now I have all of these other people's photographs in my house. Whole albums their own kids don't even want.

DD

But you're still looking at these through your own mental lens.

JH

I had this loose idea I was going to make fictional photographs by working with other photographs. After a bit, I started saying that I wasn't taking photographs; I was making photography. I had to research how to do what I wanted to do, and as soon as I began everyone suggested I make digital prints. But what was fascinating to me about the photography I was looking at out in the world were the assumptions I brought to it. If you take people off the street and interview them, they understand that painting is an imaginative act that whatever the painting depicts it didn't necessarily exist except in the painter's imagination. But if you show them a photograph, they presume this thing "happened"; they presume there was a photographer there to record it. And they presume that the event happened in some moment "before" the photograph was taken.

DD

The line between fact and fiction is easily blurred, especially with photography, especially now. What's your process? Manipulation is obviously a decisive factor.

JH

The process is one where first I get an idea in my head for a photograph. I might have gotten it from three or seven photographs I've collected or I might just get the idea and go out looking for the photographs. After I've made up my mind about the idea, I have the constituent elements scanned professionally on a high-resolution machine. Then I work with a very skilled retoucher fluent in Photoshop. We work side by side and separately in three or four sessions for each photograph.

DD

How does this collaboration play out?

JH

Sometimes I have a little drawing, sometimes a list of words and a diagram. It's things like I want this woman to be over here, but bigger and facing the other direction. I want her to have different hands. Now the hand has to cast a little shadow on the wall. Then when we add this other person, we have to work on the fact that they are each lit differently. Then when we have a kind of composite, we work on it like a painting. We darken the sky or beef up the shadow or emphasize the wires, or take others out. We put a frame around the door so the left side of the composition has more weight to it.

DD

You're thinking like a painter in the medium of photography.

JH

There are ways in which it is really like making a painting. I have one photo called *My Birth* that, needless to say, is named for the famous Frida Kahlo painting. In it, I'm a little clay child that a model-maker is sculpting and I'm holding a tiny boat. My father is below in a kind of nautical shirt and my mother has on a bathing suit. I wanted to play up the boat for those reasons but also to be a little sparkle of white against the dark body, like Tinkerbell in the cartoon.

DD

You're able to dodge?

JH

Yes, we can dodge in the Photoshop stage. And later, after I've converted the digital file into an LVT negative—which is where it reenters the world of photography—then as that negative is printed and becomes a silver gelatin print, it can be dodged and affected greatly at that point also. The person doing the printing is very important; the printer is a magician.

DD

I wondered about the photos' diminutive size. Talk to me about that.

JH

I came up with that size intuitively. I wanted the photographs to have a very factual feel. Big photography feels more made up to me. I wanted the feeling I get from small black-and-white photography. Almost reportage.

DD

That sounds right. Their size implies a certain history and pedigree, too, that's intimate and poetic. The window you look through opens to another world.

JH

At this scale it feels a little more secret and a little more past. Remembered. Not as now.

DD

The photographs' size and seemingly seamless scenarios ally you with Surrealist photography. Not a bad precedent. And your gut is right: their size jibes perfectly with your intention.

JH

And the color issue is interesting. I make so many things with a lot of color, but I just really wanted the photographs to be black and white, even when some of the elements are color photographs.

DD

Speaking about size and color, how do these variables play out in another body of work—the "butterfly maps"—which are considerably larger and more colorful?

JH

The first butterfly map, which was *All Souls (Tabuk)*—the one centered on Iraq—came to me in a dream. There wasn't really any organic process that led up to it, as with the photos. It just came into my mind full blown. When I analyzed it, whether I wanted to do it or not and what it was about, what it meant—the scale and the color were right there front and center. I wanted it to feel like an old map with living butterflies on it. So the scale flowed from the natural size of the butterflies. Their color needed to be vibrant and as true as possible and the map needed to be old, roughed up and stained.

DD

The map's political content is hard to miss, at odds with a butterfly's beauty and vulnerability.

JH

Yes, I think the pieces contrast the brevity of the butterfly's life span with the duration of these ancient cities. You'll notice the maps deemphasize nationhood and emphasize the cities. And they also contrast the beauty and delicacy of the butterflies with the frisson of political conflict, or war, or danger.

DD

A sense of place seems to connect the "Butterfly Maps" with your earlier postcard collages. Talk to me about these.

JH

I went to Mexico one summer with a girlfriend and I went out to the drugstore and came back with a pile of Mexican comic books and a ton of postcards. I began cutting up the comics with manicure scissors and collaging the elements into the postcards. I had people swimming in the water, all kinds of things. It was a very chaotic process because Mexico is hot in the summer and we constantly had the ceiling fan on—so all the little pieces were blowing around. In a couple of cases I used the same postcard twice and did two different things to it. My favorites are where I have created two different collages for two copies of the same postcard. It's similar to my "Soapstone" paintings, where I used the same room for several paintings.

DD

Variations on the card. I like the manicure scissors, and the collage process relates to what you've continued to do. Also, postcards are not only found objects; they're photo-based to boot.

JH

Yes, they are quite photographic. I hadn't thought of that before, but you are right. They are also about the same size as snapshots.

DD

Some of the Mexican postcards are funny. How does humor play out in the work? Is it one aspect of a complex personality?

JH

I suppose, yes, but it's not always there. The leaf piece I've recently made about the war in Iraq has not a scintilla of humor in it. Nor do the butterfly maps. I'm sure you would agree.
But I have definitely made things that I think are funny and I've made them because they're funny. I've also made things I thought were funny but viewers take to be scary or angry. And the opposite is true, too.

DD

There's sometimes a vast divide between internalized humor and humor that bleeds into an image. Humor is a great way to deflect something that's troubling. Humor deflates seriousness and can be used to great advantage that way.

JH

In general, I would say that humor is held in low esteem in our culture. I've always felt that if someone told me that my work was funny it was a little dismissive. When you first start out, especially as a woman artist, you want to be taken "seriously," not "funnily." As I get older, I'm less inclined to worry about what someone else's canon is. I think that humor is an incredibly important, elemental human thing, which is also one whisker away from danger, anger, repression, you know?

DD

I wonder, too, if humor is age-determined. Leon [Golub] had a remarkable sense of humor, very existential, his own kind of gallows humor, and the soft underbelly to a lot of what he did. Even the most serious "Mercenary" paintings have humorous undertones.

JH

Recently I've learned that cartoons in the New Yorker are often drawn and written by two different people. So the humor isn't just coming from one person's "sense of humor" being perfectly expressed, but from the imperfect alignment of two differing sensibilities. That friction is part of their collaboration.

DD

Sounds like an absurd encounter between two predisposed minds.

JH

Yes, if you think of it that way, it is basically tension. Then it is a classic Shakespearean idea of what makes a great work of art. So then I can relax about it, if I go that route.

DD

Humor offers relief; look at stand-up comedy. The audience relaxes in the process because they're in on the joke; it makes them feel good.

JH

And because the comedian is bearing their anger for them. The comedian is basically saying to the audience, "Here, I'll take your anger and hold it for an hour."

DD

There are many analogs to the way you think. You mentioned cooking, surely an art of mixing and recombining.

JH

Yes, cooking is an interest of mine. And although I think of it as a hobby, there are things that I have learned about art making from cooking. I remember an interview Julia Child gave years ago. She described having dinner at a French woman's house in the country. The main course was lamb, and Julia described the woman pouring some of the juices from the roasting pan into the salad dressing. Her explanation was that although a meal should have variety and contrast, it should also be possessed of a certain subliminal continuity.

DD

I was thinking about your musical analogy, hip-hop and sampling. And of course there's jazz, an art of brilliant improvisation. You're well attuned to working this way.

JH

I'm a mixer, not just in terms of images but also in terms of methodologies. I use the found and the felt, the improvisational and the strategic. One of the things I admire most about John Ashbery's work is the seamless way in which he fuses overheard, almost lapidary, pieces of language with his own personal feelings—whether silly, melancholic, self-mocking—whatever, with larger supra-personal ideas. It's a bricolage of all those things and the reader barely knows where one ends and the other begins. The constant switching and layering of voice is both playful and a profound statement on the complexity of all of our inner lives. And our outer lives, too, for that matter.

DD

I'd be hard pressed to summarize all that we've talked about. That said, a few things do stand out: that the work in general abounds with visual information, the product of your creative curiosity at any given moment; and that each painting and work on paper, once conceived, becomes polysemous, something else, above and beyond who you are.

JH

You know, in general, I am always more engaged in extending than summarizing. Your point about works becoming something "above and beyond" is the heart of the matter. When things go well, there is more there than I even know, maybe than I will ever know. That will be the interesting part for me.

CATALOGUE

PREMONITION, 1990

1 Gouache, graphite, and rubber stamps on rice paper, $24\frac{1}{4}$ x $38\frac{3}{4}$ inches

Collection of the artist

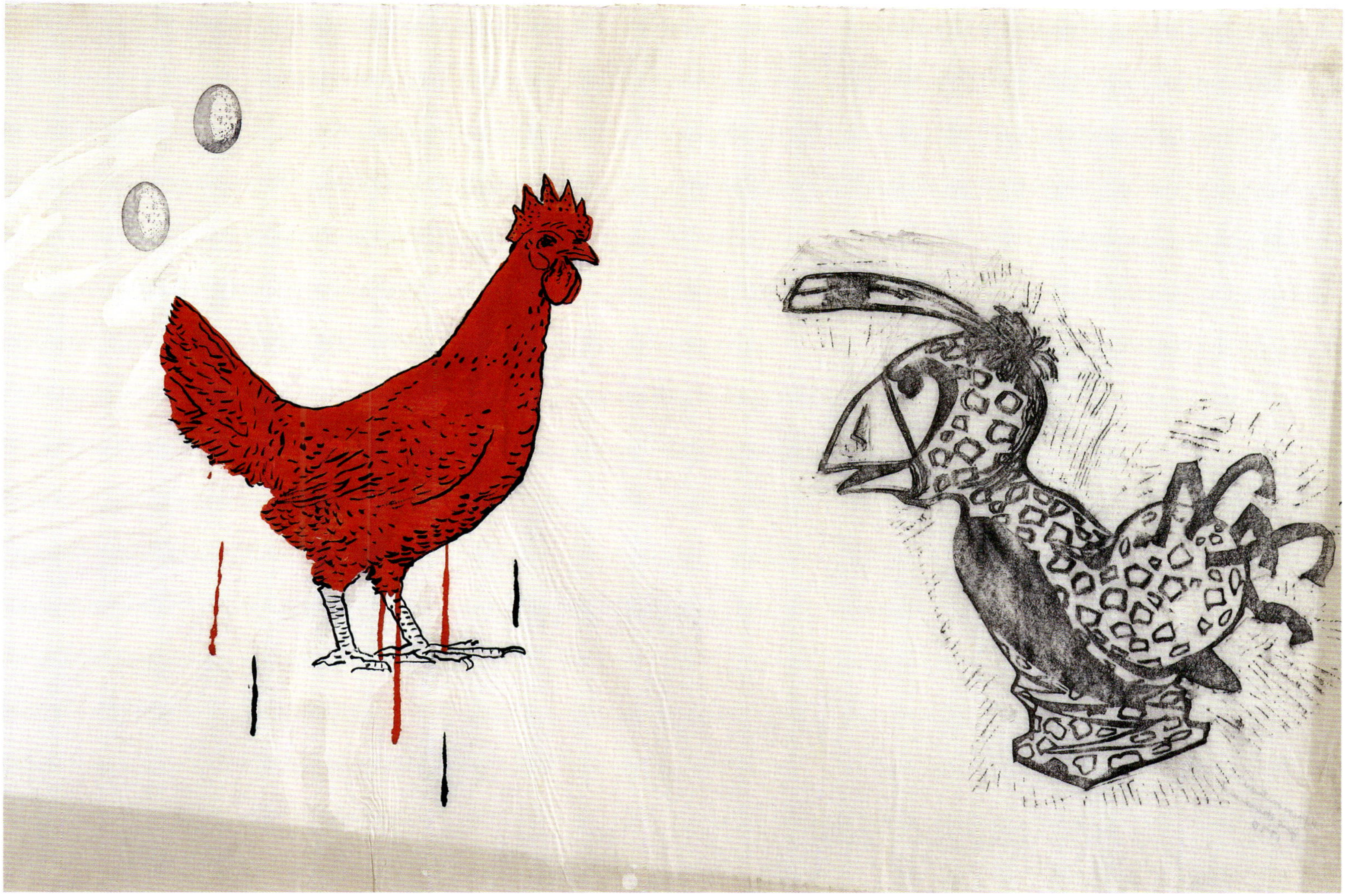

AFFINITY, 1991

2 Acrylic, tempera, gouache, graphite, and rubber stamp on rice paper, $24^1/2$ x $38^1/4$ inches

Collection of the artist

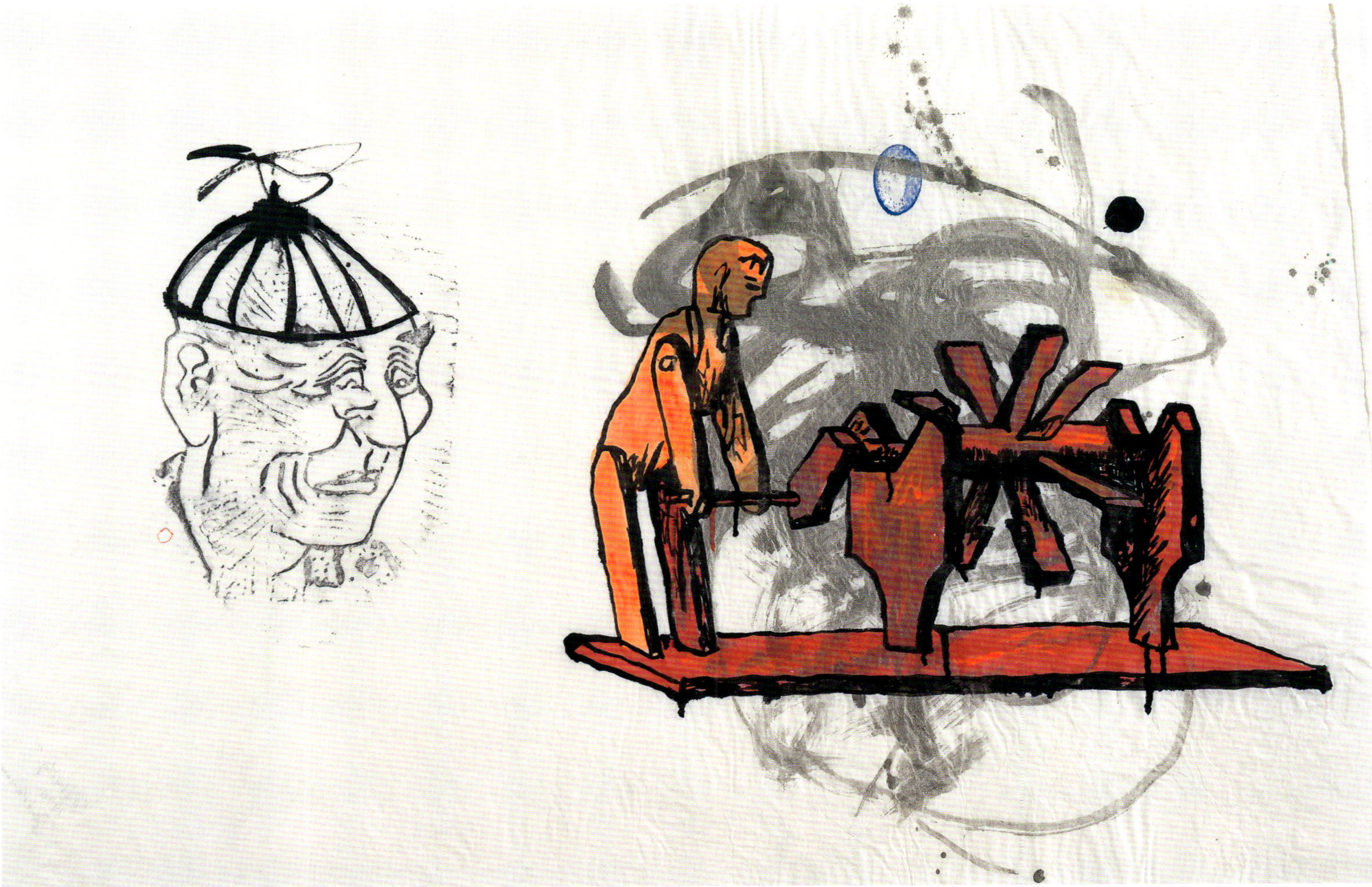

ELECTRIC KACHINA, 1997

3 Acrylic, gouache, graphite, pastel, solvent transfers, color Xerox, and linoleum block prints on collaged Japanese papers, $34^{1}/_{2}$ x 31 inches

Private collection, New York

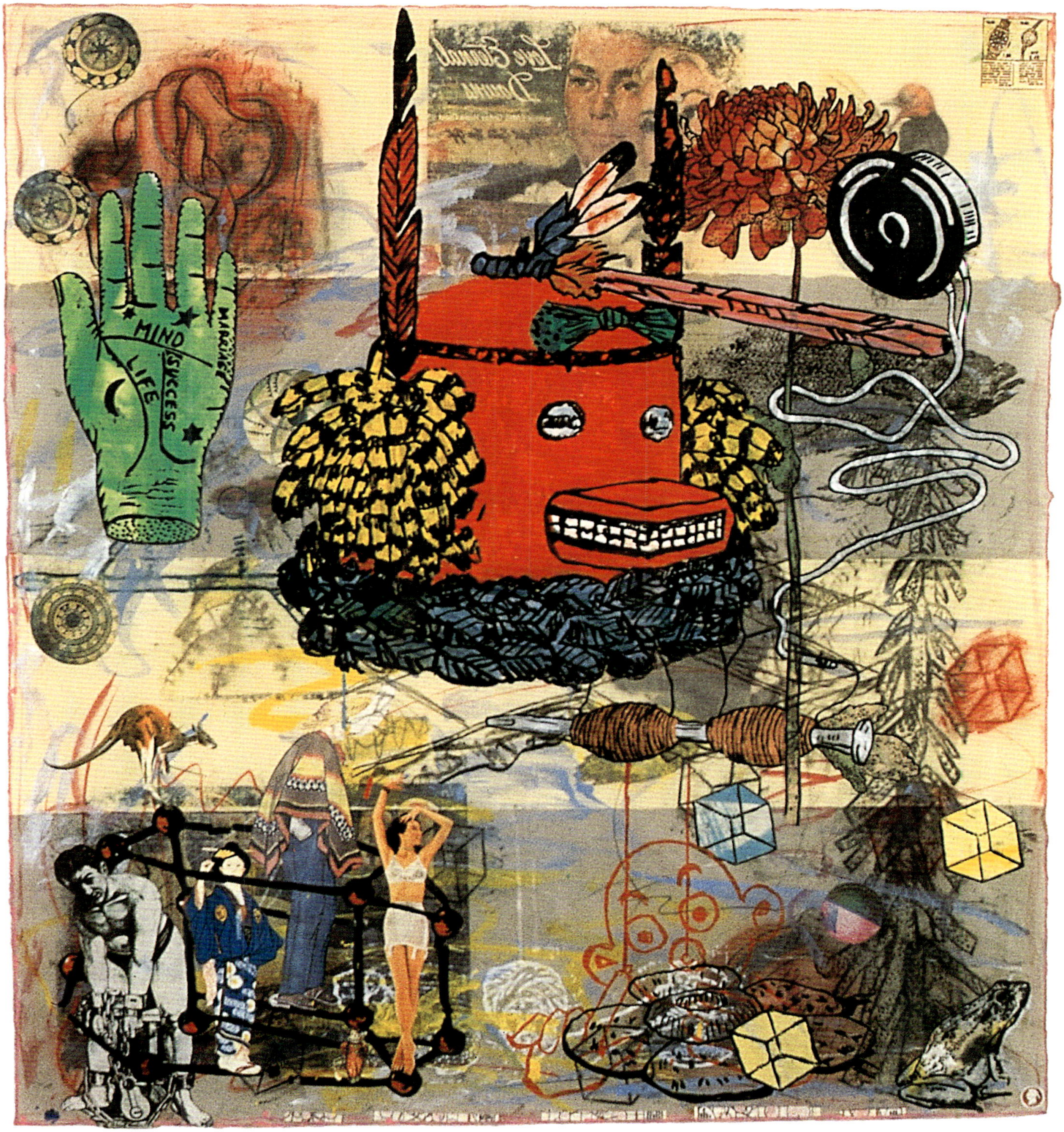
MIND
LIFE
SUCCESS

ELECTRIC DOLLHOUSE, 1998

4 Acrylic, gouache, graphite, crayon, solvent transfers, color Xerox, linoleum block prints, and Van Dyke prints on collaged Japanese papers, 36 x 31 inches

Collection of Paul and Mary Delle Stelzer, New York

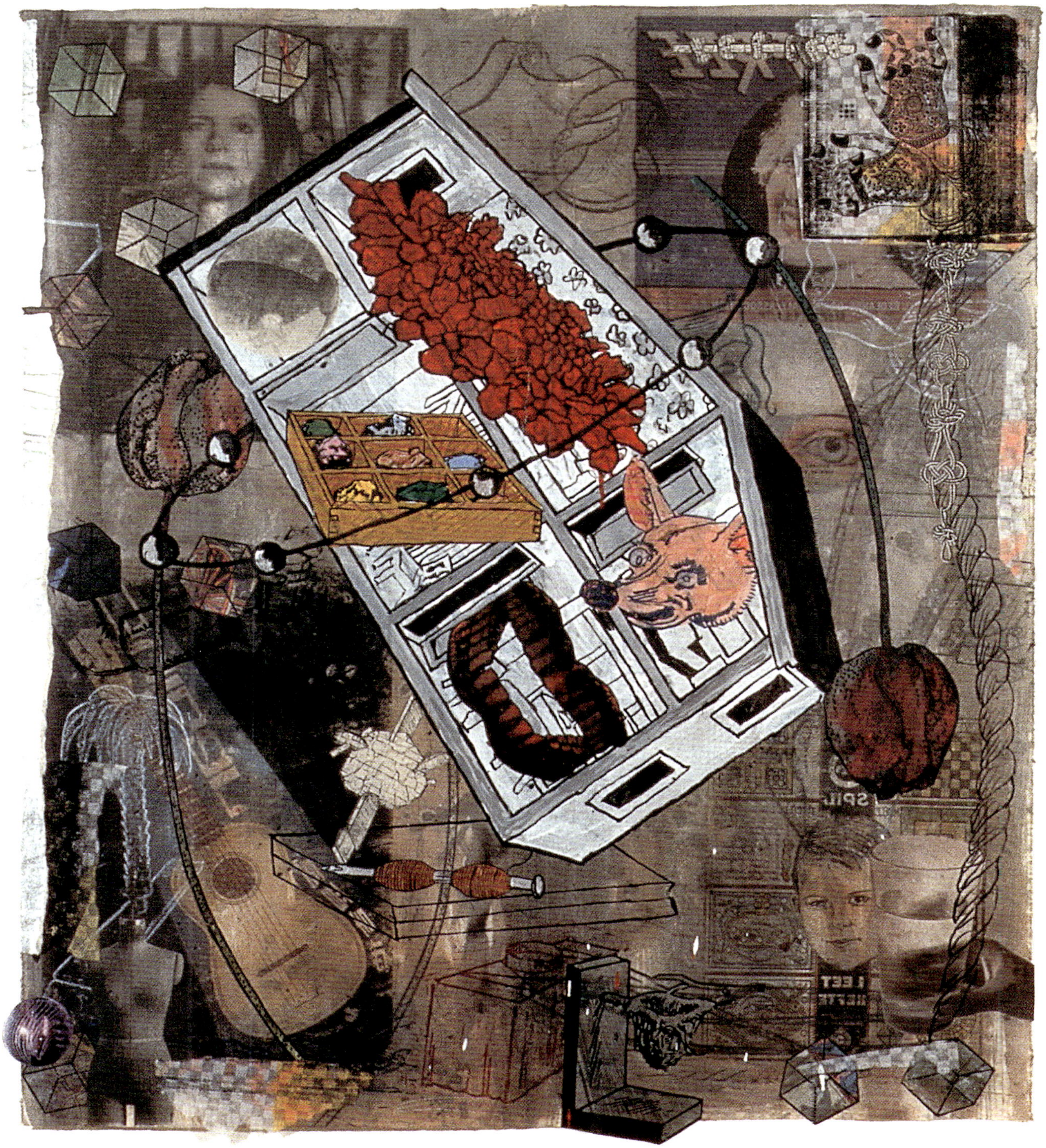

PAST TIME, 1998

5 Acrylic, gouache, graphite, crayon, solvent transfers, color Xerox, linoleum block prints, and relief print on collaged Japanese papers, 35 x 30 inches

Private collection, Winnetka, Illinois

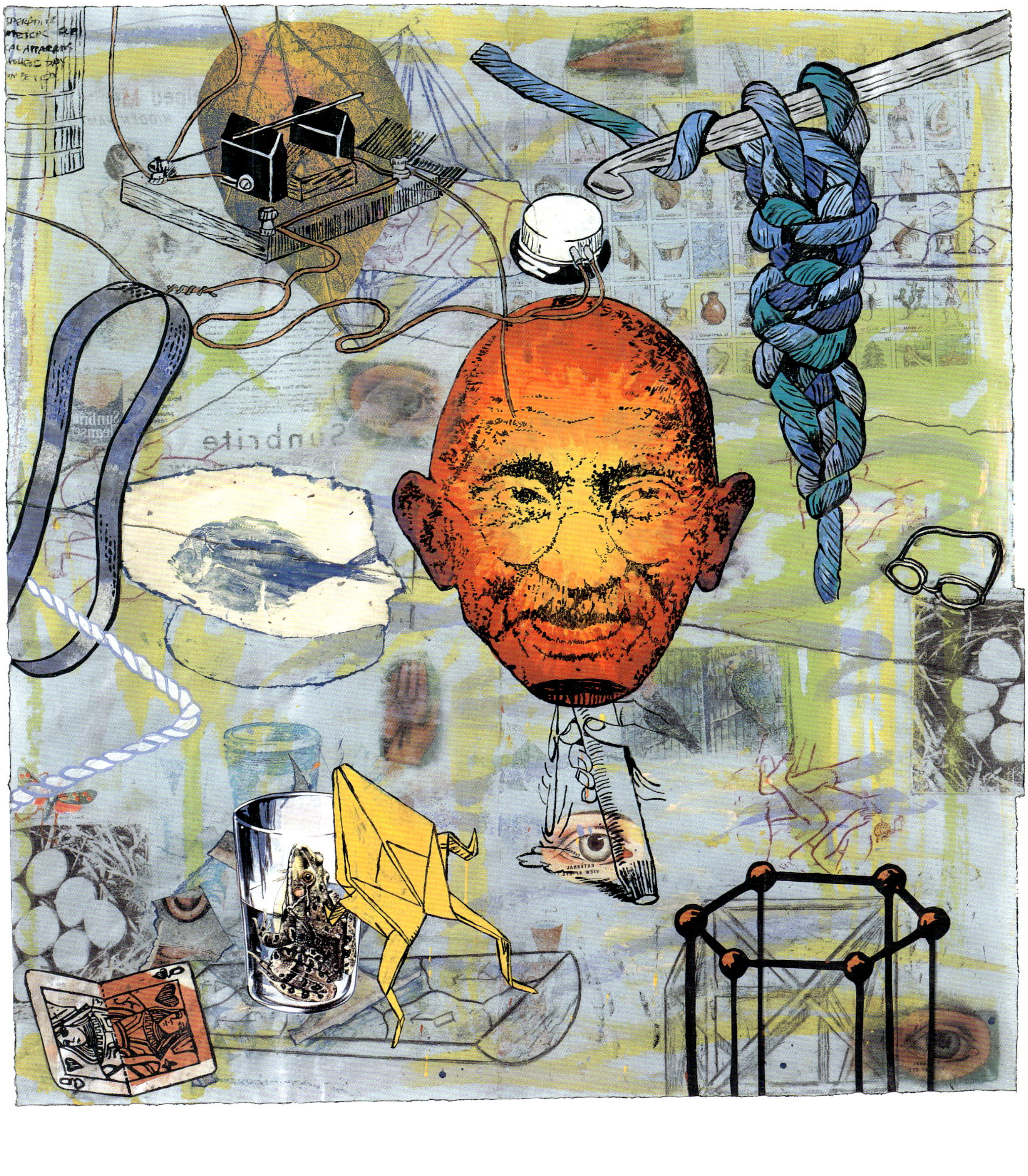

DOG DANCE, 1998

6 Acrylic, gouache, graphite, crayon, solvent transfers, color Xerox, linoleum block prints, and rubber stamps on collaged Japanese papers, 38 x 30 1/2 inches

Private collection, New York

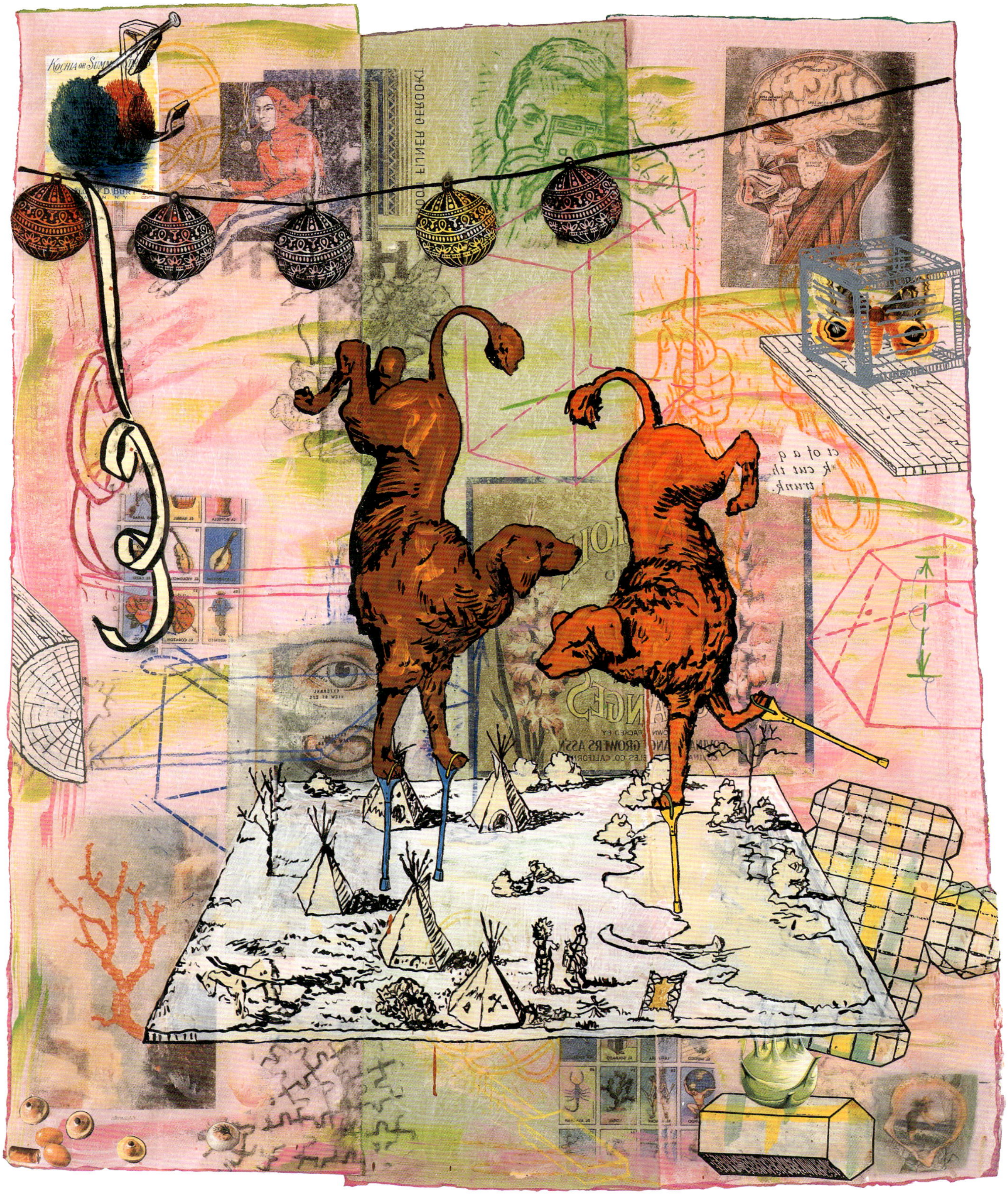

STILL LIFE WITH SEAL, 1999

7 Acrylic, gouache, graphite, crayon, solvent transfers, color Xerox, linoleum block prints, and rubber stamps on collaged Japanese papers, $35^{1}/_{2}$ x $29^{1}/_{2}$ inches

Collection of Beth Rudin DeWoody, New York

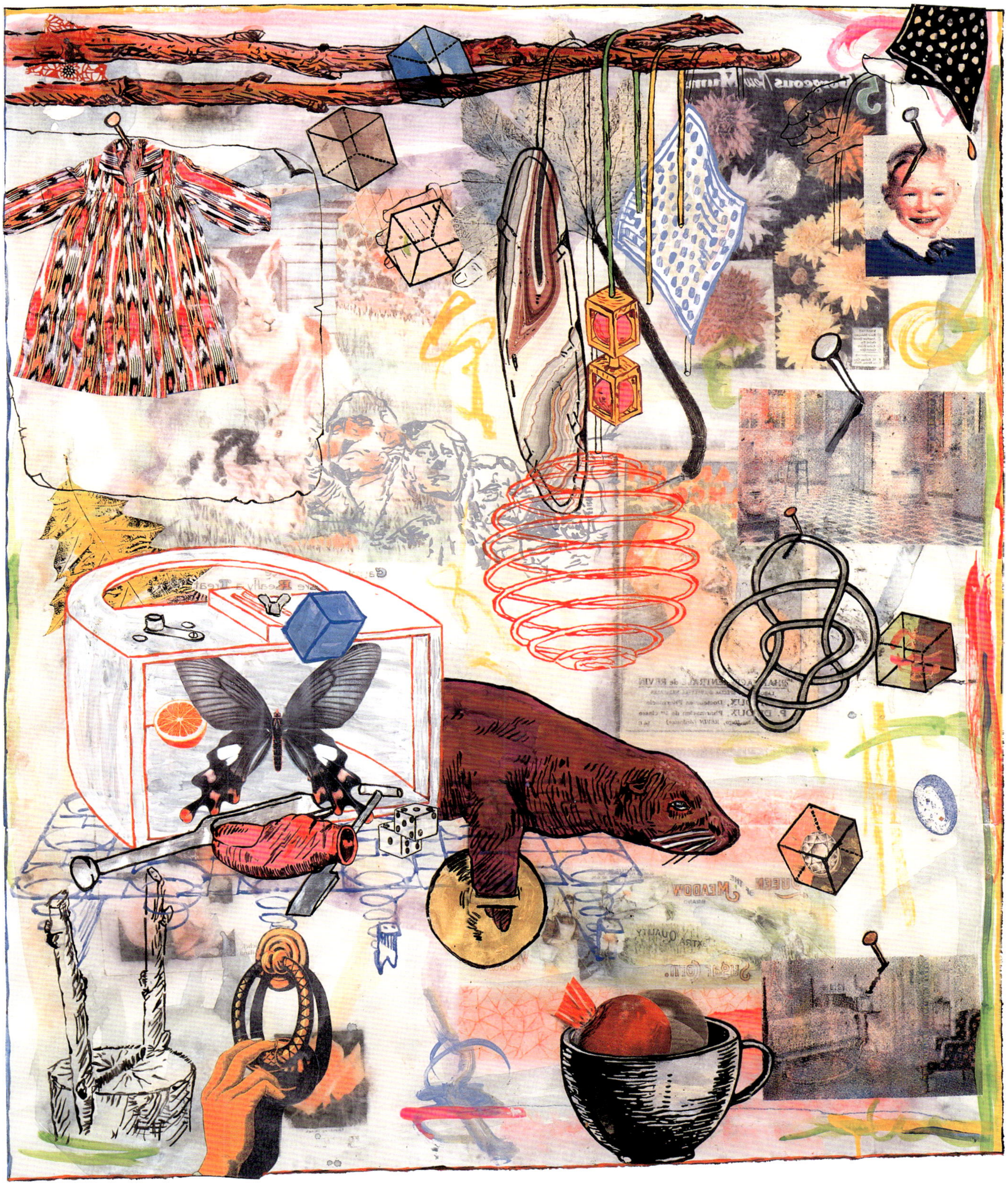

MARTIN HOUSE ME, 1999

8 Acrylic, gouache, graphite, crayon, solvent transfers, color Xerox, linoleum block prints, lithographs, and leaf prints on collaged Japanese papers, 38 x 30 1/4 inches

Collection of Betsy and Frank Babb, Tucson, Arizona

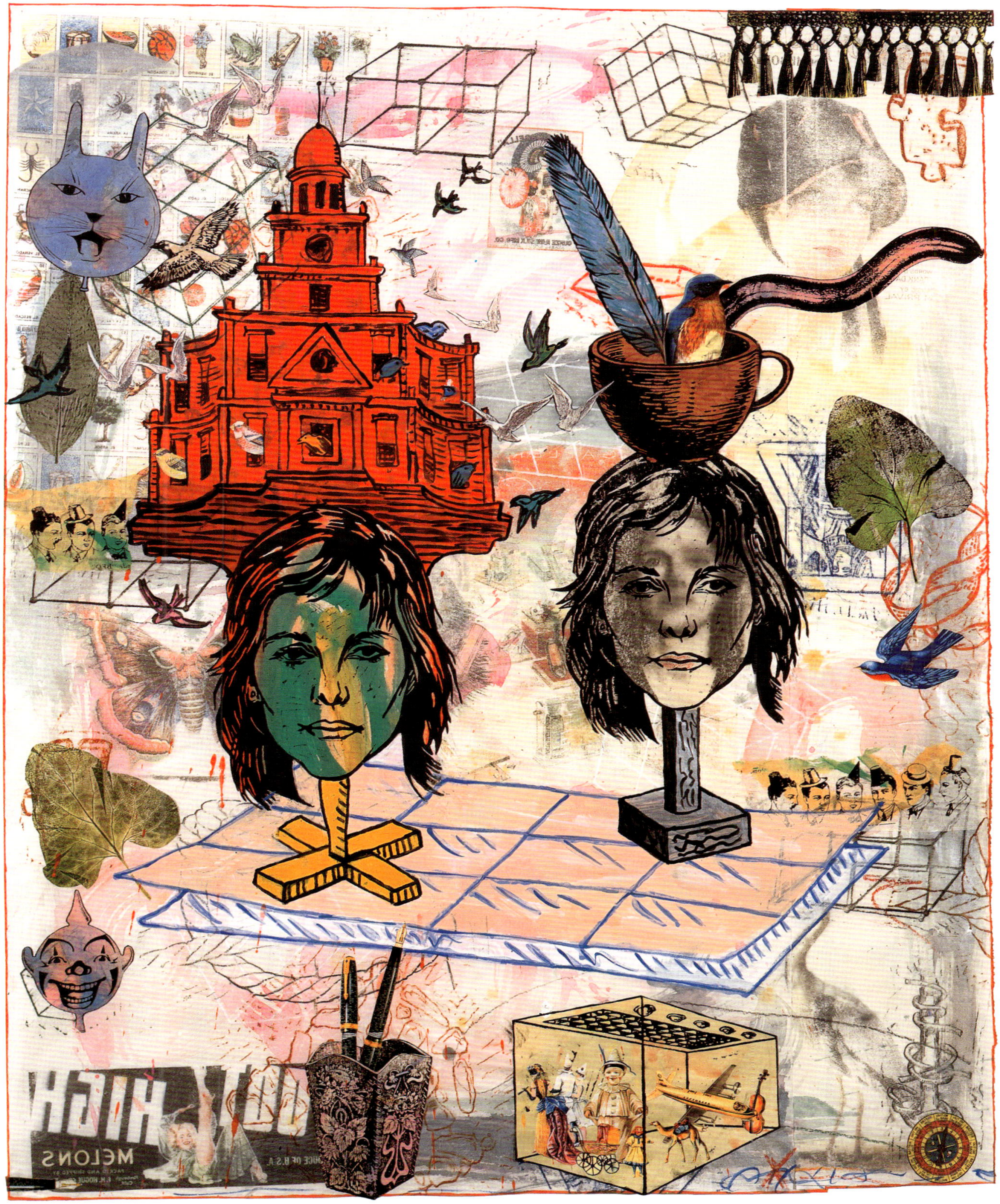

THE CRUSH OF CIRCUMSTANCE, 1999

9 Acrylic, gouache, graphite, crayon, solvent transfers, color Xerox, linoleum block prints, lithographs, and rubber stamps on collaged Japanese papers, 37 x 32 inches

Collection of Byron and Eileen Cohen, Kansas City, Missouri

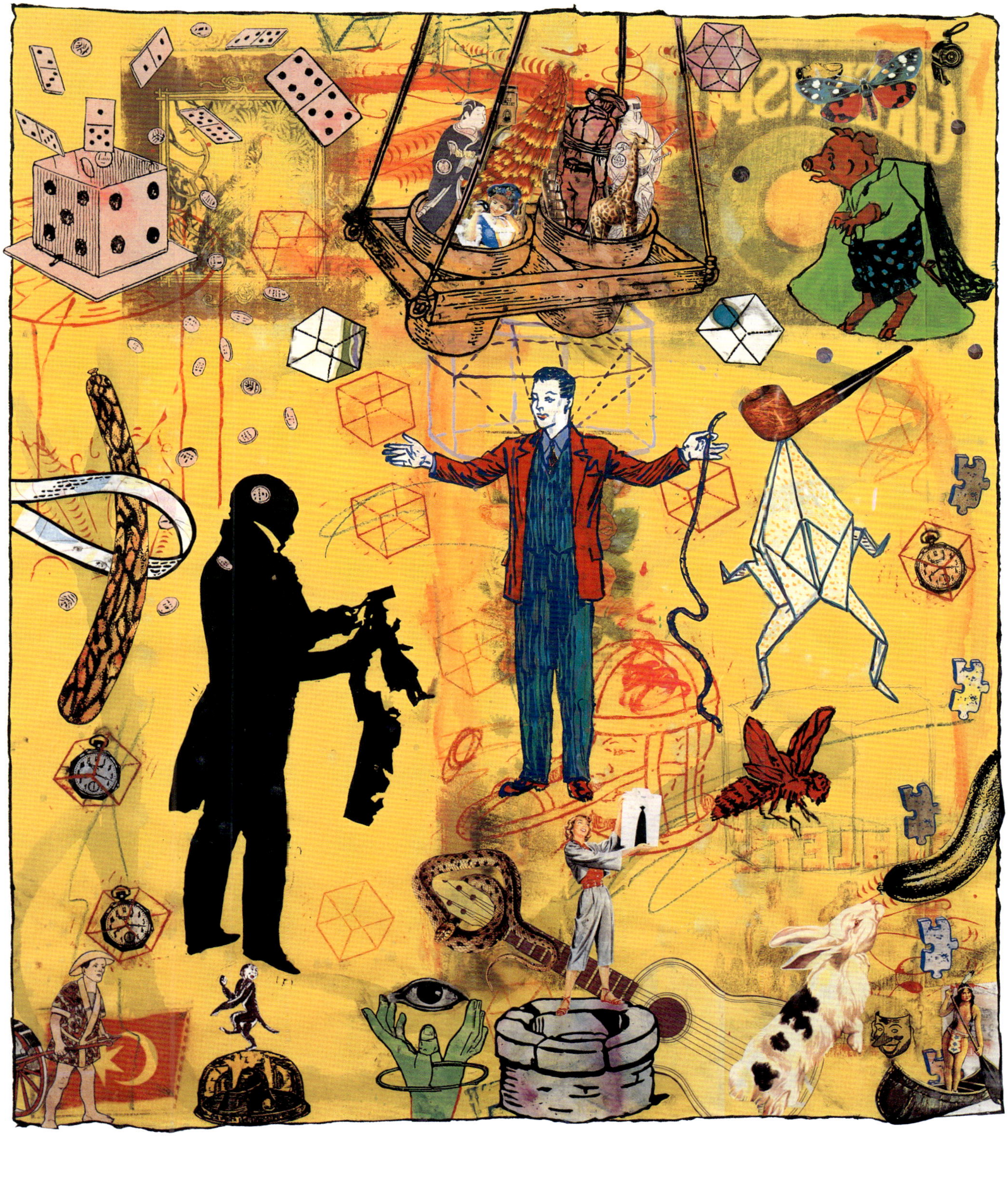

10 THE CRUSH OF CIRCUMSTANCE #2, 1999

Acrylic, gouache, graphite, crayon, solvent transfers, color Xerox, linoleum block prints, lithographs, and rubber stamps on collaged Japanese papers, 38 x 32 inches

Private collection, Barcelona

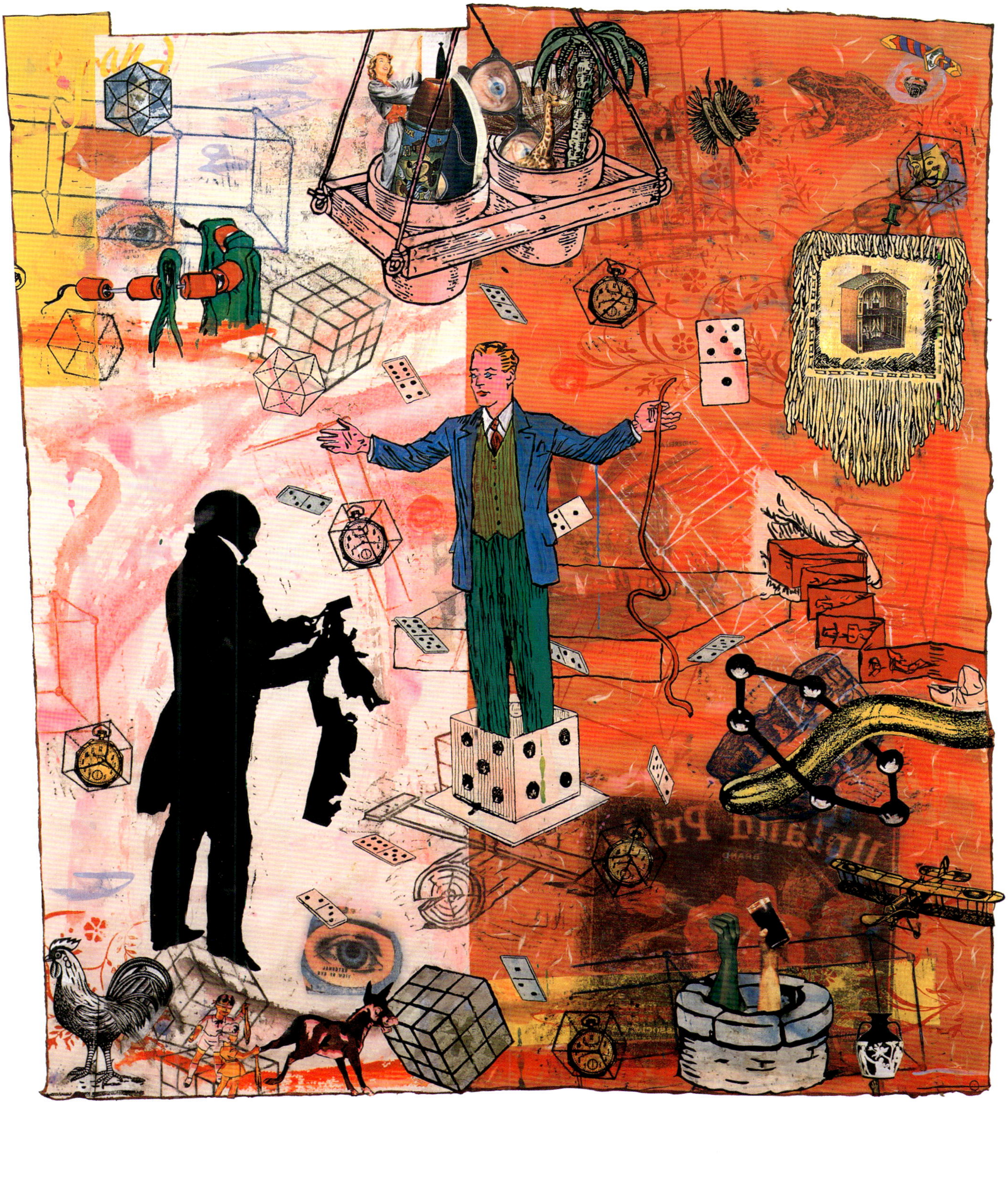

BLACK BIRD DRAWING, 2002

11 Acrylic, gouache, graphite, crayon, solvent transfers, color Xerox, and linoleum block prints on collaged Japanese papers, 35 1/4 x 33 inches

Collection of Kimberly and Robert Fischer, Detroit

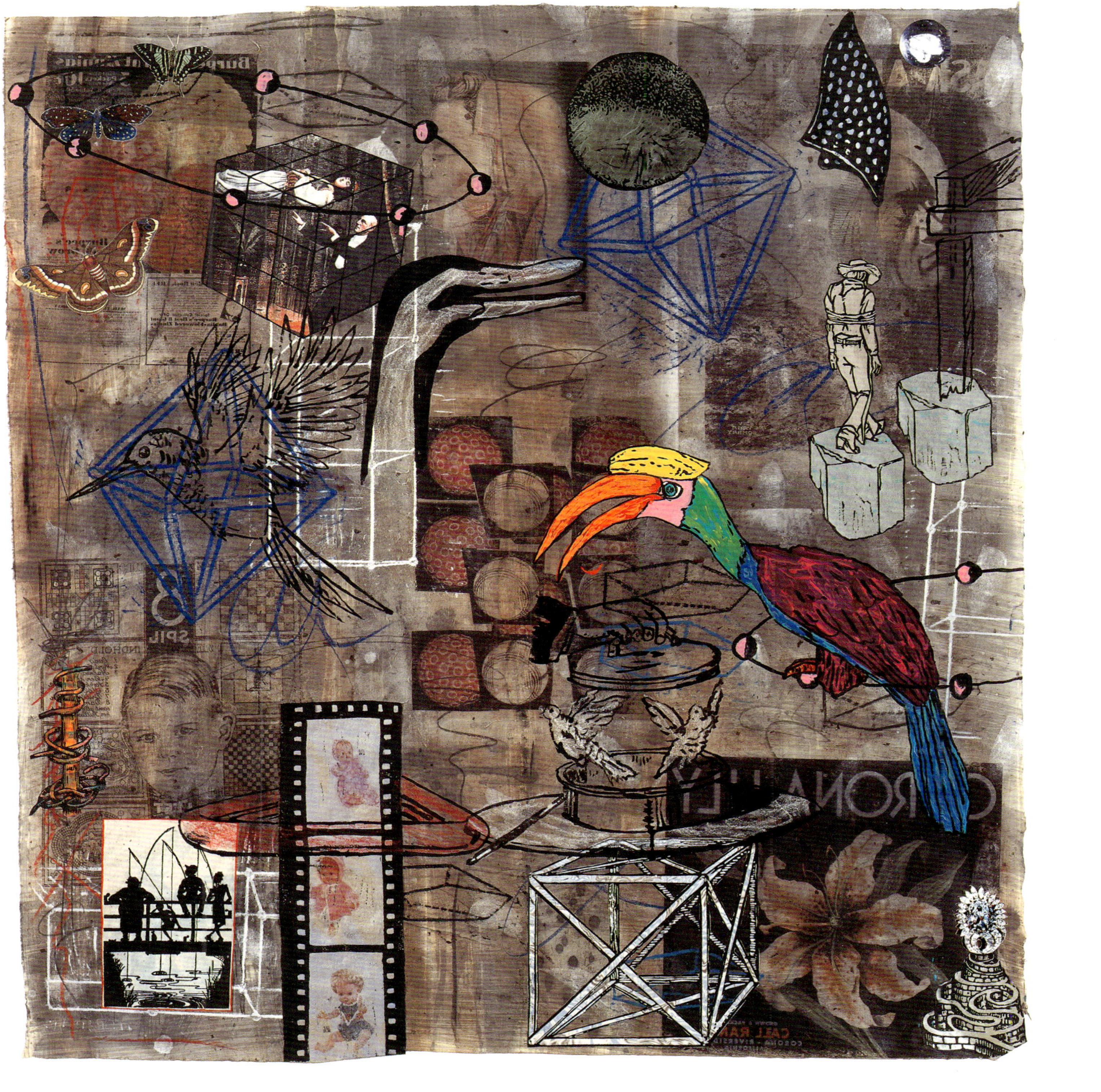

TWELVE WISHES, 2000

12 Acrylic and gouache on antique Chinese notebook pages, 47 x 40 inches

Collection of Sally and Wynn Kramarsky, New York

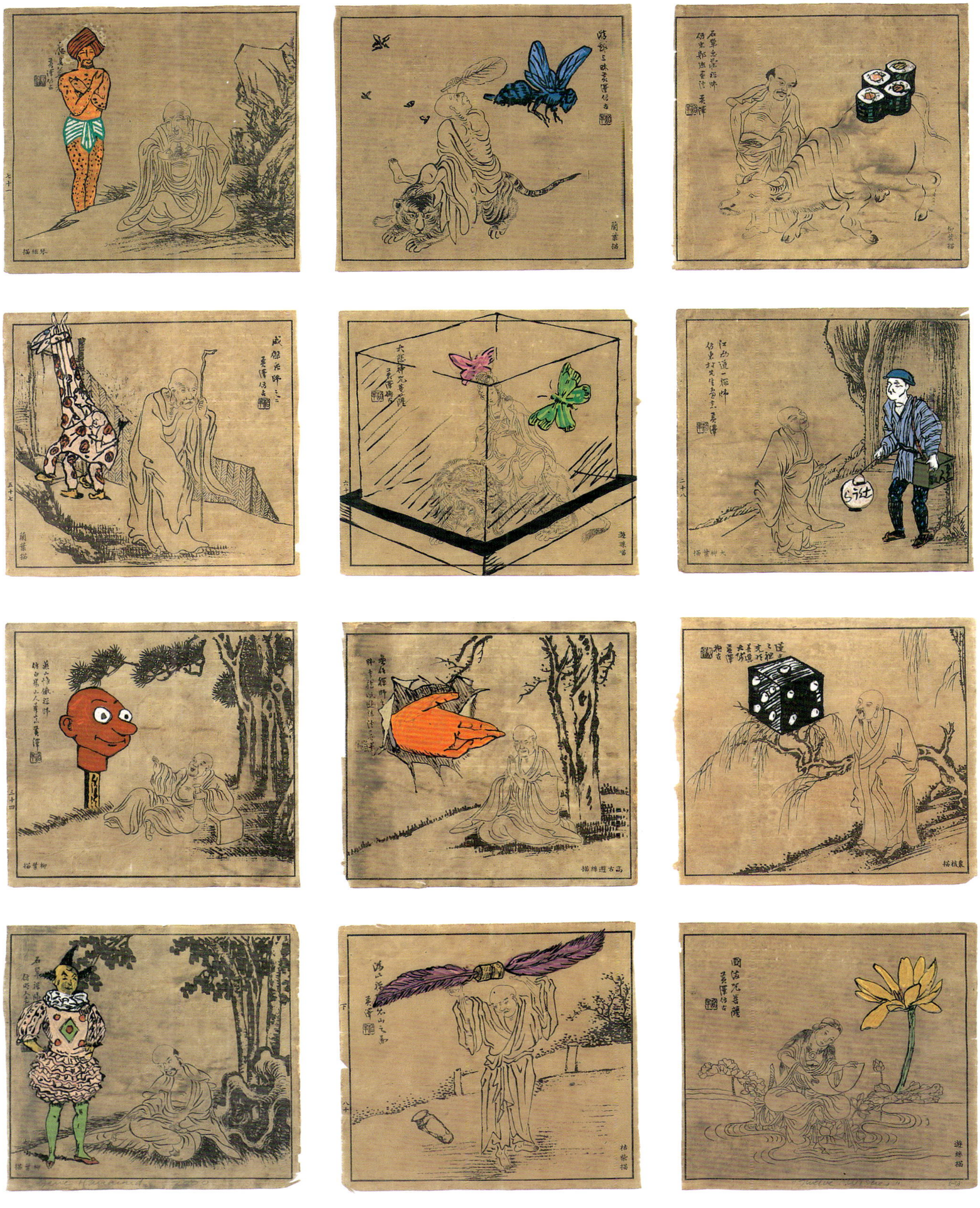

CHALK TALK, 2000

13 Acrylic, chalk, blackboard paint, and gesso on handmade papers, 44 x 78 inches

Collection of Guy and Nora Barron, Bloomfield Hills, Michigan

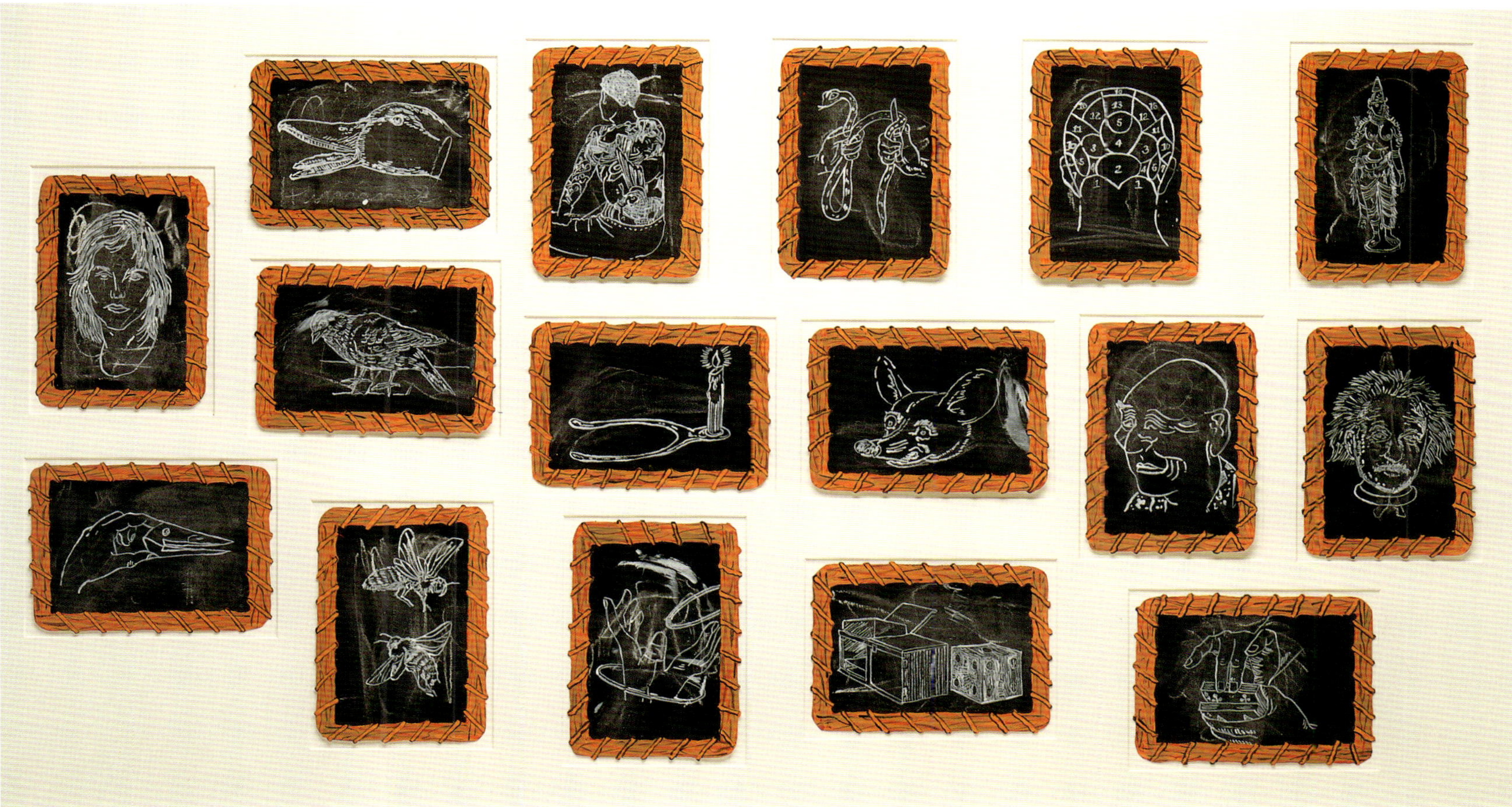

BACKSTAGE: SECRETS OF SCENE PAINTING, 2001

14 Acrylic, gouache, watercolor, rubber stamps, color Xerox, and lithographs on mixed papers, 20 x 30 inches

Collection of Mr. and Mrs. Judson P. Reis, New York

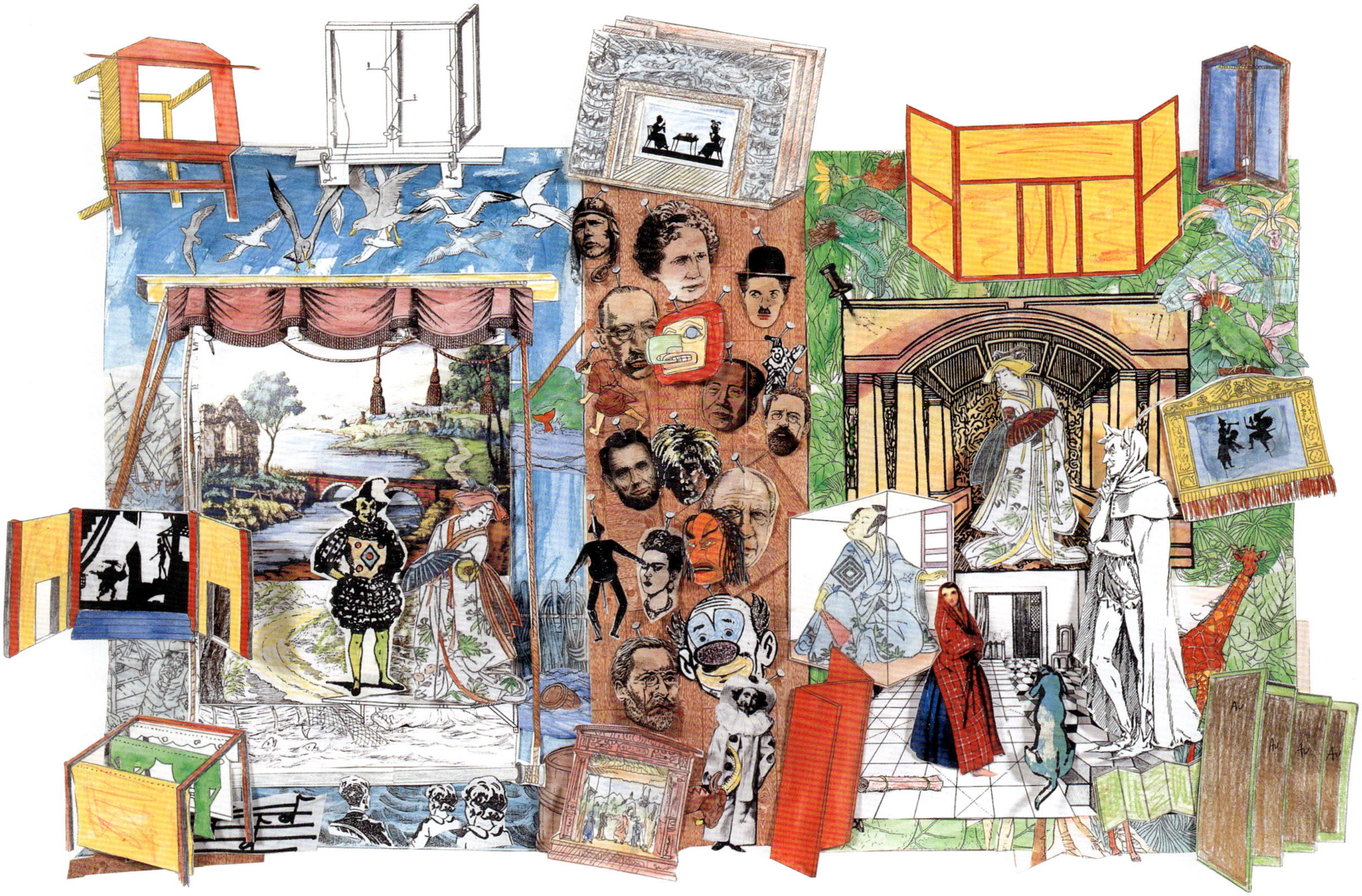

SCRAPBOOK (SHIP IN BOTTLE), 2003

15 Acrylic, gouache, watercolor, lithographs, rubber stamps, color Xerox, and found Mexican valentine on assorted Japanese papers with French marbled paper, archival book board, and bookbinder's thread, 26 x 39 x 2 1/2 inches

Collection of Brooke and Daniel Neidich, New York

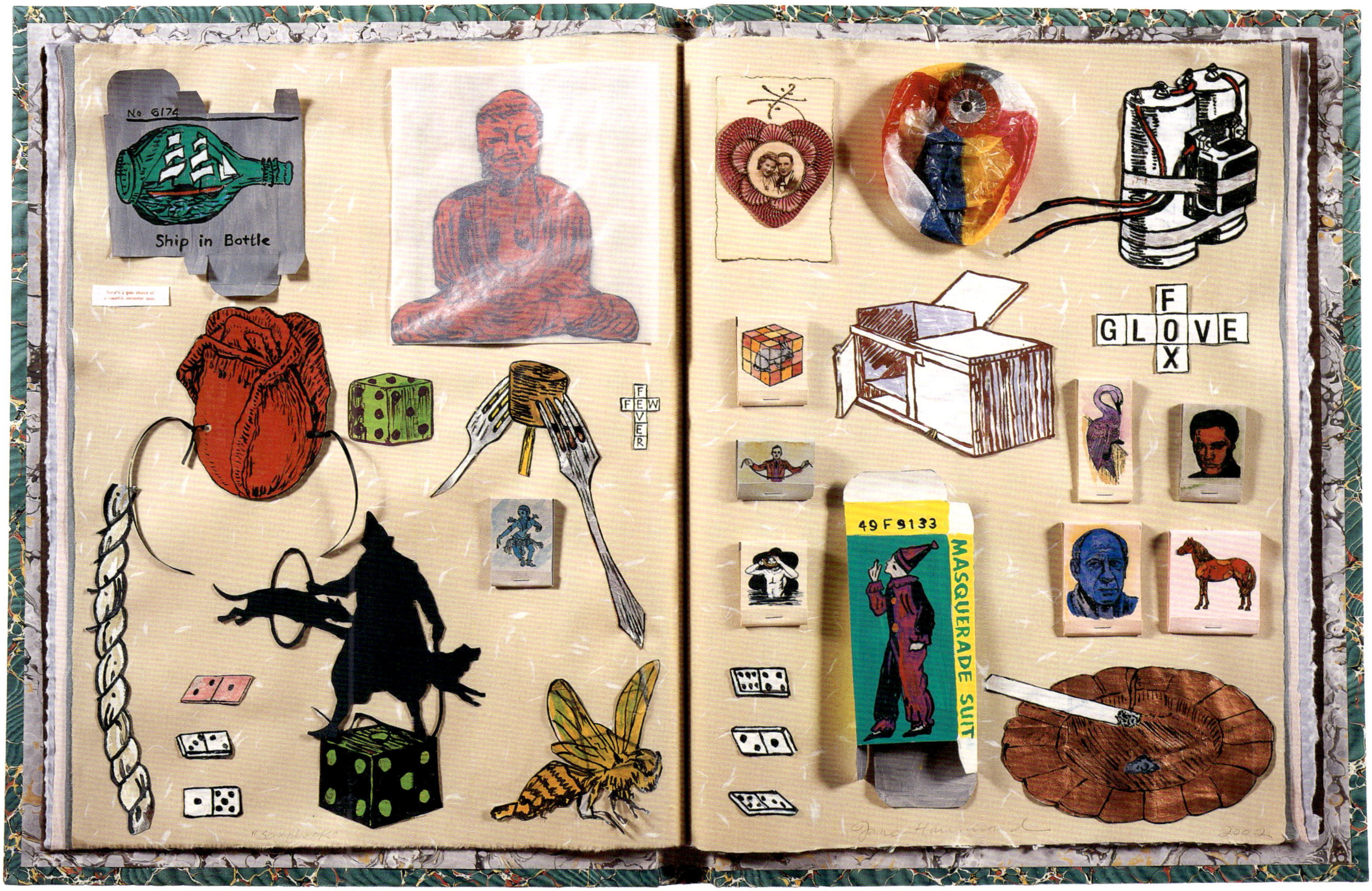
No 6174
Ship in Bottle
FEW
FEVER
GLOVE
FOX
49 F 9133
MASQUERADE SUIT

16 **SCRAPBOOK (*1000* YEN), 2003**

Acrylic, gouache, watercolor, linoleum block prints, rubber stamps, lithographs, digital prints, color Xerox, found plastic toy, glassine, thread, and postage stamps on assorted Japanese papers with French marbled paper, archival book board, and bookbinder's thread, $25^{3}/8$ x $42^{3}/4$ x $2^{1}/2$ inches

Collection of Sunny and Brad Goldberg, Mamaroneck, New York

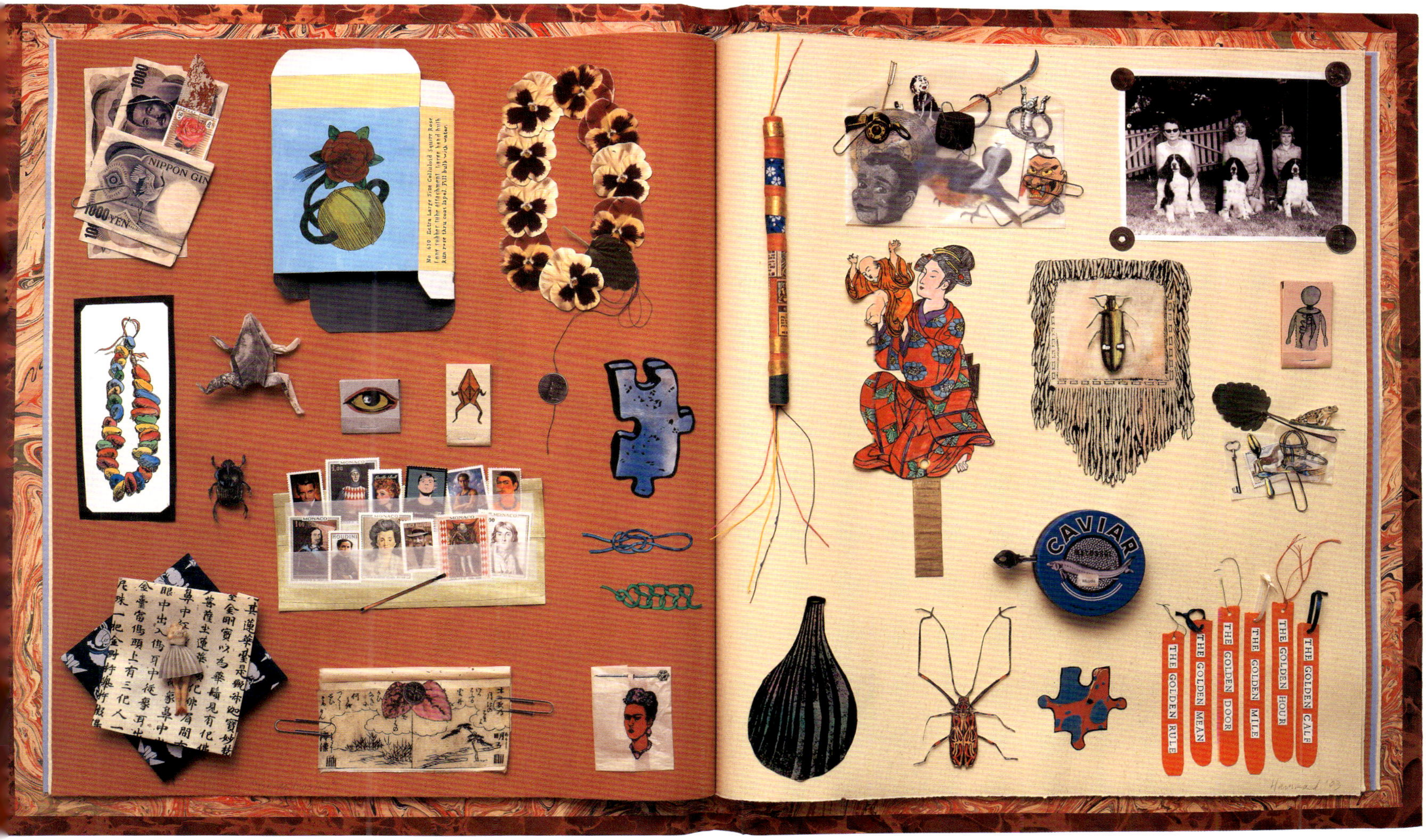
NIPPON GIN
1000 YEN
CAVIAR
THE GOLDEN RULE
THE GOLDEN MEAN
THE GOLDEN DOOR
THE GOLDEN MILE
THE GOLDEN HOUR
THE GOLDEN CALF

17 **CONVERGENCE OF STARS, 2003**

Acrylic, gouache, graphite, and solvent transfers on Japanese paper and heavy rag paper with bamboo pole, 65 x 71 inches

Courtesy of the artist and Galerie Lelong, New York

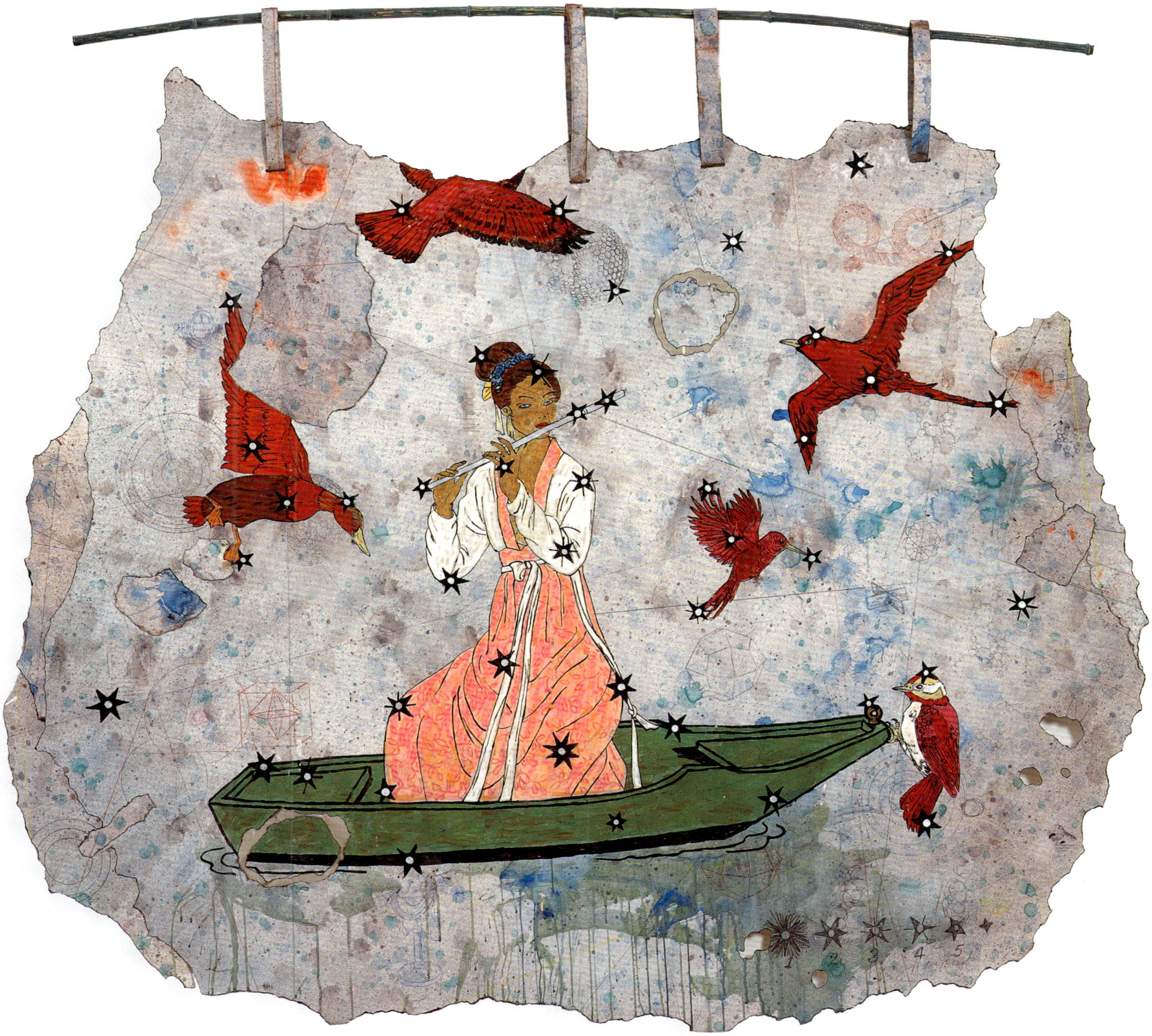

EXTRAVAGANT REFLEX, 2003–4

18 Feathers from feather boas and rubber stamps on assorted papers, 24 1/4 x 44 inches

Courtesy of the artist and Galerie Lelong, New York

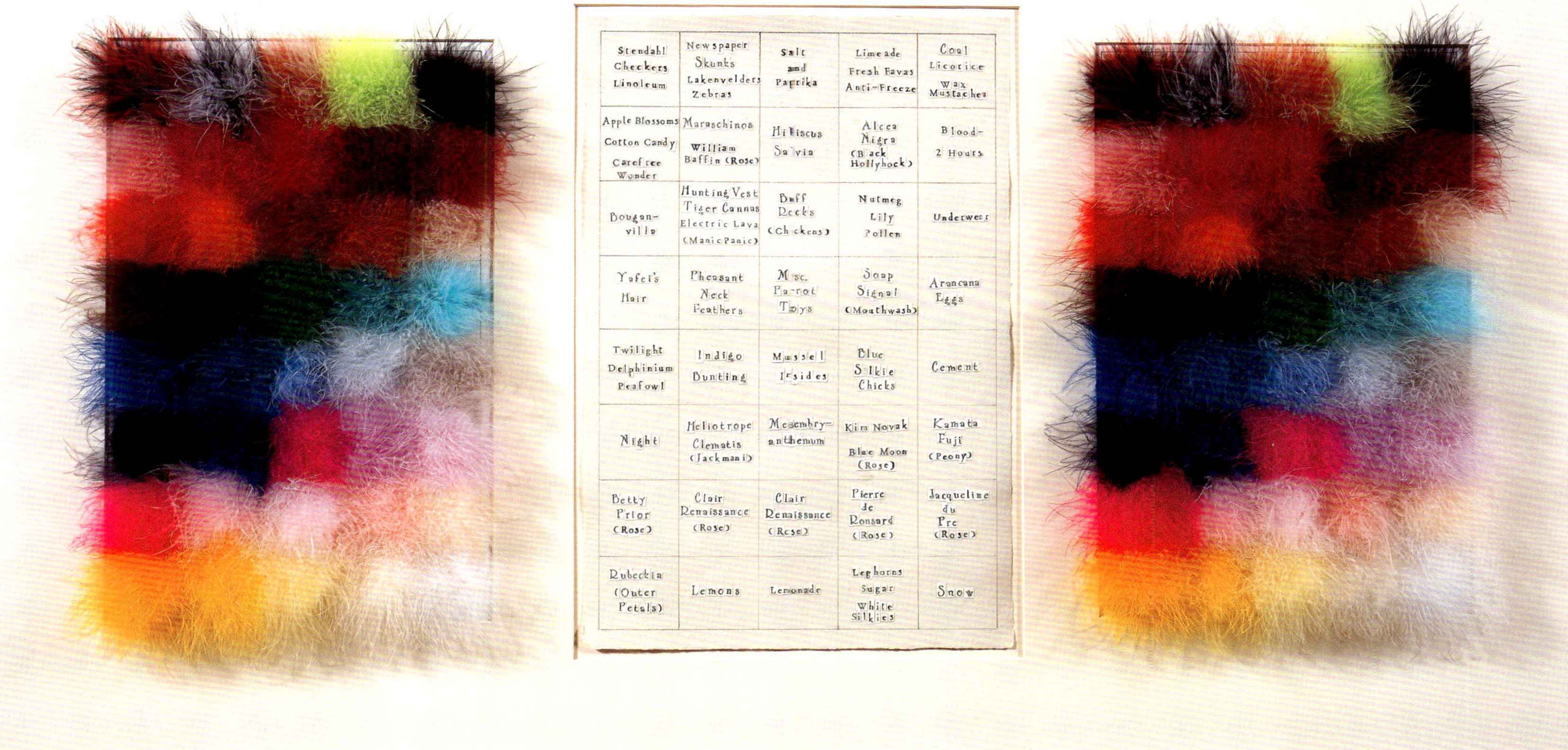
Stendahl Checkers Linoleum
Newspaper Skunks Lakenvelders Zebras
Salt and Paprika
Limeade Fresh Favas Anti-Freeze
Coal Licorice Wax Mustaches
Apple Blossoms Cotton Candy Carefree Wonder
Maraschinos William Baffin (Rose)
Hibiscus Salvia
Alcea Nigra (Black Hollyhock)
Blood- 2 Hours
Bougan- villa
Hunting Vest Tiger Cannas Electric Lava (Manic Panic)
Buff Rocks (Chickens)
Nutmeg Lily Pollen
Underwear
Yafei's Hair
Pheasant Neck Feathers
Misc. Parrot Toys
Soap Signal (Mouthwash)
Arancana Eggs
Twilight Delphinium Peafowl
Indigo Bunting
Mussel Insides
Blue Silkie Chicks
Cement
Night
Heliotrope Clematis (Jackmani)
Mesembry- anthemum
Kim Novak Blue Moon (Rose)
Kamata Fuji (Peony)
Betty Prior (Rose)
Clair Renaissance (Rose)
Clair Renaissance (Rose)
Pierre de Ronsard (Rose)
Jacqueline du Pre (Rose)
Rubeckia (Outer Petals)
Lemons
Lemonade
Leghorns Sugar White Silkies
Snow

FALLEN, 2004–ONGOING

19 Archival digital inkjet prints on archival paper with acrylic, gouache, matte medium, Jade glue, fiberglass strands, and Sumi ink on a pedestal of high-density foam, cotton, muslin, cotton thread, foam core, and handmade cotton rag paper, 11 x 154 x 89 inches

Whitney Museum of American Art, New York

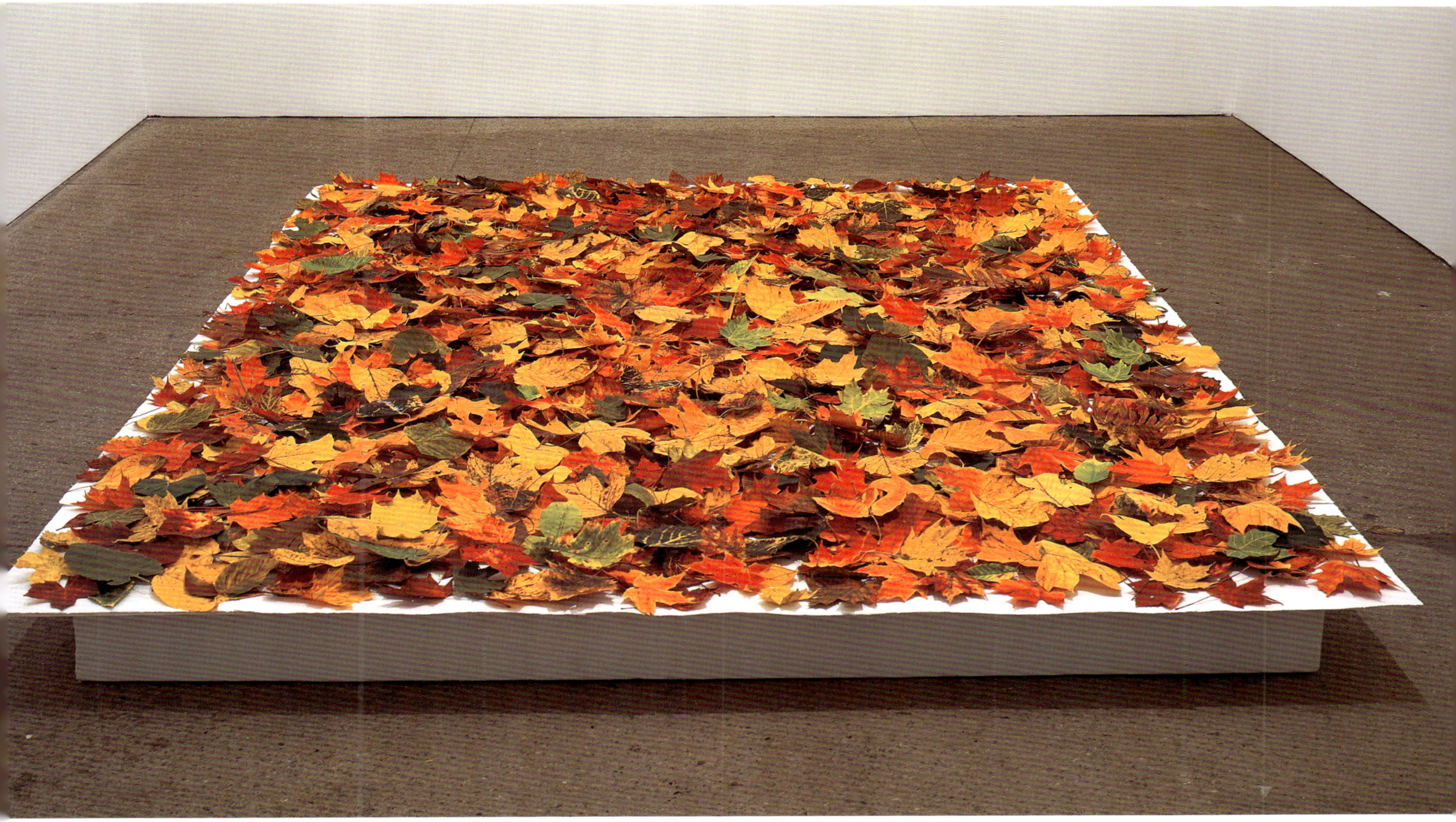

Detail, *Fallen*, 2004–ongoing

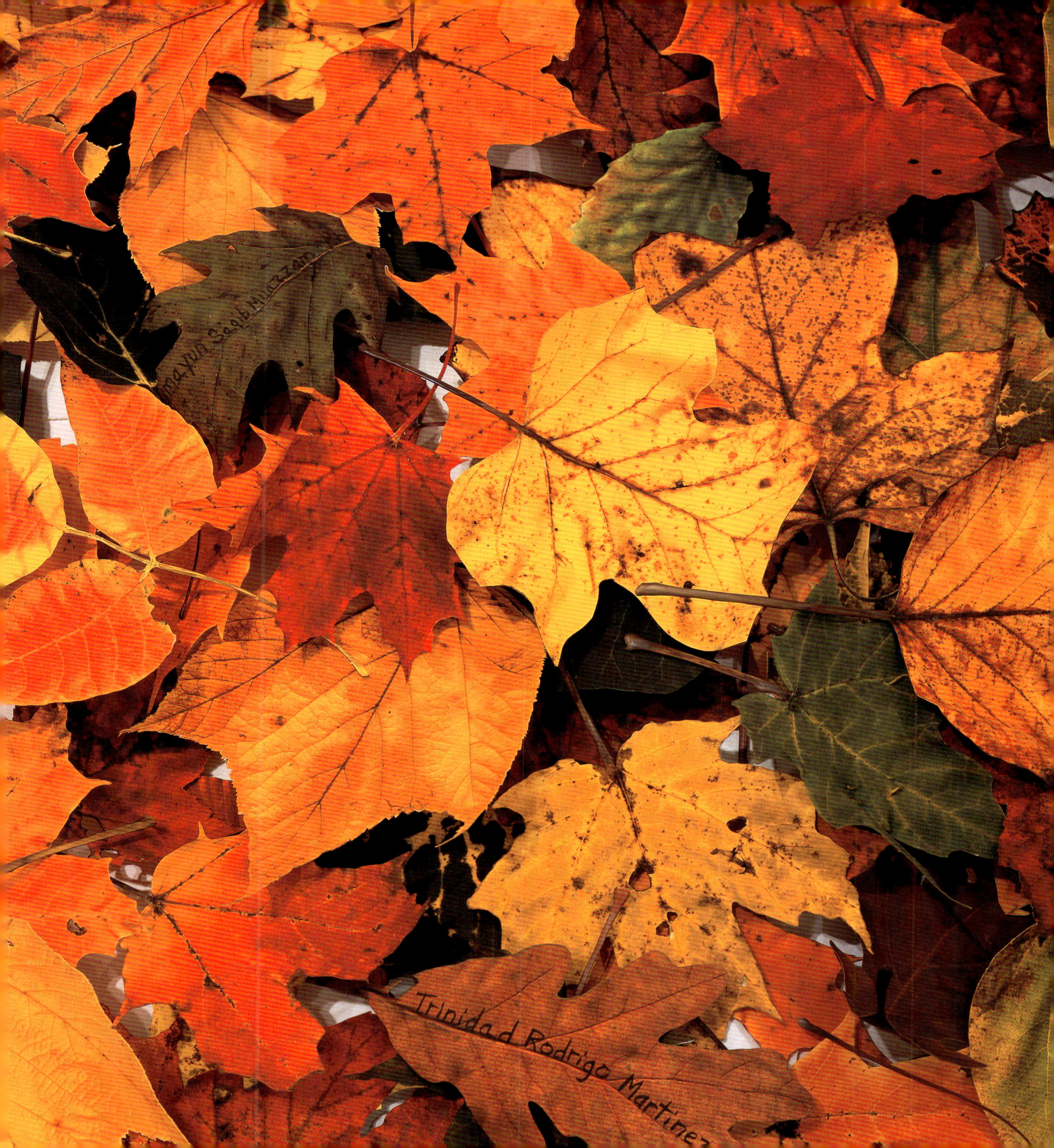
Trinidad Rodrigo Martinez

20 **UNTITLED (BLUE TEEPEE), 2000**

Watercolor and rubber stamps with block printing ink on dyed gampi papers, 20 x 21 inches

Collection of Viretta Brady, New York

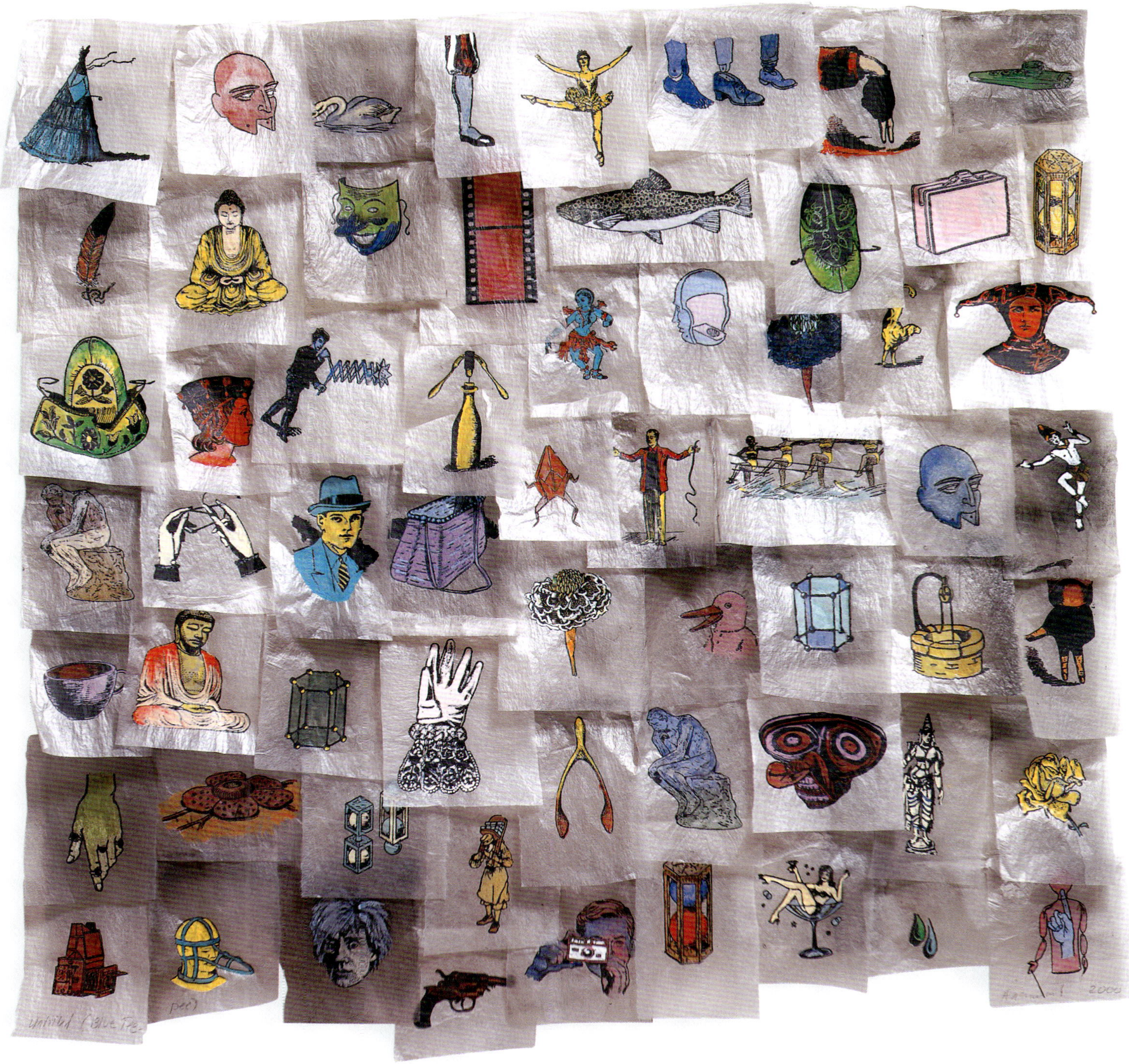

21 **UNTITLED (RED FROG #2), 2000**

Watercolor and rubber stamps with block printing ink on gampi papers, 29 x 32 inches

The Metropolitan Museum of Art, John B. Turner Fund, 2000 (2000.658)

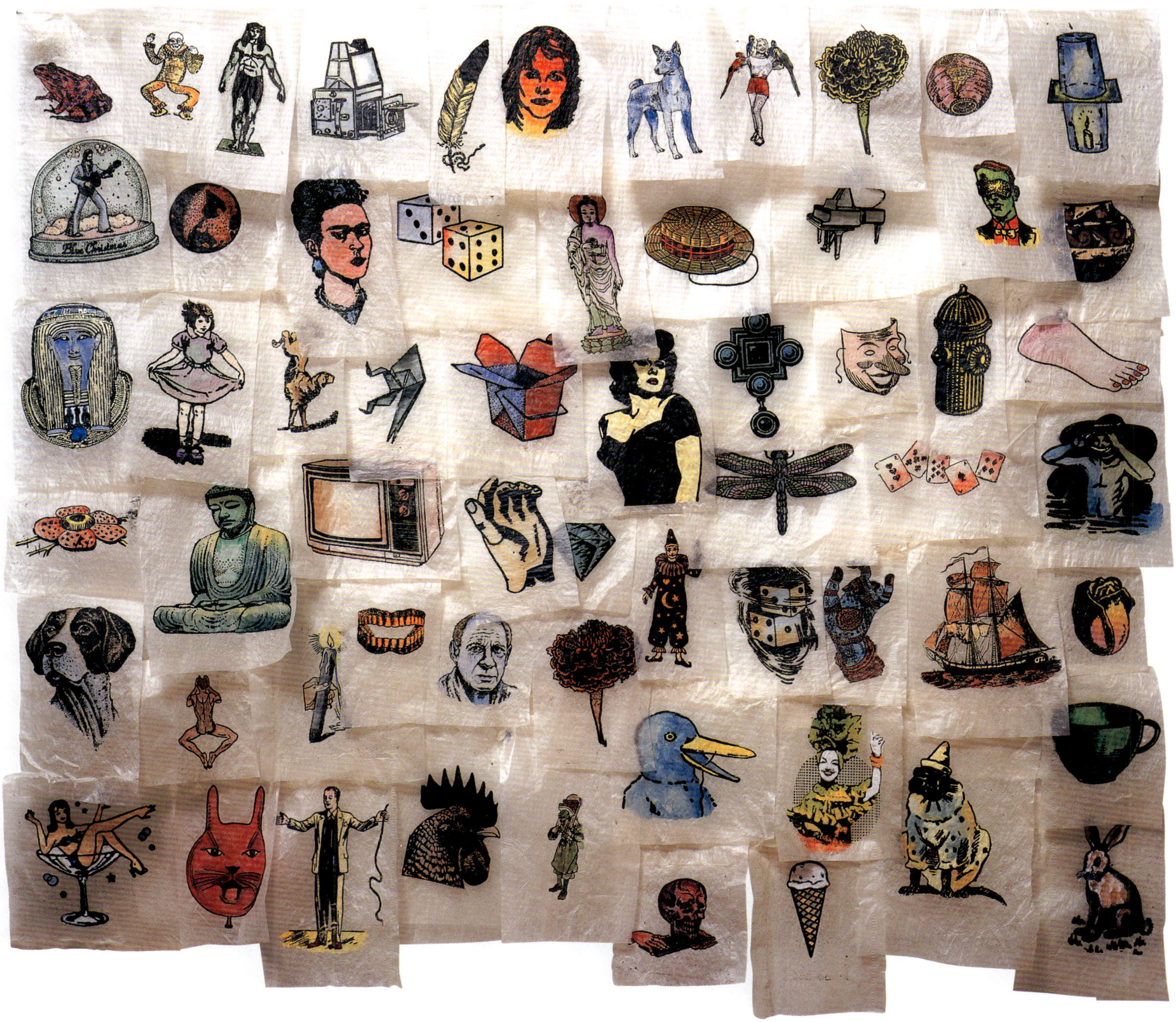
Blue Christmas

22 **UNTITLED (PINK PIANO), 2001**

Watercolor and rubber stamps with block printing ink on gampi papers, 24 1/2 x 26 1/4 inches

Collection of Jim and Beth Kempner, Scotch Plains, New Jersey

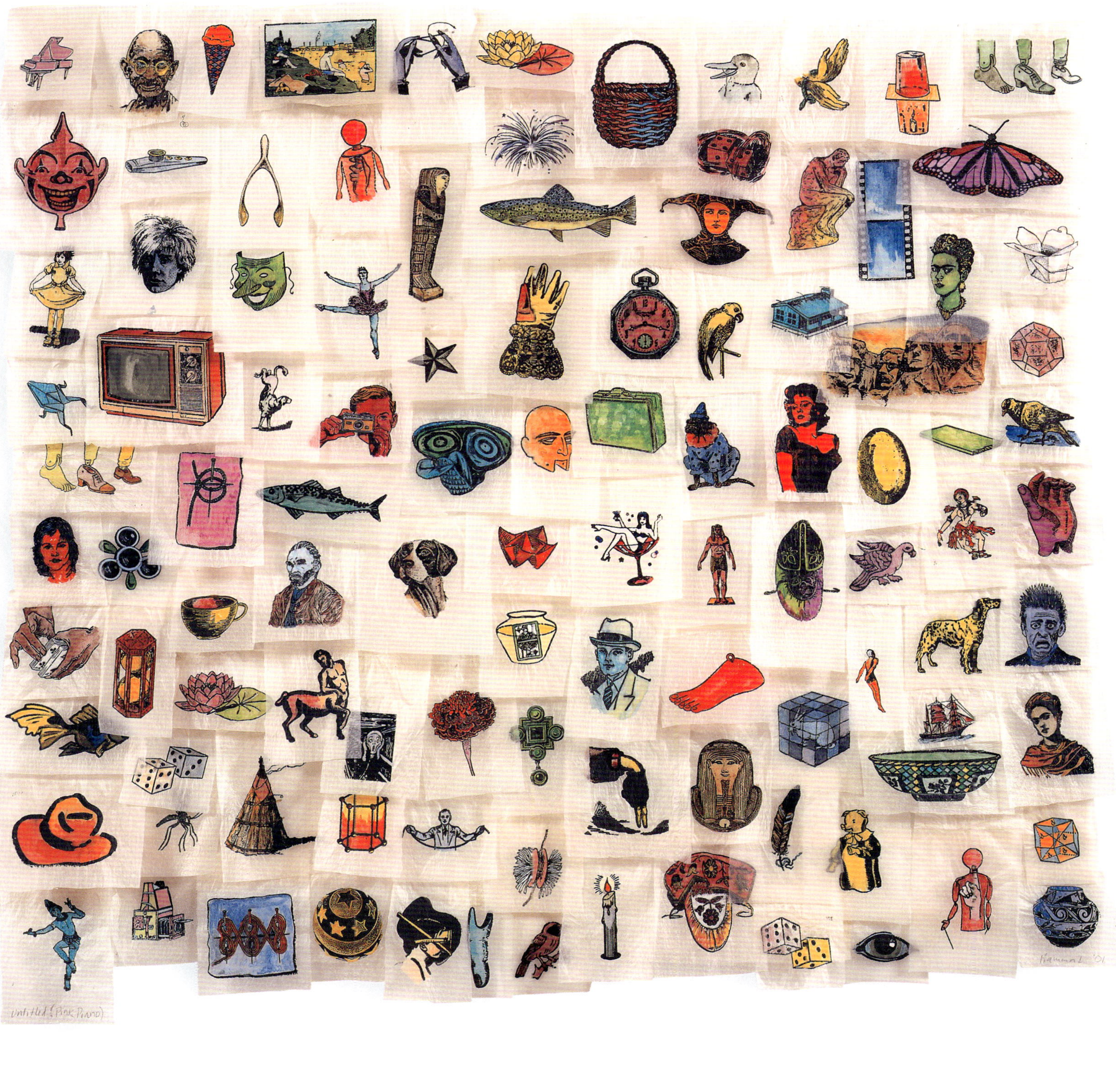
Untitled (Pink Piano)

CLOWN SUIT 1, 1994

23 Acrylic, gouache, solvent transfers, color Xerox, rubber stamps with block printing ink, and lithographs on assorted Japanese papers, 60 x 40 x 10 inches

Collection of Ruth Lingen, New York

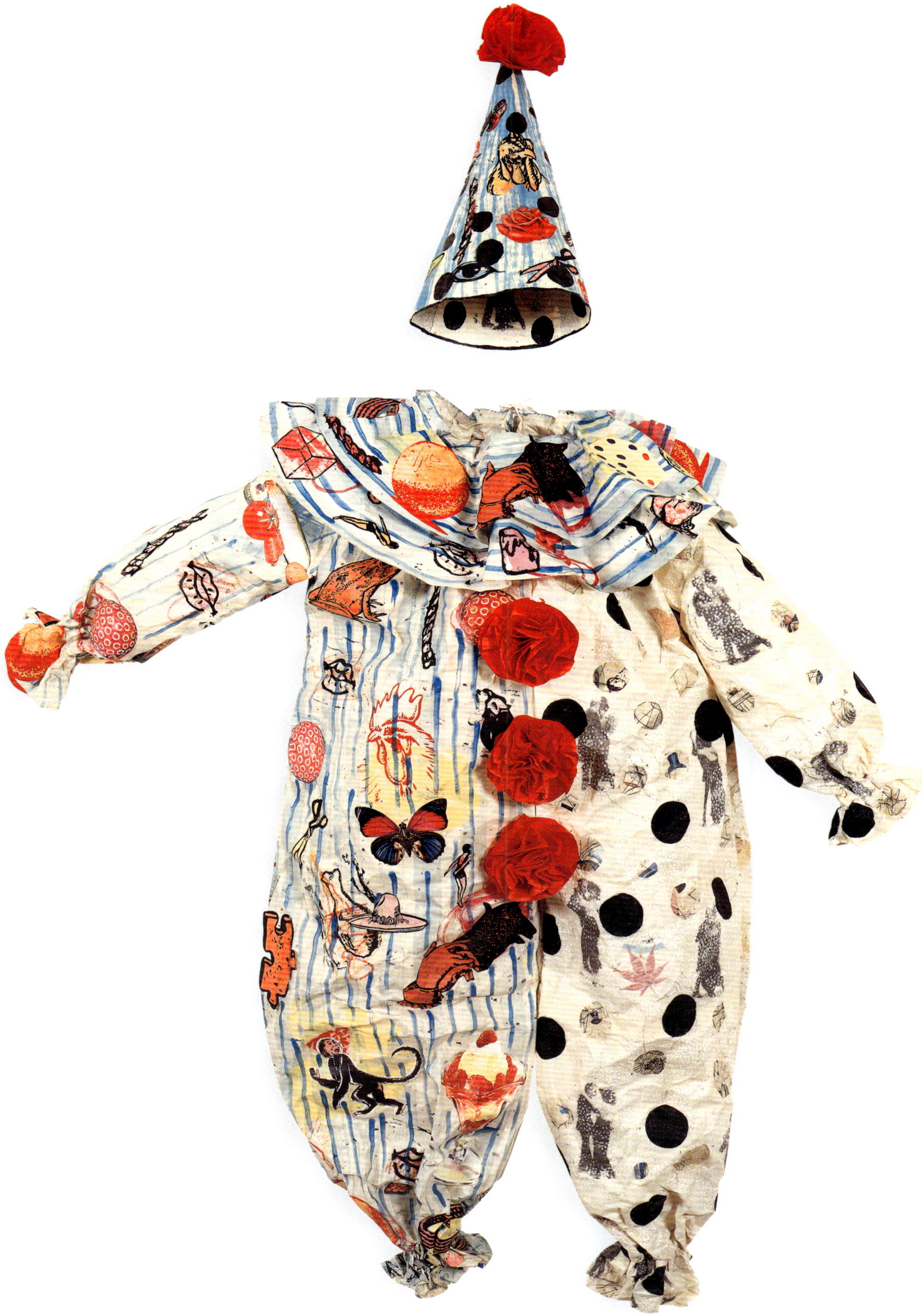

CLOWN SUIT 2, 1994

24 Acrylic, gouache, watercolor, and rubber stamps with block printing ink on assorted Japanese papers, 60 x 40 x 10 inches

Private collection, New York

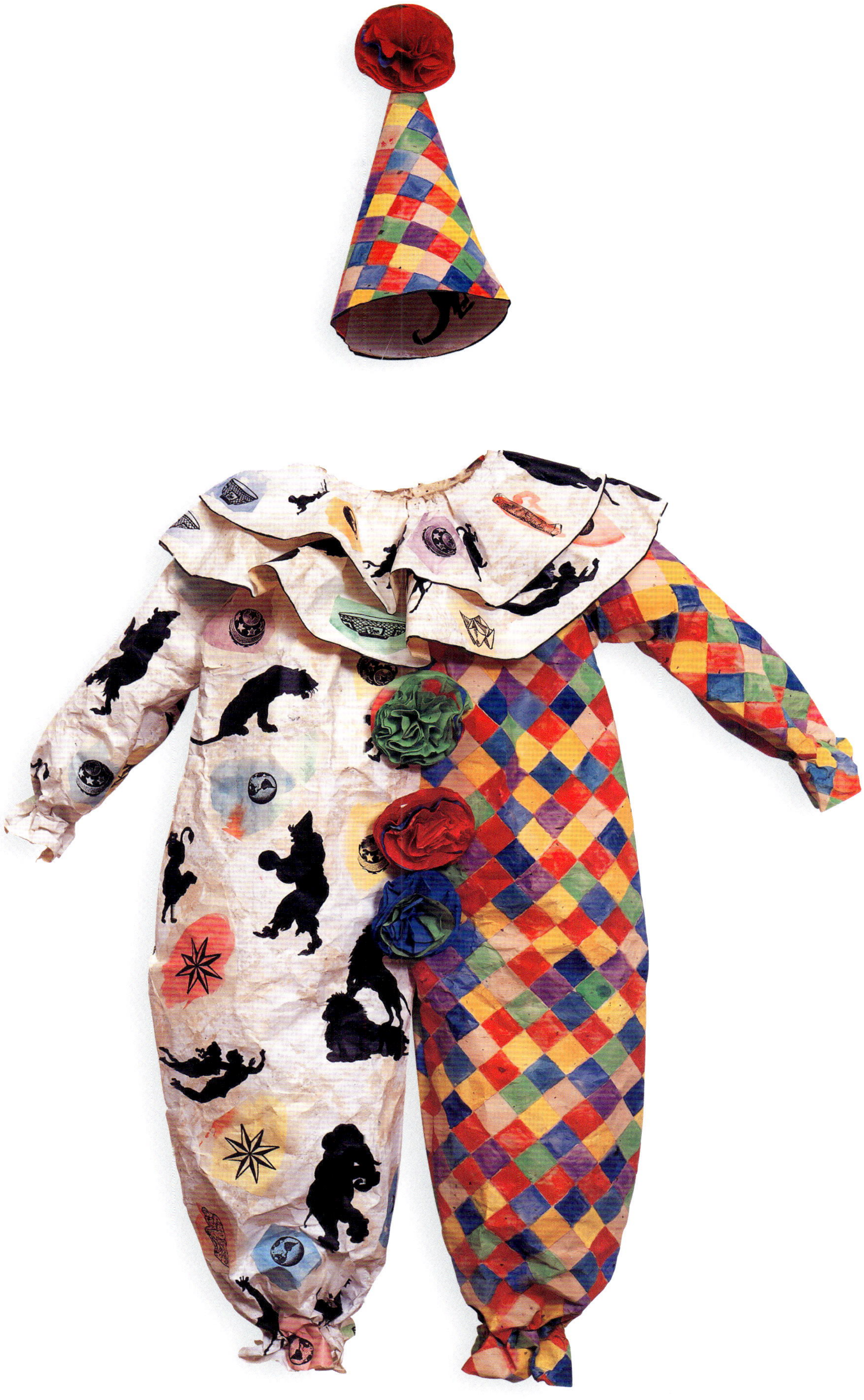

CLOWN SUITS *3*, 1995

25 Acrylic, gouache, linoleum block prints, rubber stamps with block printing ink, and color Xerox on assorted Japanese papers, 60 x 35 x 9 inches

Private collection, New York

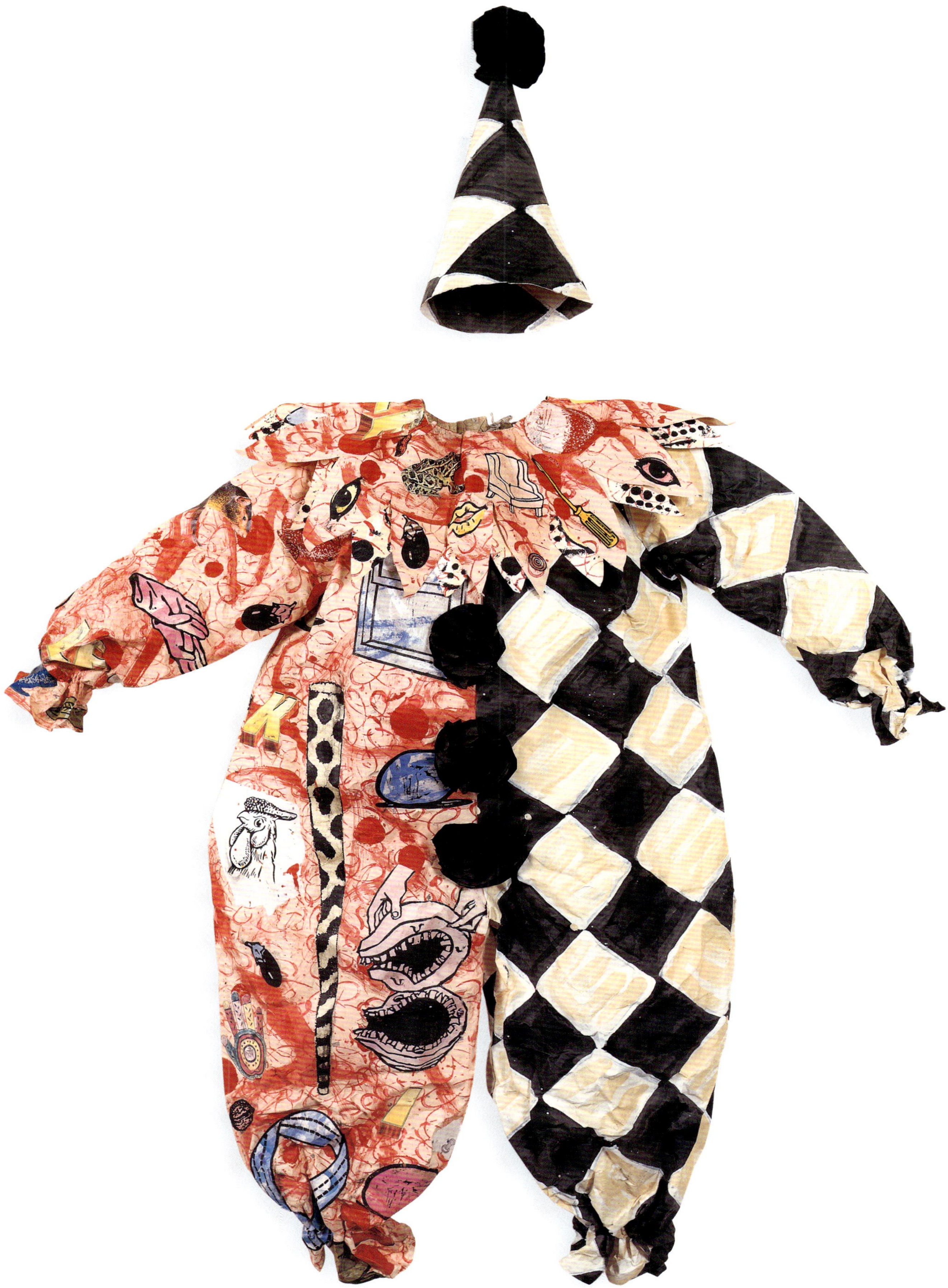

MEXICAN POSTCARD #3 (FROM A SET OF 46 POSTCARDS), 1993

26 Mexican comics collaged onto Mexican postcard, 4 x 6 inches

Collection of the artist

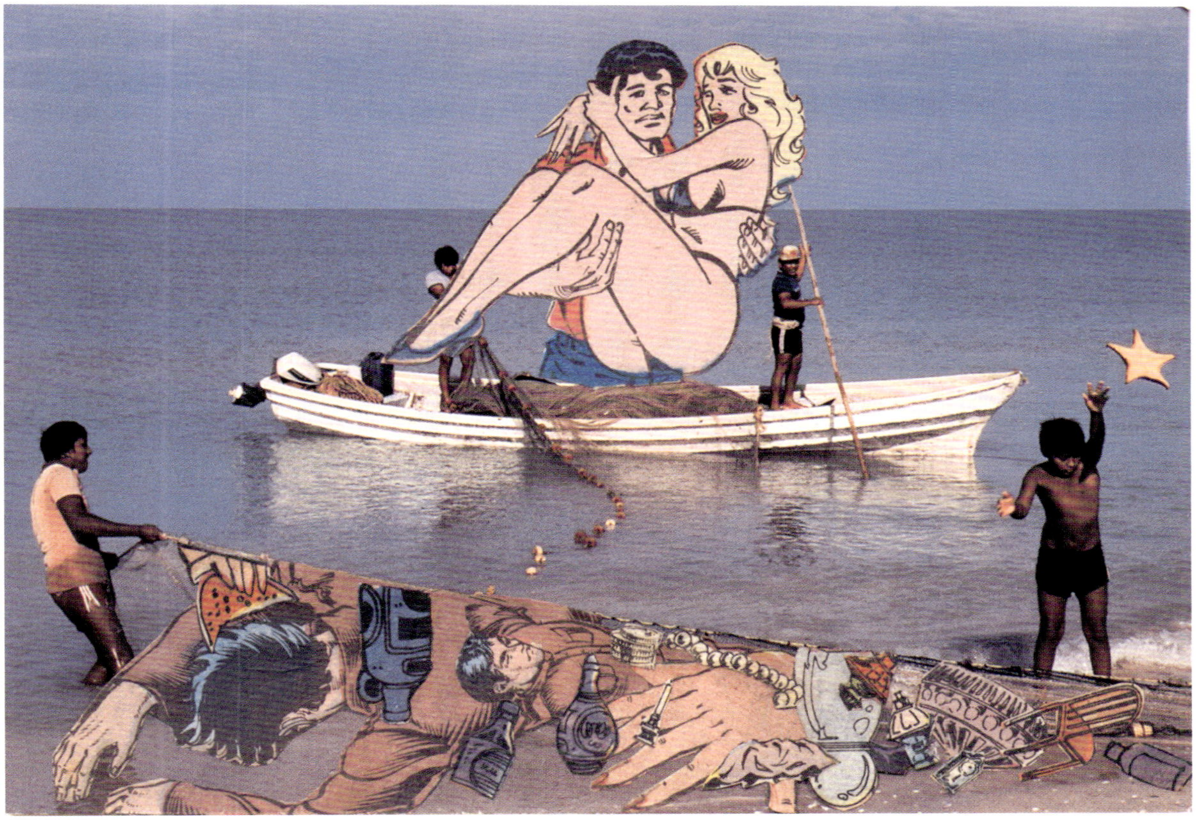

MEXICAN POSTCARD #4 (FROM A SET OF 46 POSTCARDS), 1993

27 Mexican comics collaged onto Mexican postcard, $5^{7}/_{8}$ x $4^{1}/_{8}$ inches

Collection of the artist

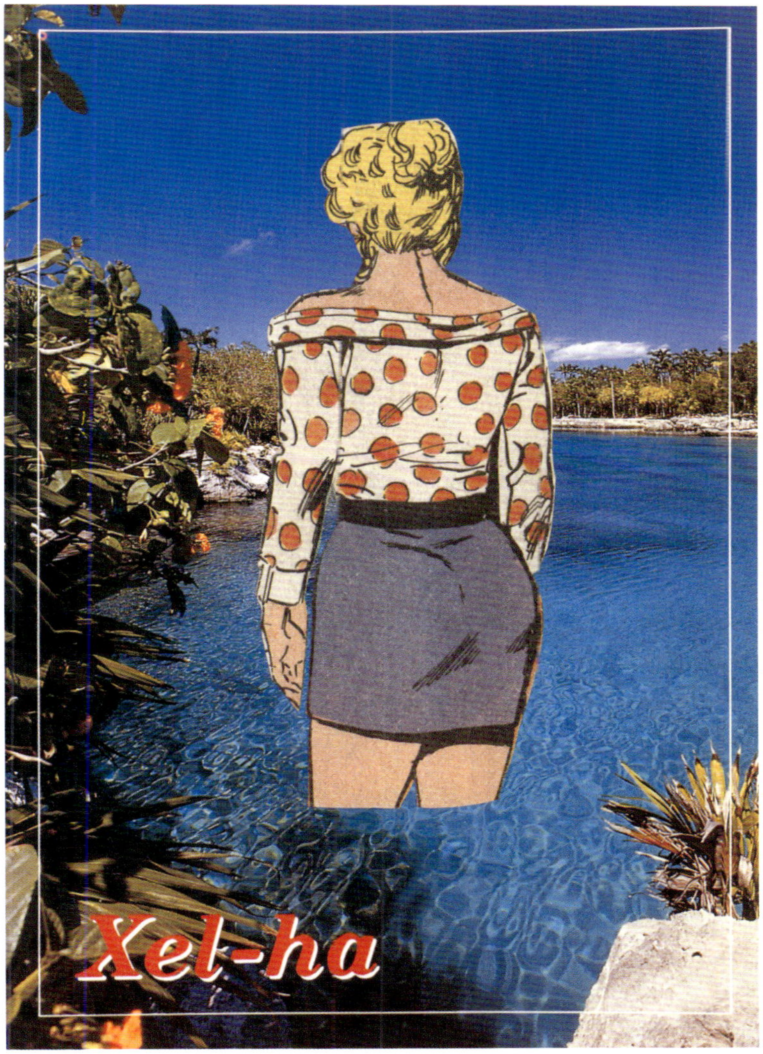
Xel-ha

28 **MEXICAN POSTCARD #5 (FROM A SET OF 46 POSTCARDS), 1993**

Mexican comics collaged onto Mexican postcard, $4^{1}/2$ x $6^{1}/2$ inches

Collection of the artist

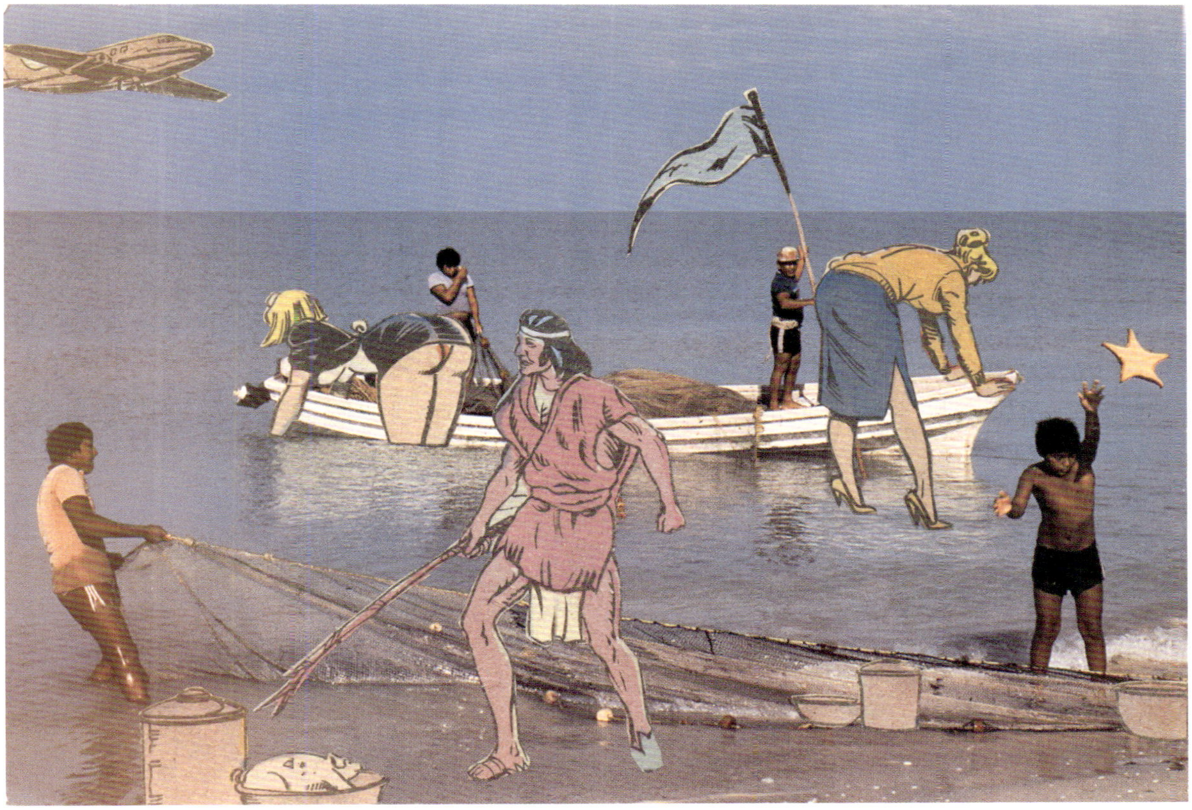

MATCHBOOKS (RED FACE), 2003

29 Watercolor and rubber stamps with block printing ink on rag paper, 19 x 18 1/4 x 1 3/4 inches

Collection of Guy and Nora Barron, Bloomfield Hills, Michigan

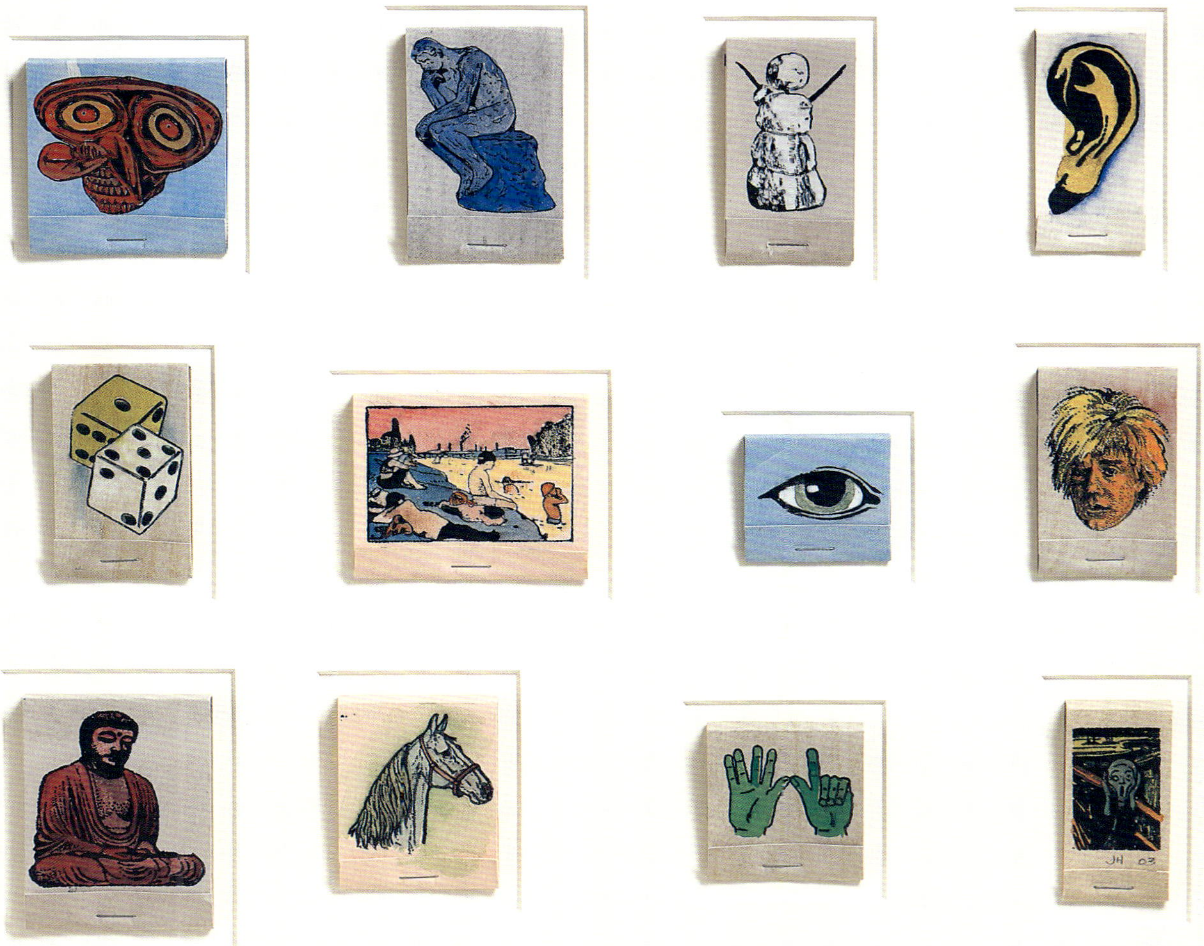
JH 03

ALL SOULS (HEFEI), 2004–5

30 Acrylic, gouache, graphite, colored pencil, metal leaf, archival digital prints, rice paper, and horsehair on assorted handmade papers, 57 x 62 1/2 x 3 inches

Collection of Susan and Arthur Fleischer, Jr., New York

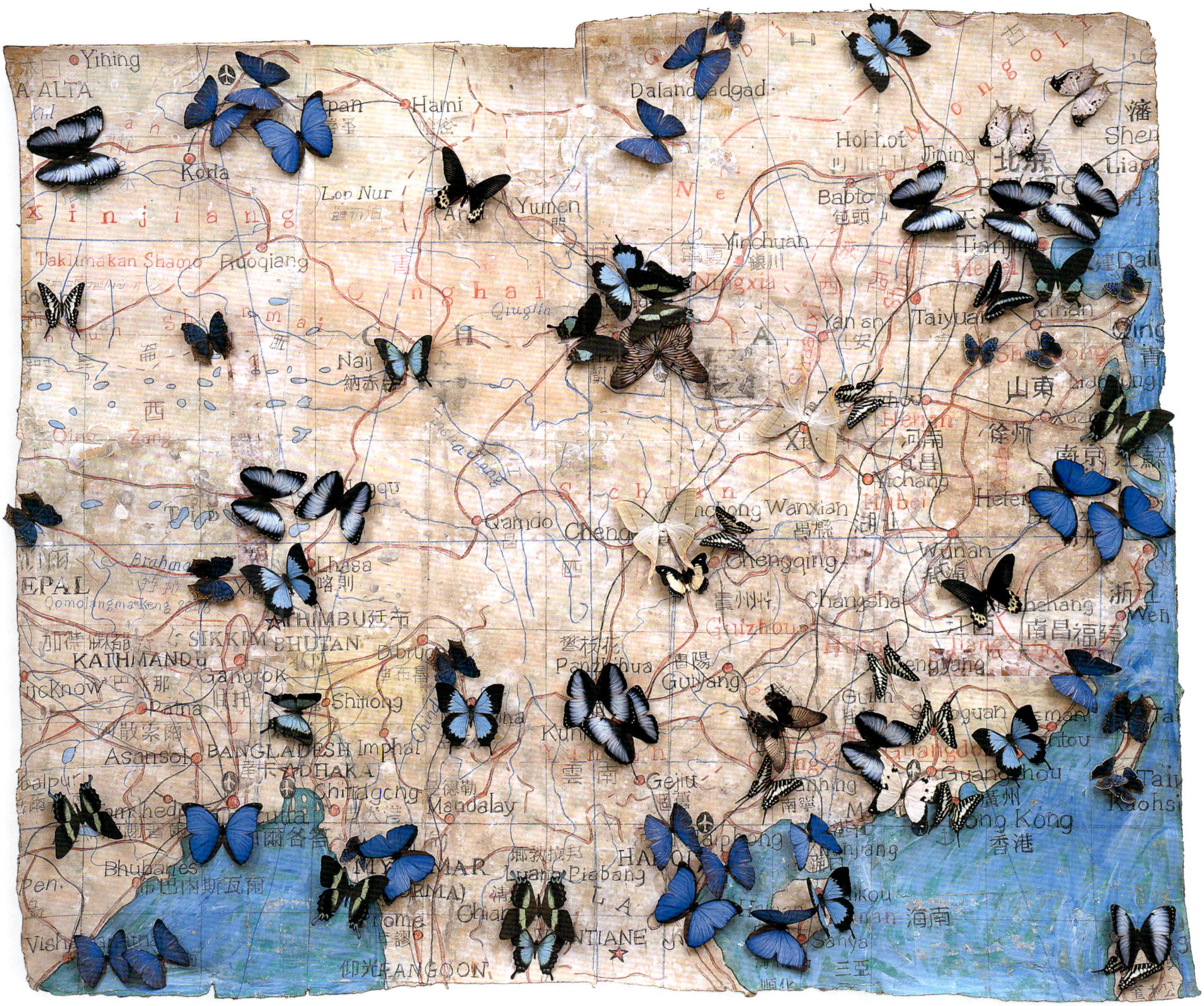
Yining
Hami
Dalandzadgad
Hohhot
Jining
Korla
Lop Nur
Yumen
Baotou
Yinchuan
Tianjin
Taklimakan Shamo
Ruoqiang
Qinghai
Ningxia
Yan an
Taiyuan
山東
Qamdo
Wanxian
Yichang
Hefei
Lhasa
Chongqing
Wuhan
EPAL
Changsha
Guizhou
THIMBU
SIKKIM
BHUTAN
KATHMANDU
Gangtok
Guiyang
Asansol
BANGLADESH
Imphal
雲南
Gejiu
Mandalay
Guangzhou
Hong Kong
香港
Bhubanes
Luang Prabang
Kaohsi
海南
Sanya
三亞
RANGOON

Detail, *All Souls (Hefei)*, 2004–5

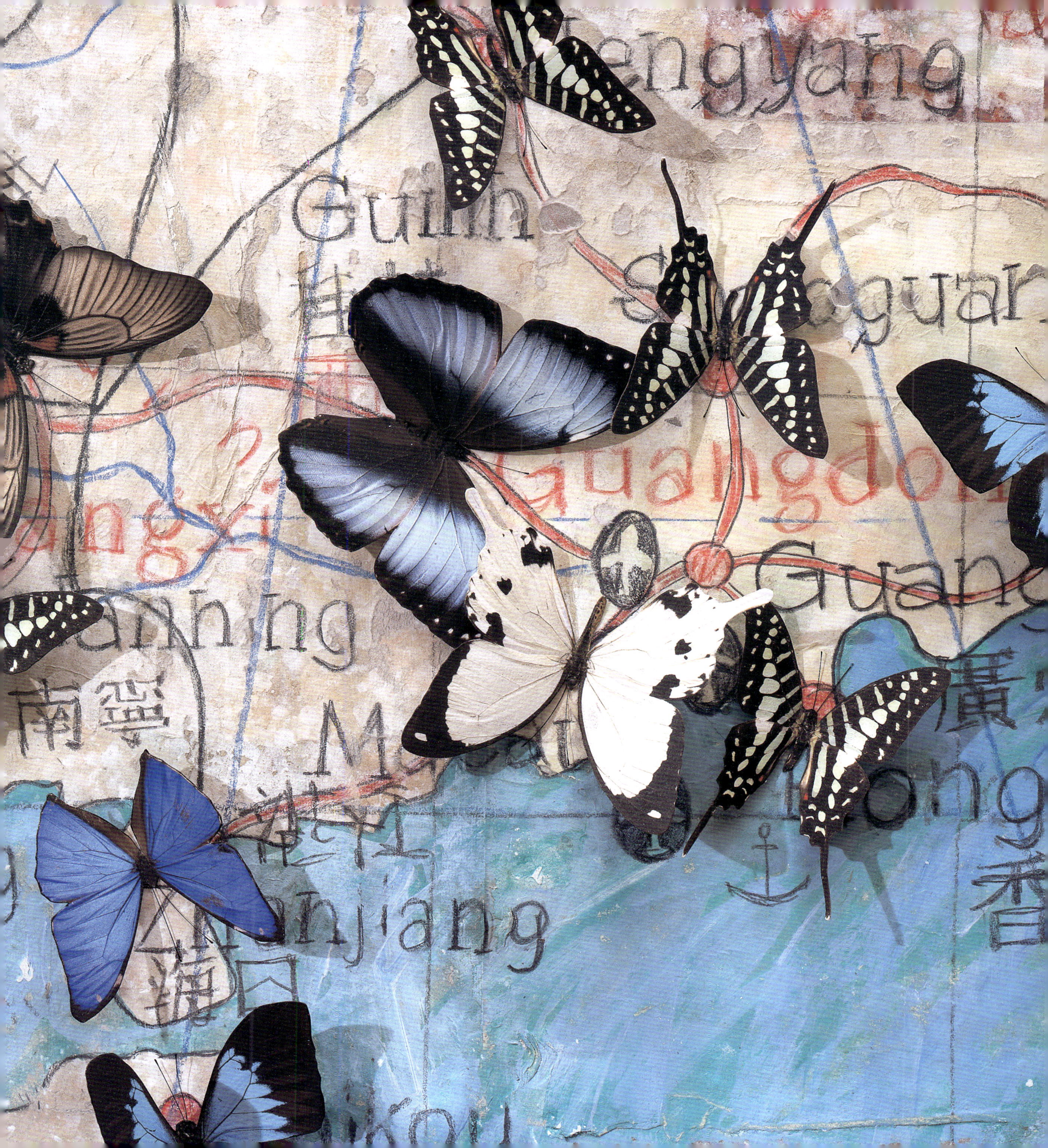
南寧

ALL SOULS (CORDOBA), 2005

31 Acrylic, gouache, Flashe, graphite, iridescent pigment, colored pencil, archival digital prints, rice paper, and horsehair on assorted handmade papers, $46^{1}/_{2}$ x 58 x 5 inches

Collection of Jo Ann and Peter Wood, New Hampshire

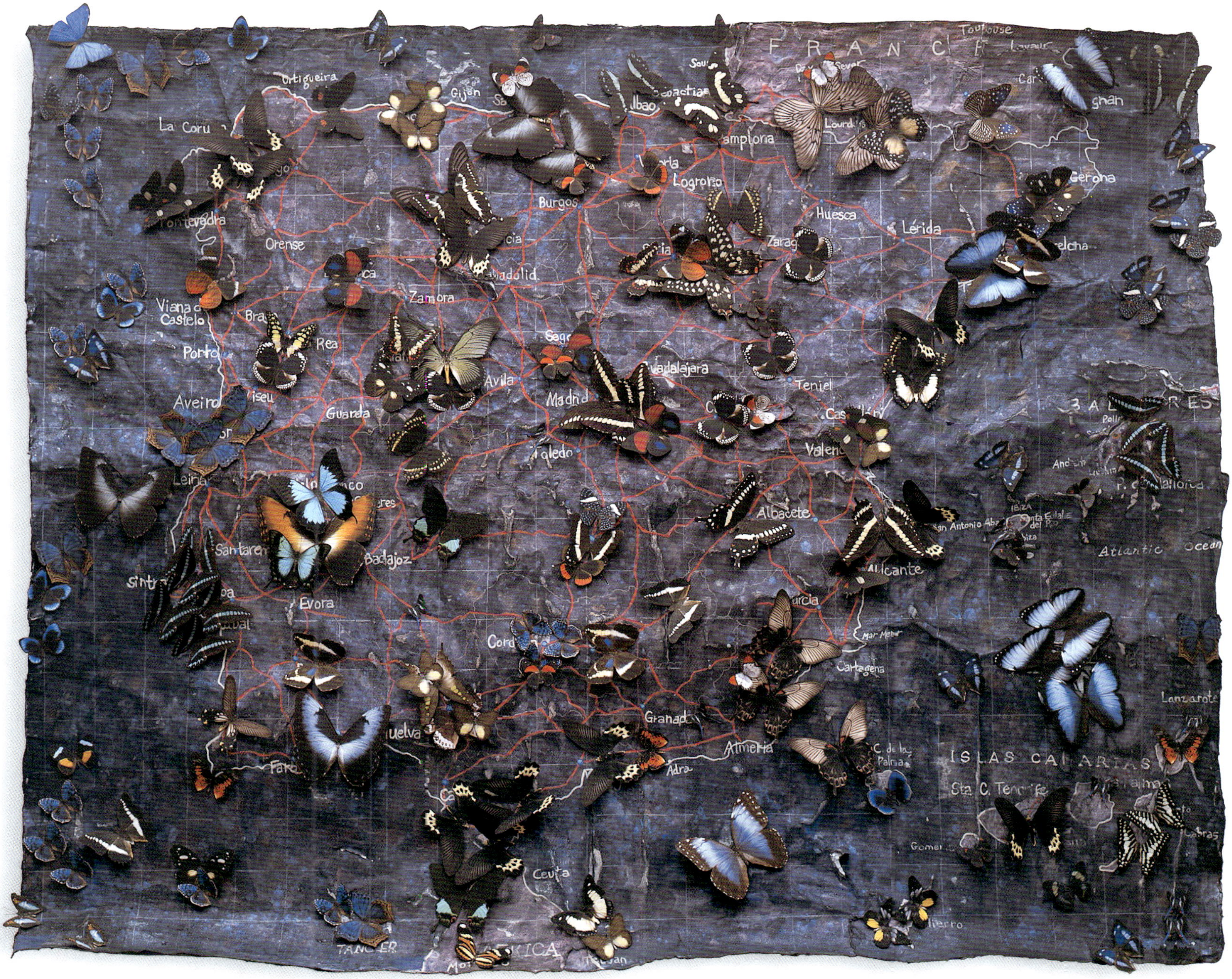
FRANCE
Toulouse
Lavaur
Ortigueira
Gijon
Logroño
Burgos
Huesca
Lérida
Gerona
Orense
Zamora
Castelo
Rea
Avila
Madrid
Aveiro
Guarda
Albacete
Badajoz
Evora
Cartagena
Mar Menor
Almeria
Adra
Ceuta
TANGER
IBIZA
Atlantic Ocean
Lanzarote

Detail, *All Souls (Cordoba)*, 2005

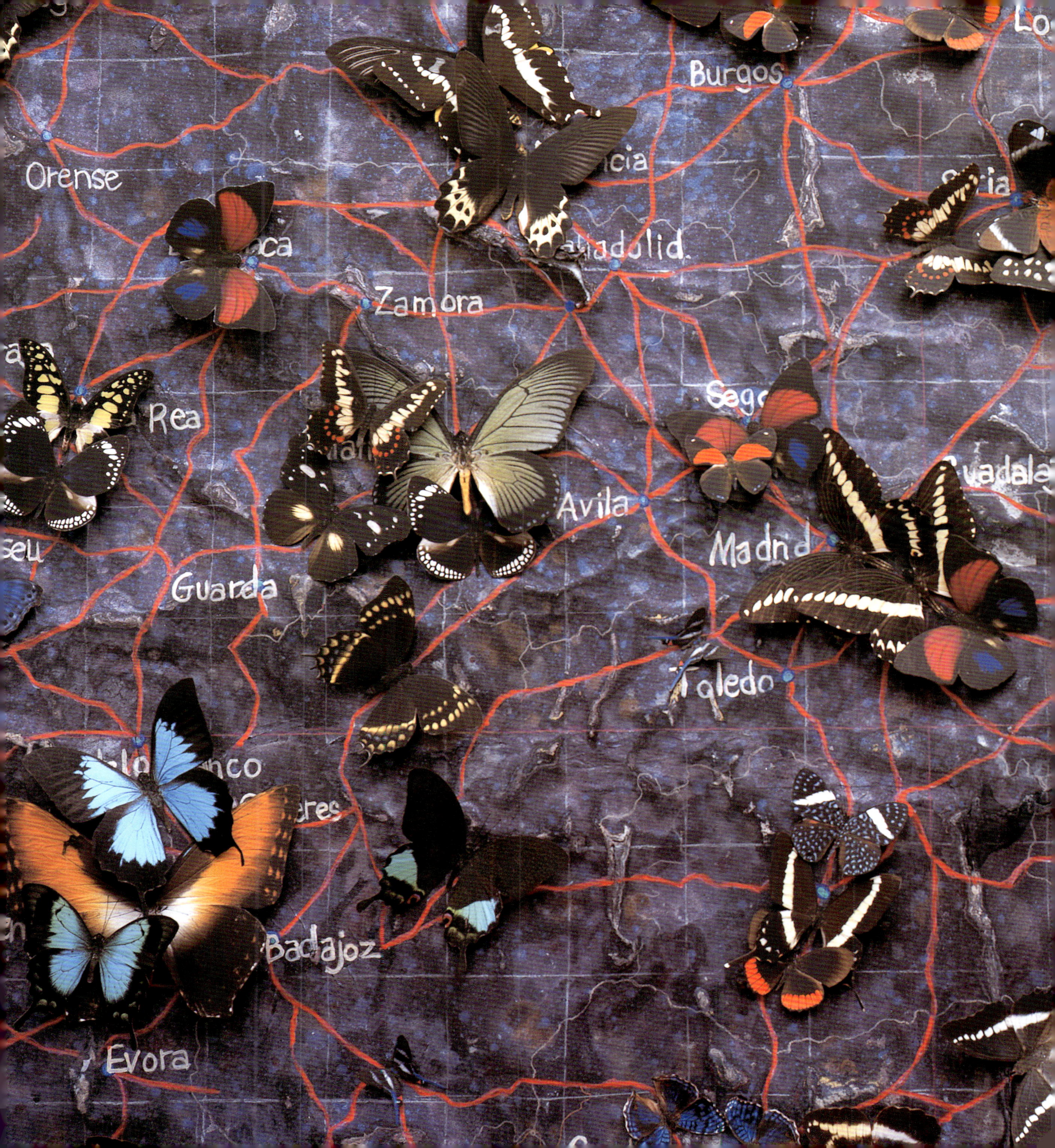
Burgos
Orense
Zamora
Avila
Madrid
Guarda
Toledo
Badajoz
Evora

FULL HOUSE, 1992–93

32 Intaglio print with silkscreen, lithography, and collage, $78^{1}/_{2}$ x 51 inches, edition of 32, published by Universal Limited Art Editions, Inc.

Courtesy of Universal Limited Art Editions, Inc., Bay Shore, New York

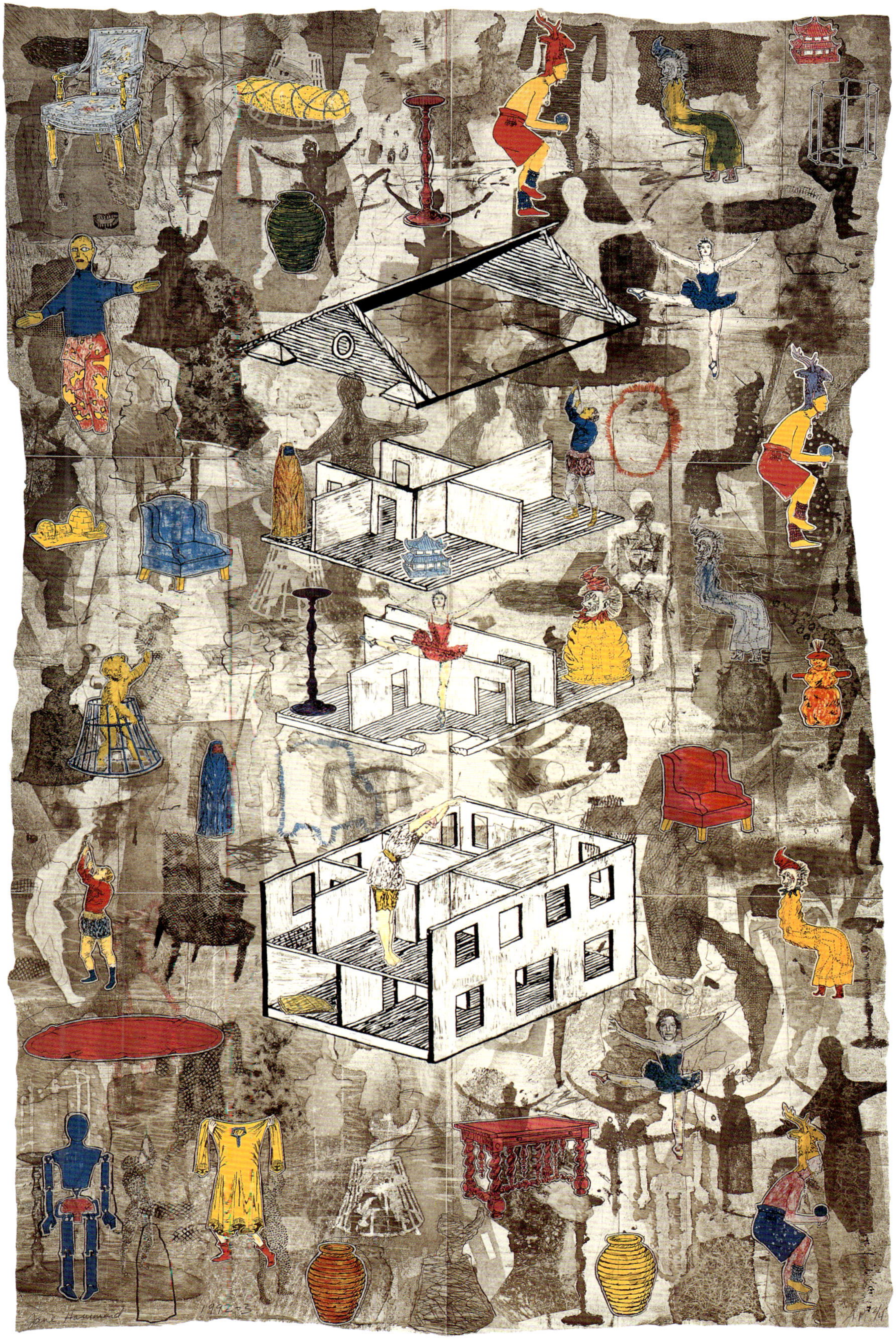

CLOWN SUIT, 1995

33 Three-dimensional, twenty-four-color lithograph with silkscreen and collage, 55 x 46 1/2 x 10 inches, edition of 45, published by Universal Limited Art Editions, Inc.

Courtesy of Universal Limited Art Editions, Inc., Bay Shore, New York

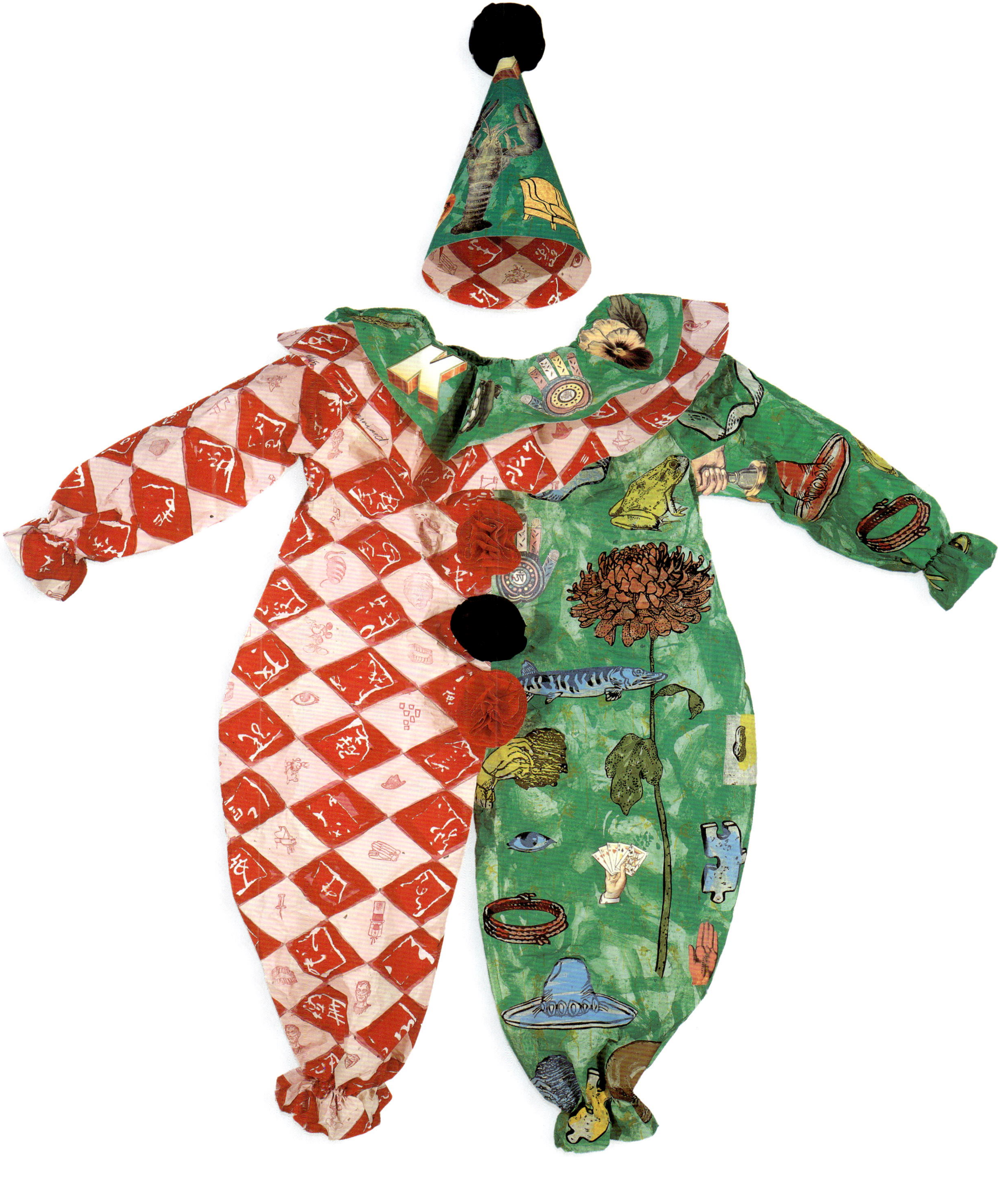

THE WONDERFULNESS OF DOWNTOWN, 1997

34 Thirty-nine-color silkscreen with lithography and collage on collaged Japanese papers, $59^{1}/_{2}$ x 62 inches, edition of 50, published by Universal Limited Art Editions, Inc.

Mount Holyoke College Art Museum, South Hadley, Massachusetts, Henry Rox Memorial Fund for the Purchase of Works by Contemporary Women Artists

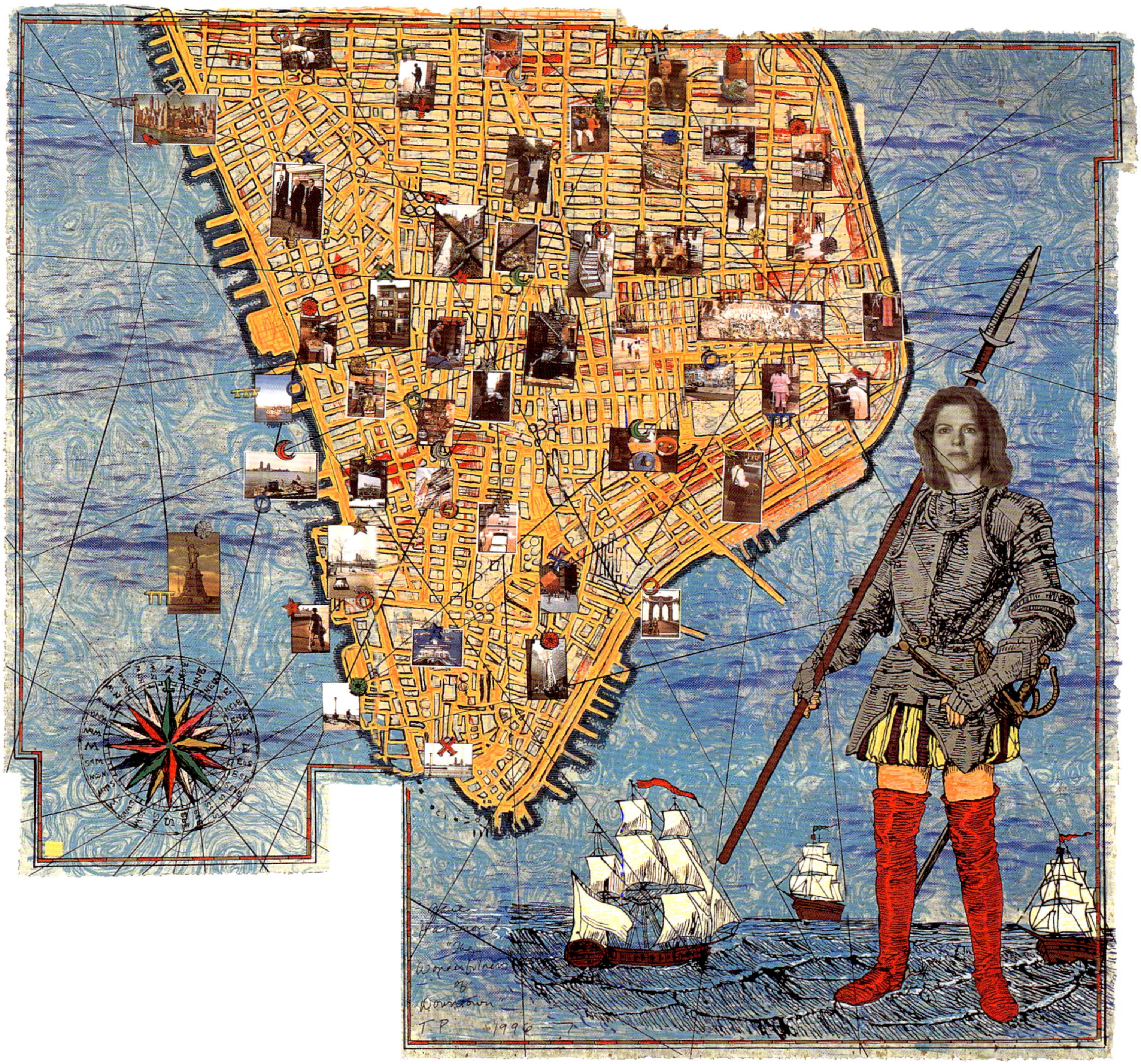
Jane Hammond
"The
Wonderfulness
of
Downtown"
T.P. 1996–7

35 **FROM THE GOOSE TO THE GIRL, 1999**

Iris and relief print with pochoir and hand-coloring on Arches paper, 27 x 26 3/8 inches, edition of 25, published by Pace Editions, Inc.

Courtesy of the artist and Pace Editions, Inc., New York

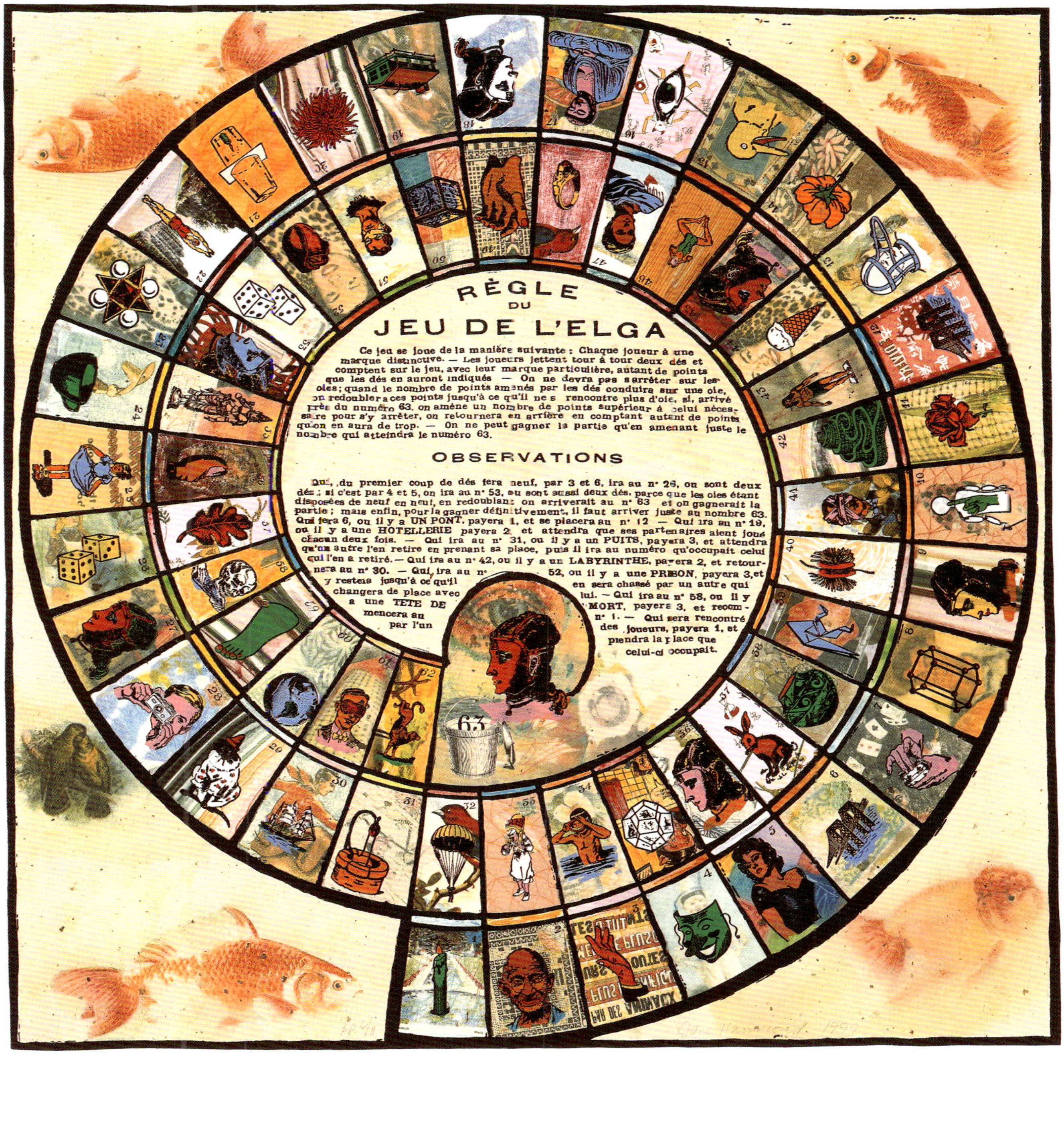
RÈGLE
DU
JEU DE L'ELGA
Ce jeu se joue de la manière suivante : Chaque joueur à une
marque distinctive. — Les joueurs jettent tour à tour deux dés et
comptent sur le jeu, avec leur marque particulière, autant de points
que les dés en auront indiqués — On ne devra pas s'arrêter sur les
oies; quand le nombre de points amenés par les dés conduira sur une oie,
on redoublera ces points jusqu'à ce qu'il ne se rencontre plus d'oie, si, arrivé
près du numéro 63, on amène un nombre de points supérieur à celui néces-
saire pour s'y arrêter, on retournera en arrière en comptant autant de points
qu'on en aura de trop. — On ne peut gagner la partie qu'en amenant juste le
nombre qui atteindra le numéro 63.
OBSERVATIONS
Qui, du premier coup de dés fera neuf, par 3 et 6, ira au n° 26, ou sont deux
dés ; si c'est par 4 et 5, on ira au n° 53, ou sont aussi deux dés, parce que les oies étant
disposées de neuf en neuf, en redoublant on arriverait au n° 63 et on gagnerait la
partie ; mais enfin, pour la gagner définitivement, il faut arriver juste au nombre 63.
Qui fera 6, ou il y a UN PONT, payera 1, et se placera au n° 12 — Qui ira au n° 19,
ou il y a une HOTELLERIE payera 2 et attendra que ses partenaires aient joué
chacun deux fois. — Qui ira au n° 31, ou il y a un PUITS, payera 3, et attendra
qu'un autre l'en retire en prenant sa place, puis il ira au numéro qu'occupait celui
qui l'en a retiré. — Qui ira au n° 42, ou il y a un LABYRINTHE, payera 2, et retour-
nera au n° 30. — Qui ira au n° 52, ou il y a une PRISON, payera 3, et
y restera jusqu'à ce qu'il en sera chassé par un autre qui
changera de place avec lui. — Qui ira au n° 58, ou il y
a une TETE DE MORT, payera 3, et recom-
mencera au n° 1. — Qui sera rencontré
par l'un des joueurs, payera 1, et
prendra la place que
celui-ci occupait.
63

SIX SETS (individually titled FAITH, INSIGHT, KINSHIP, PATIENCE, PERCEPTION, FAIRNESS), 2001

36 Suite of six Iris and relief prints with collage, hand-coloring, wood veneer, and silver foil on Arches paper, 22 x 19 inches each, edition of 15, published by Pace Editions, Inc.

Courtesy of the artist and Pace Editions, Inc., New York

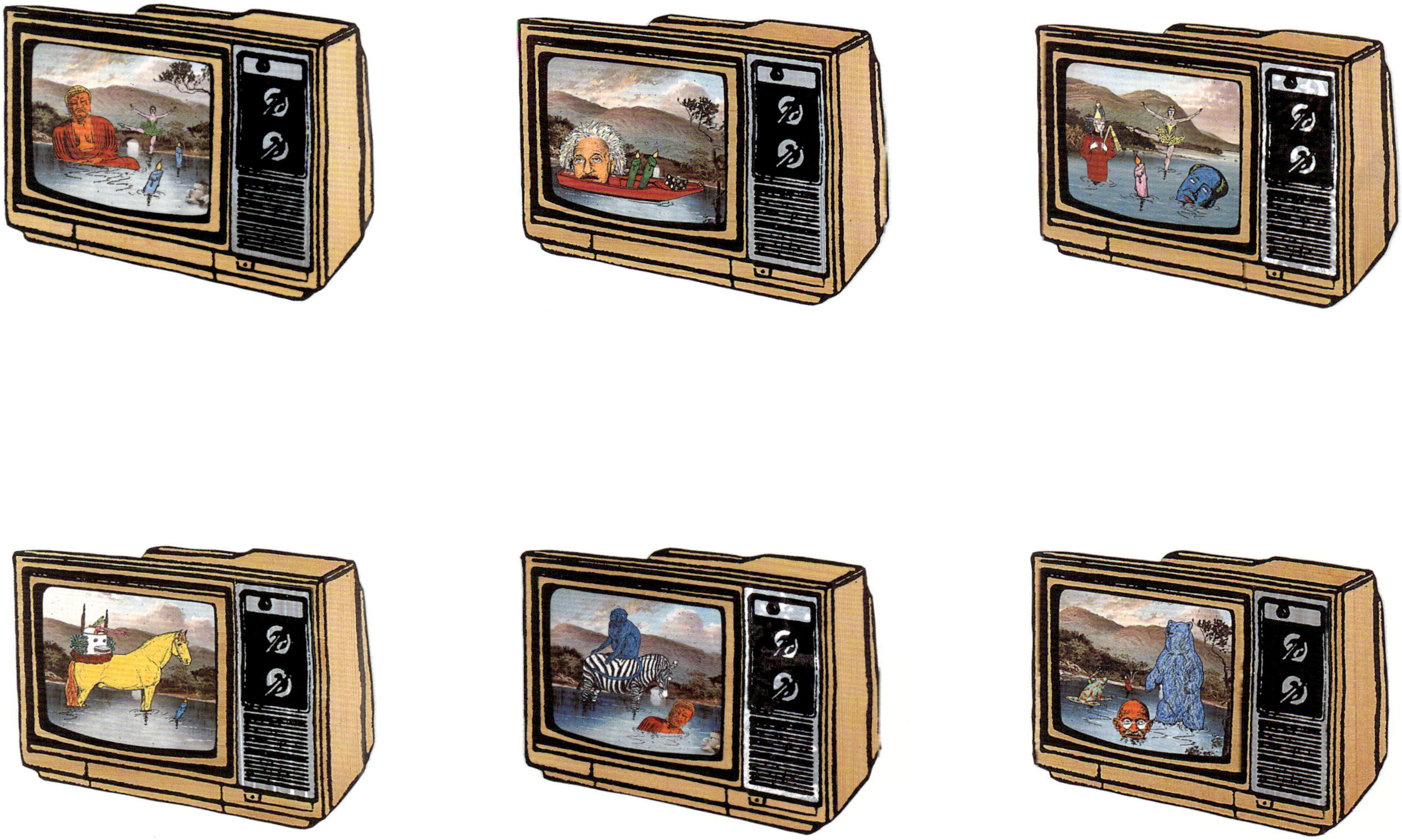

TABULA ROSA, 2001

37 Digital inkjet print on custom-made Japanese paper, 74 x 29 1/2 inches, edition of 43, published by Universal Limited Art Editions, Inc.

Courtesy of Universal Limited Art Editions, Inc., Bay Shore, New York

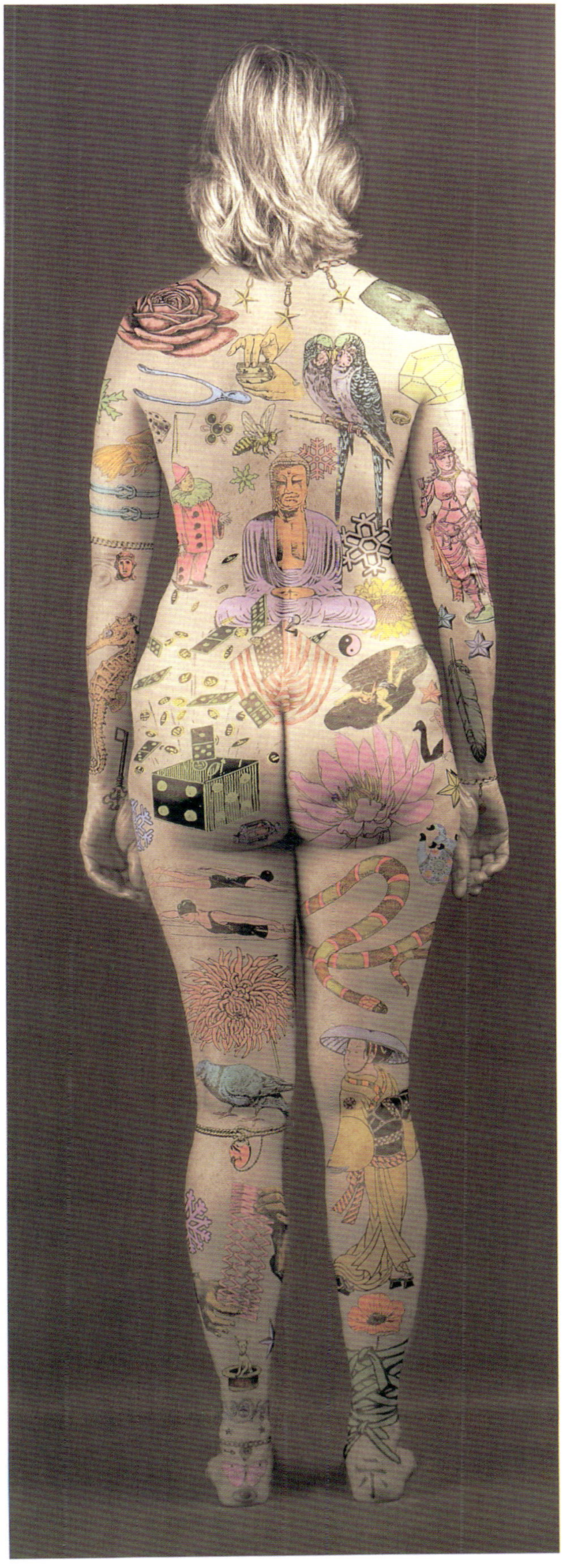

SCRAPBOOK, 2003

38 Three-dimensional, pigmented inkjet print with woodblock, collage, and hand-coloring, 38 x 42 x 2 inches, edition of 43, published by Universal Limited Art Editions, Inc.

Mount Holyoke College Art Museum, South Hadley, Massachusetts,

Henry Rox Memorial Fund for the Purchase of Works by Contemporary Women Artists

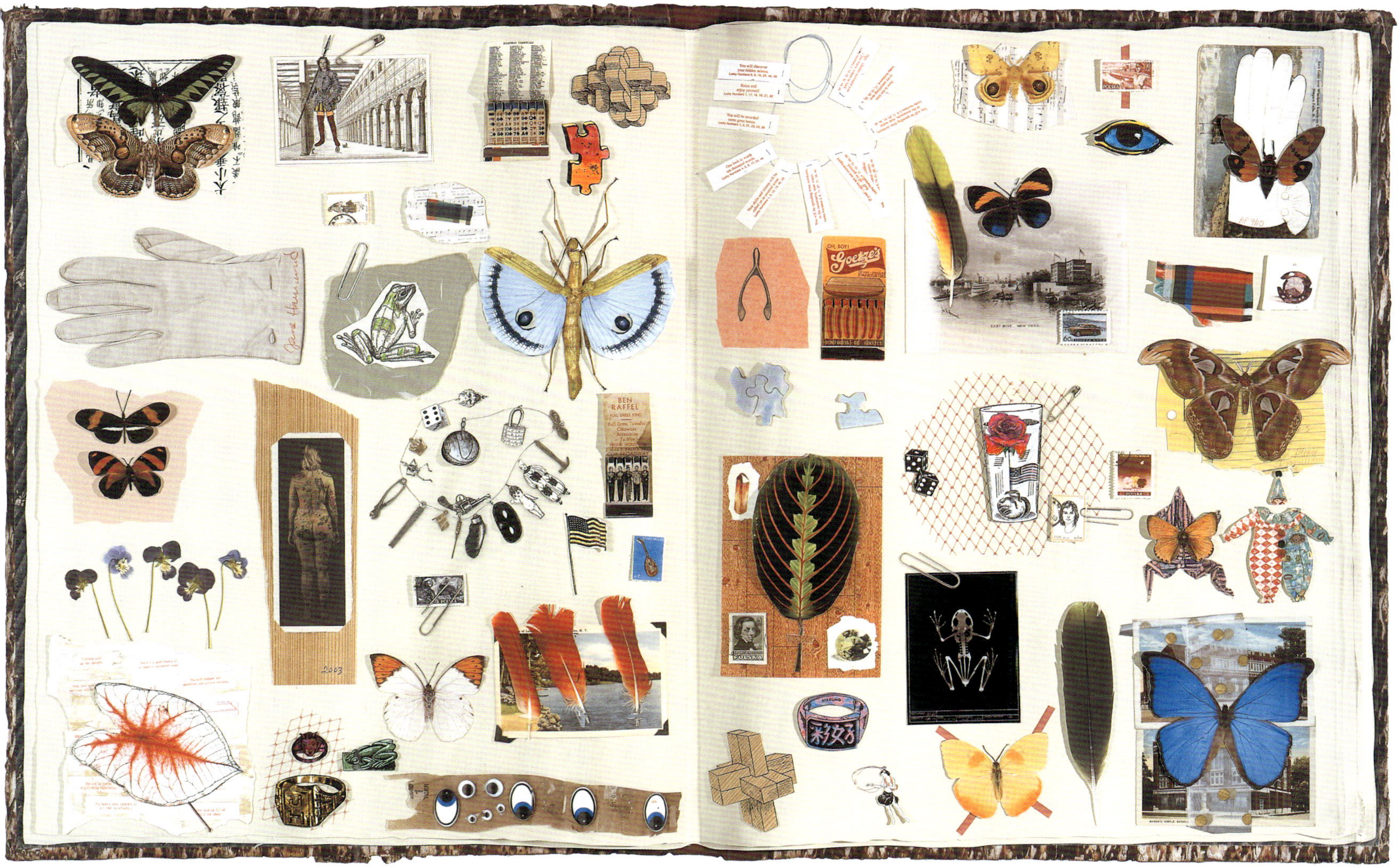

39 **MY HEAVENS!, 2004**

Twelve-color lithograph with silver Mylar and collage on amate paper, 30 x 51 inches, edition of 40, published by Shark's Ink

Collection of Bud and Barbara Shark, Lyons, Colorado

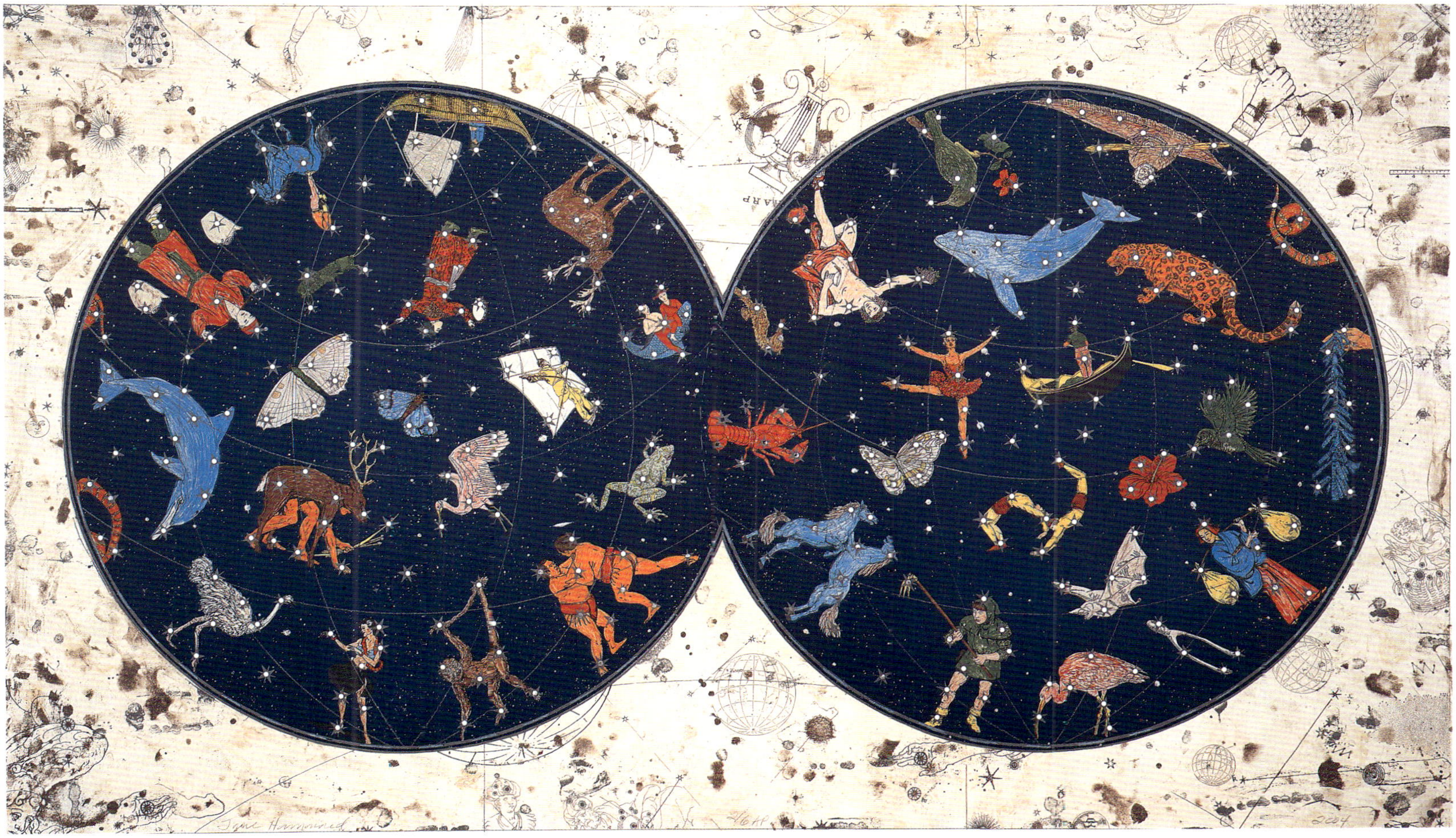

MAYSVILLE (1931), 2005

40 Selenium-toned silver gelatin print, 14 x 11 inches, edition of 5

Courtesy of the artist and Galerie Lelong, New York

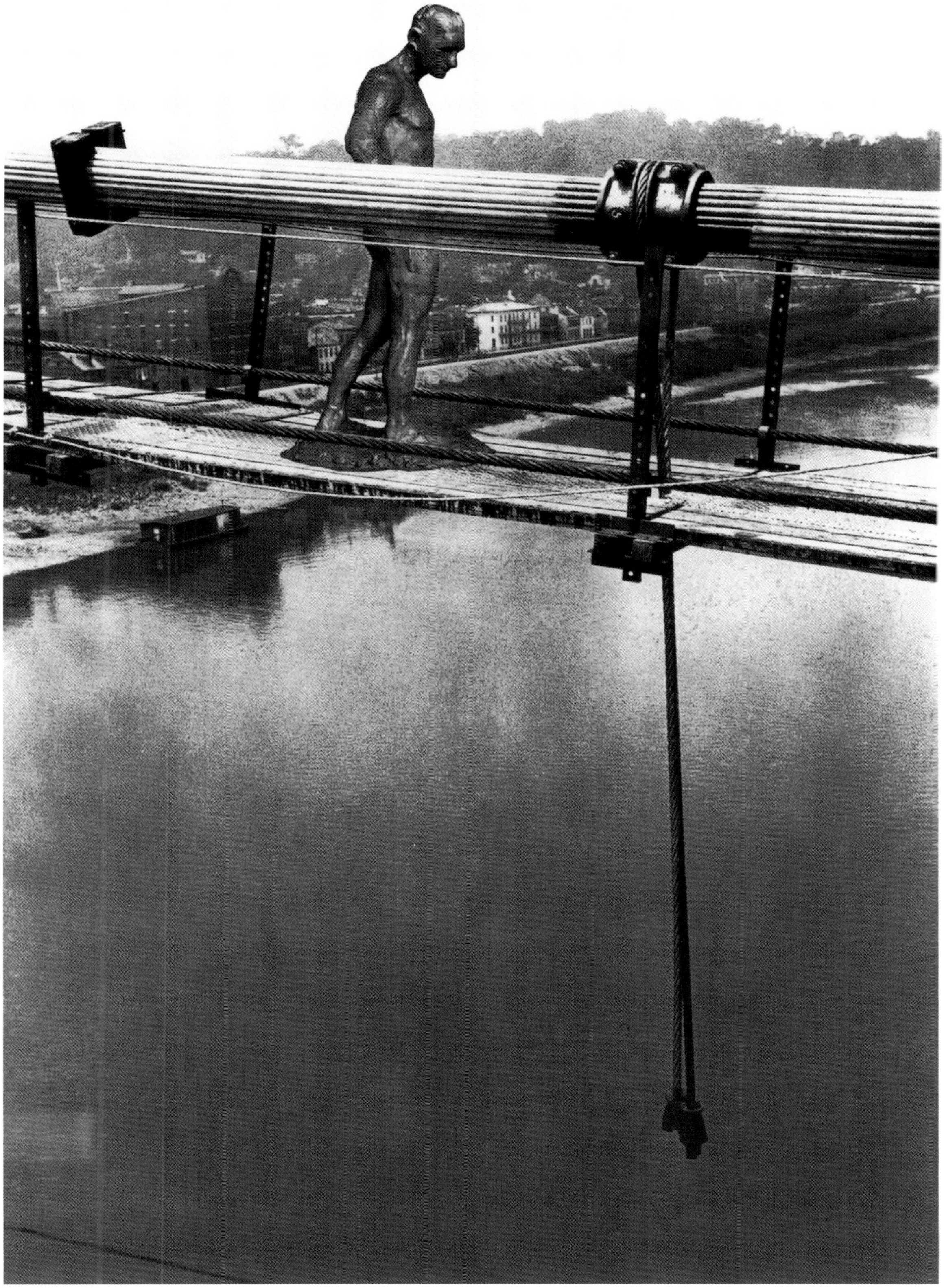

41 **CHAI WAN, 2005**

Selenium-toned silver gelatin print, 11 x 14 inches, edition of 5

Courtesy of the artist and Galerie Lelong, New York

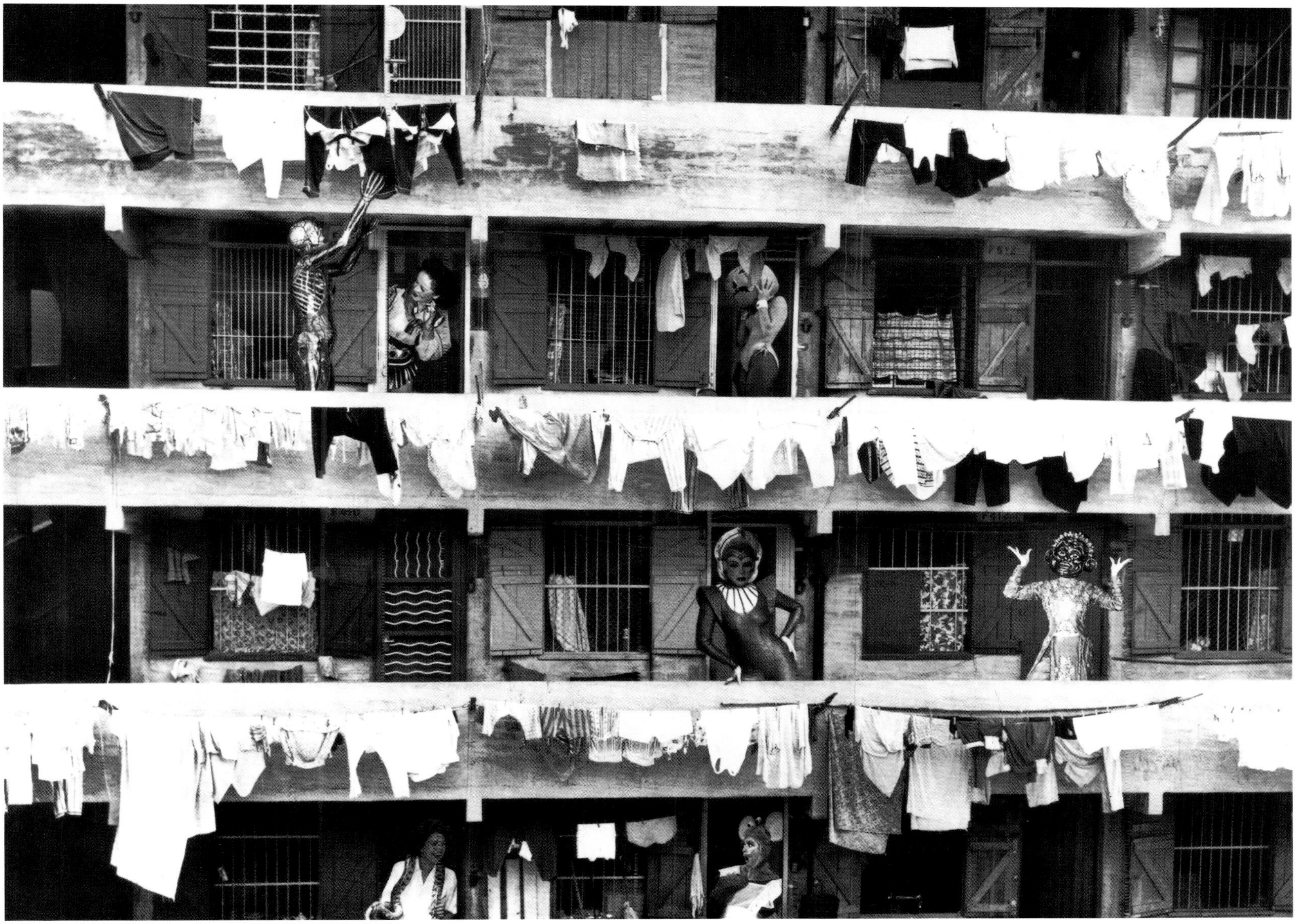

MAHDIA (TUNISIAN MEN HONOR MY MOTHER AND HER POPPIES), 2005

42 Selenium-toned silver gelatin print, 11 x 14 inches, edition of 5

Courtesy of the artist and Galerie Lelong, New York

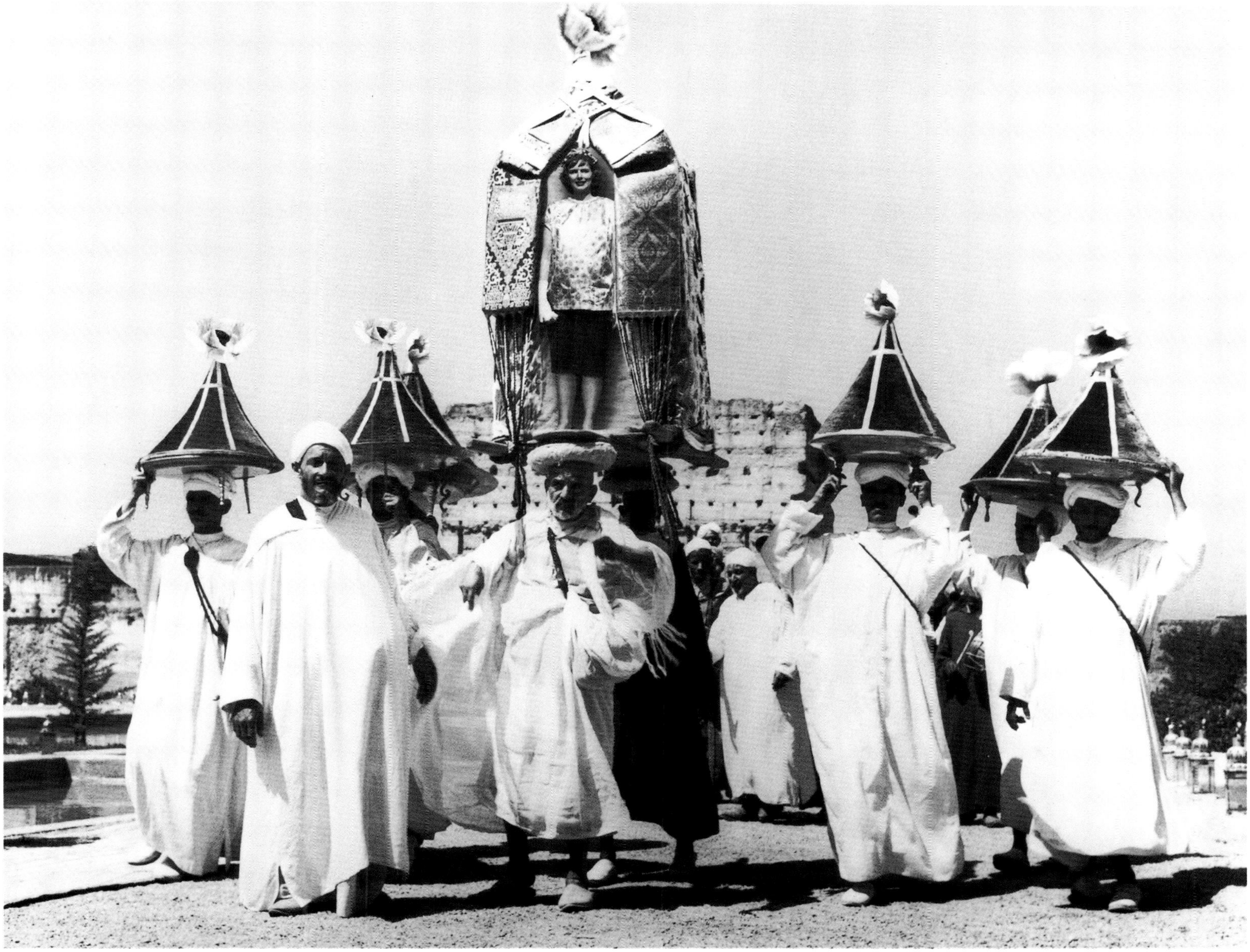

PERPETUAL LOVE, 2005

43 Selenium-toned silver gelatin print, 11 x 14 inches, edition of 5

Courtesy of the artist and Galerie Lelong, New York

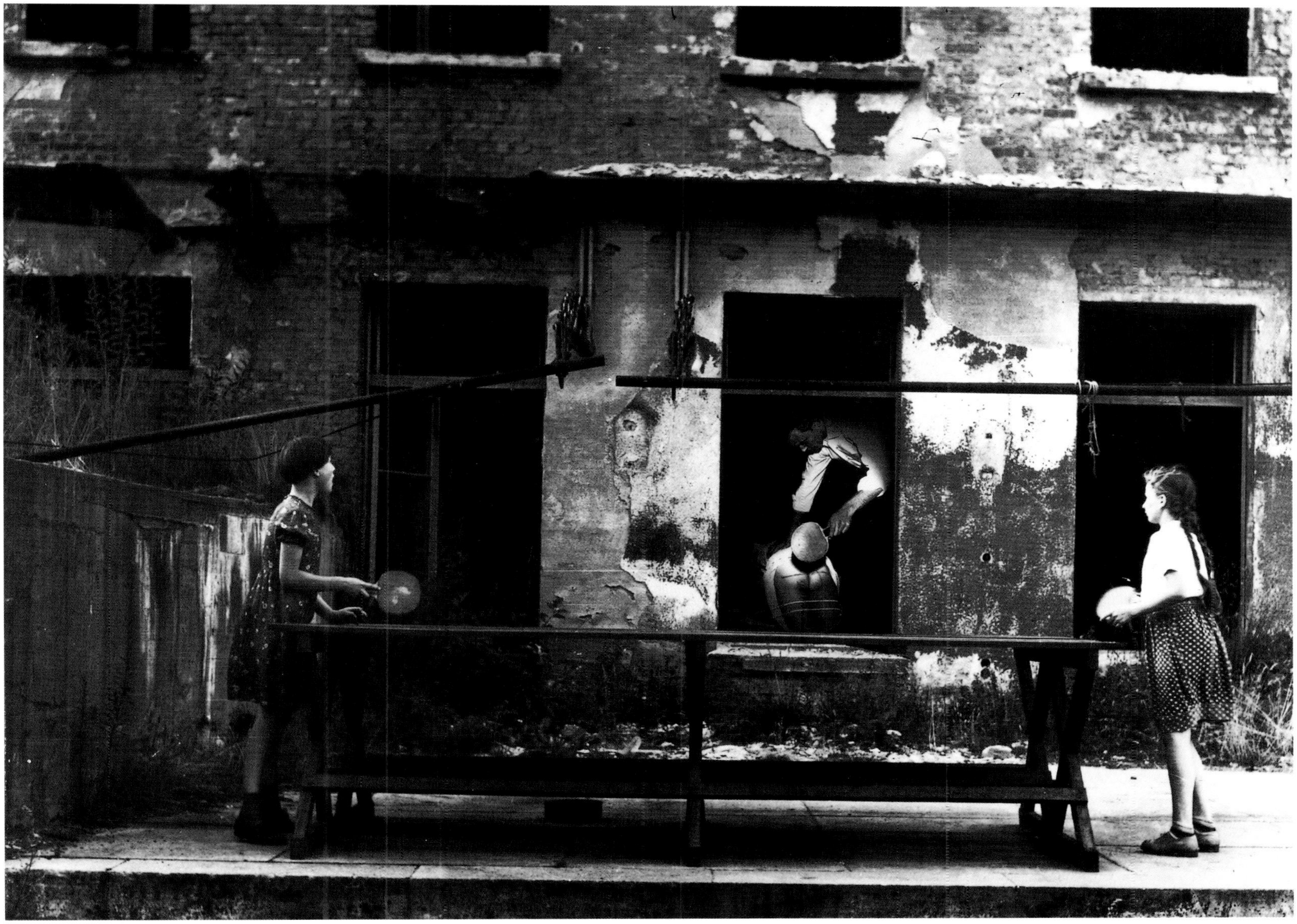

44 **MY BIRTH, 2005**

Selenium-toned silver gelatin print, 11 x 14 inches, edition of 5

Courtesy of the artist and Galerie Lelong, New York

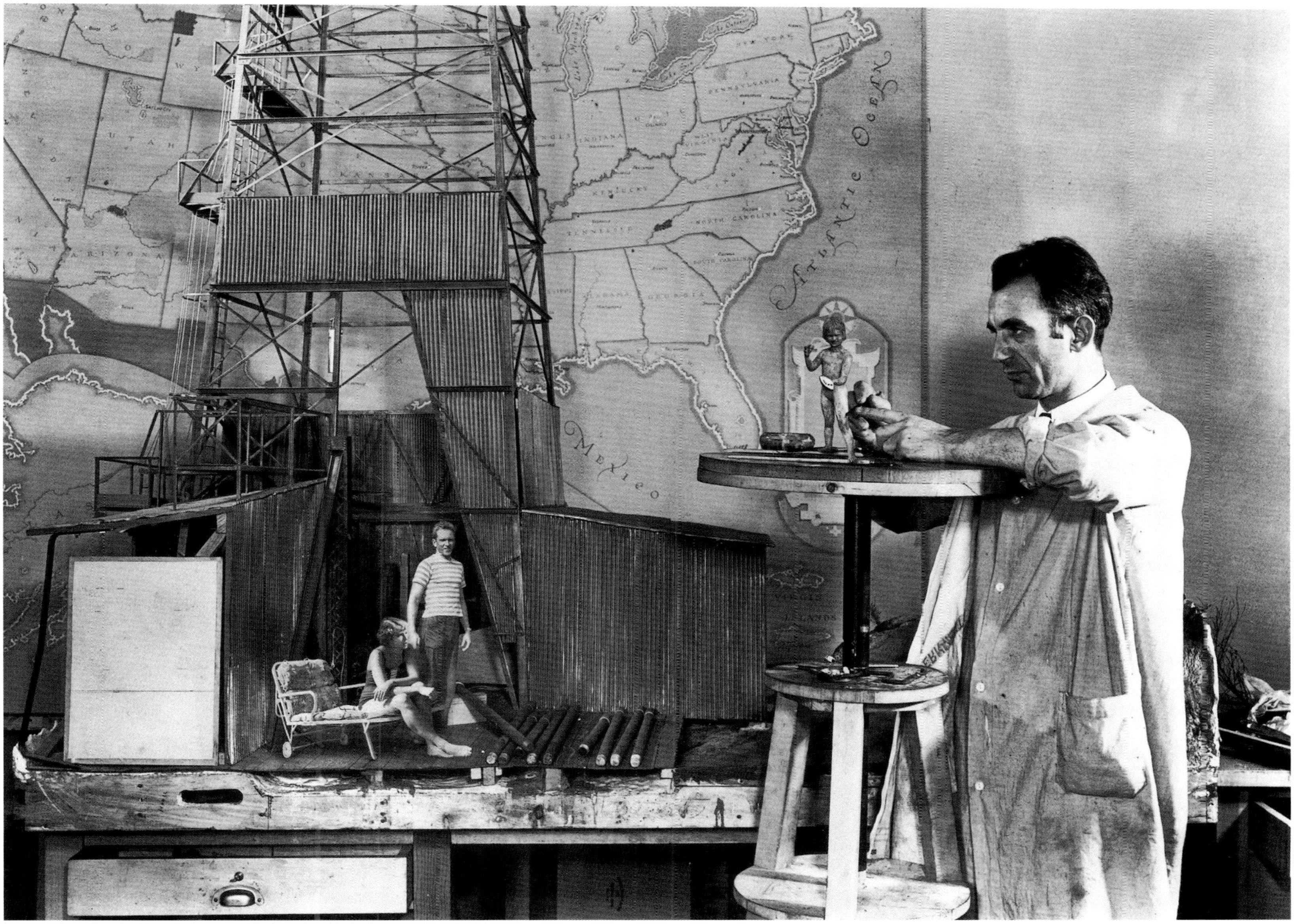
NEW YORK
PENNSYLVANIA
INDIANA
UTAH
ARIZONA
ATLANTIC OCEAN
Mexico

45 **THIRTY-TWO (FOR JEFF KOONS), 2005**

Selenium-toned silver gelatin print, 11 x 14 inches, edition of 5

Courtesy of the artist and Galerie Lelong, New York

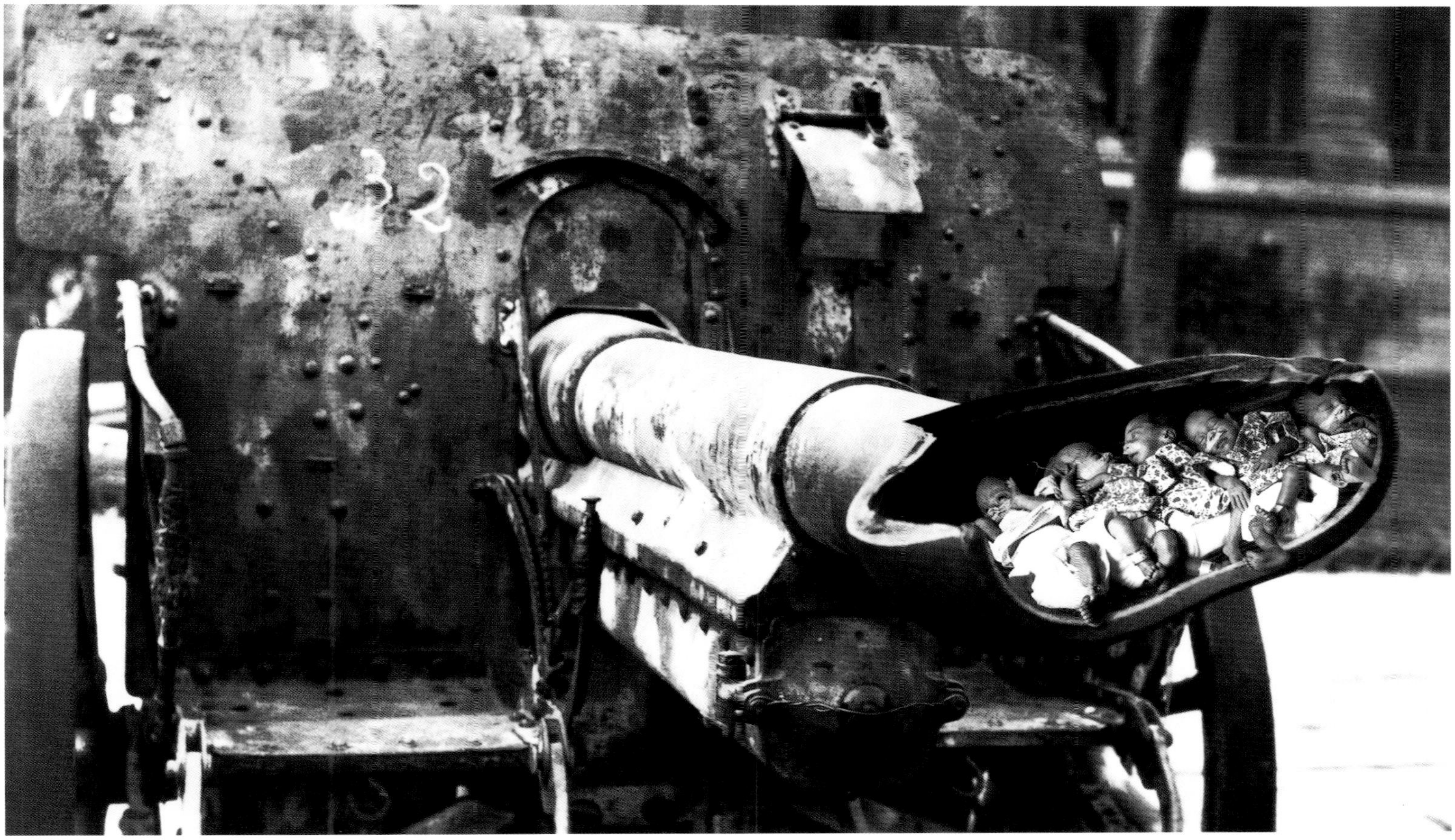
VIS
32

46 **MECHANIC FALLS, 2005**

Selenium-toned silver gelatin print, 11 x 14 inches, edition of 5

Courtesy of the artist and Galerie Lelong, New York

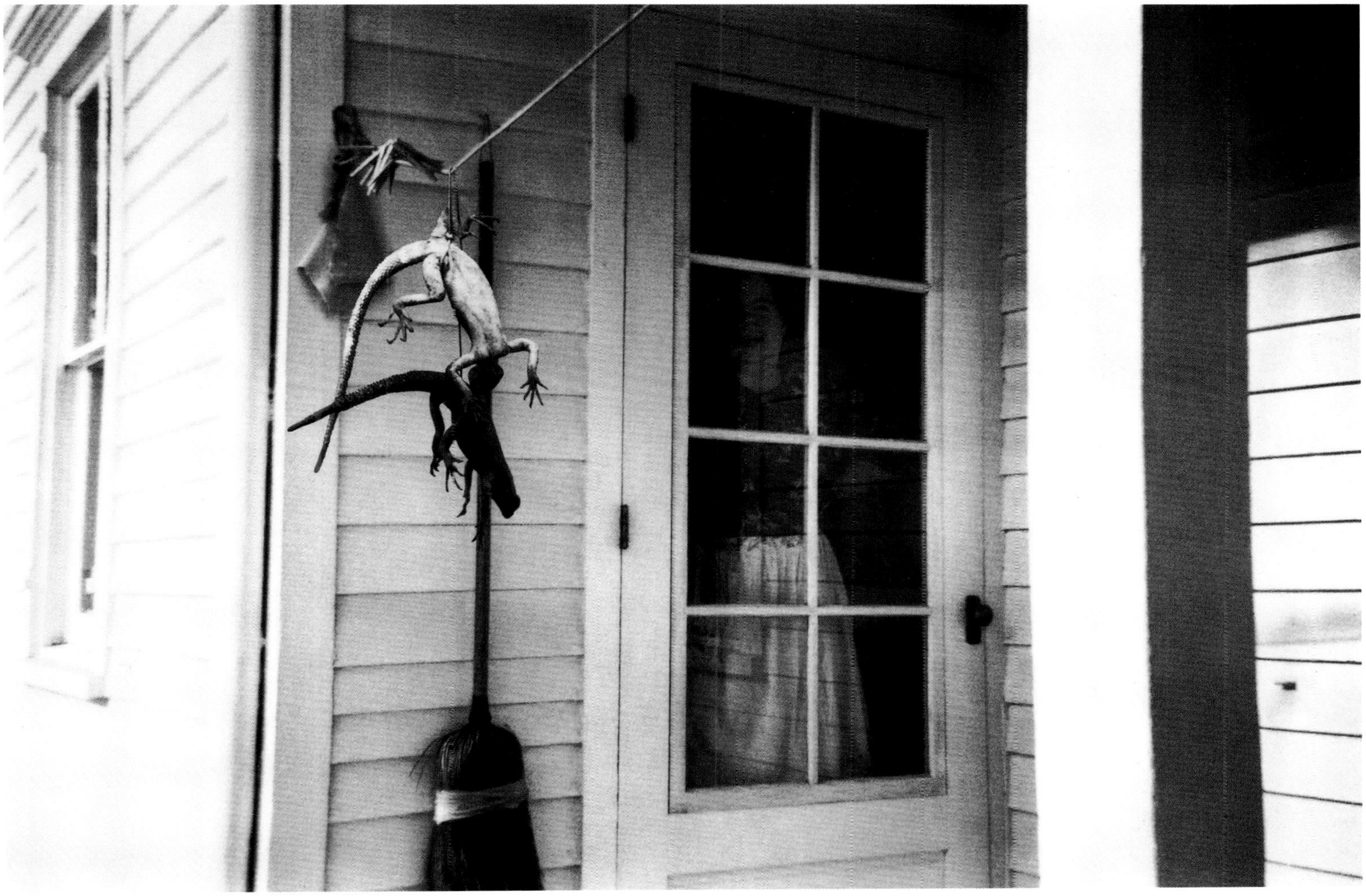

47 **FRIENDLY BEAST, 2005**

Selenium-toned silver gelatin print, 14 x 11 inches, edition of 5

Courtesy of the artist and Galerie Lelong, New York

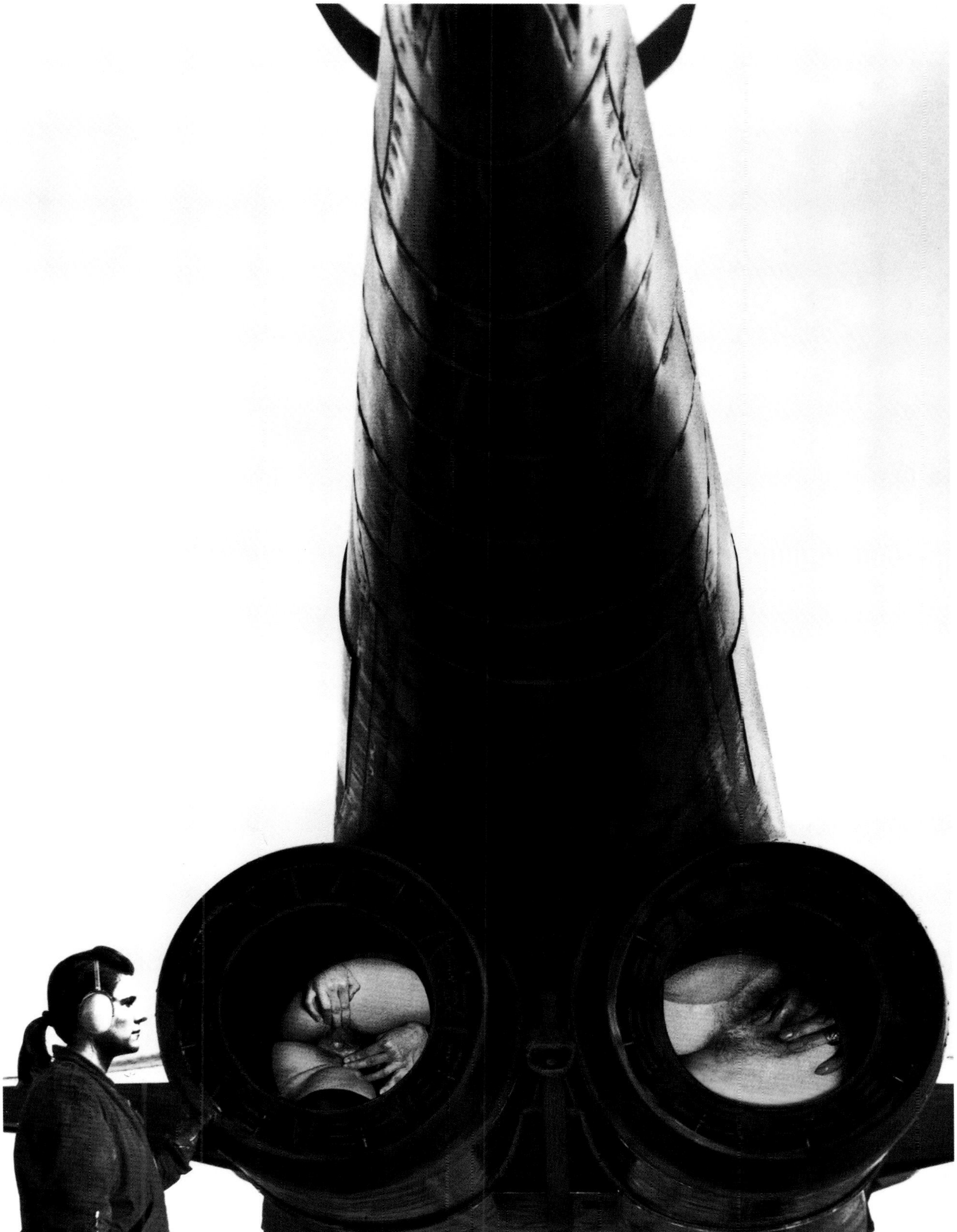

48 | **TOUR ROYALE, 2005**

Selenium-toned silver gelatin print, 11 x 14 inches, edition of 5

Courtesy of the artist and Galerie Lelong, New York

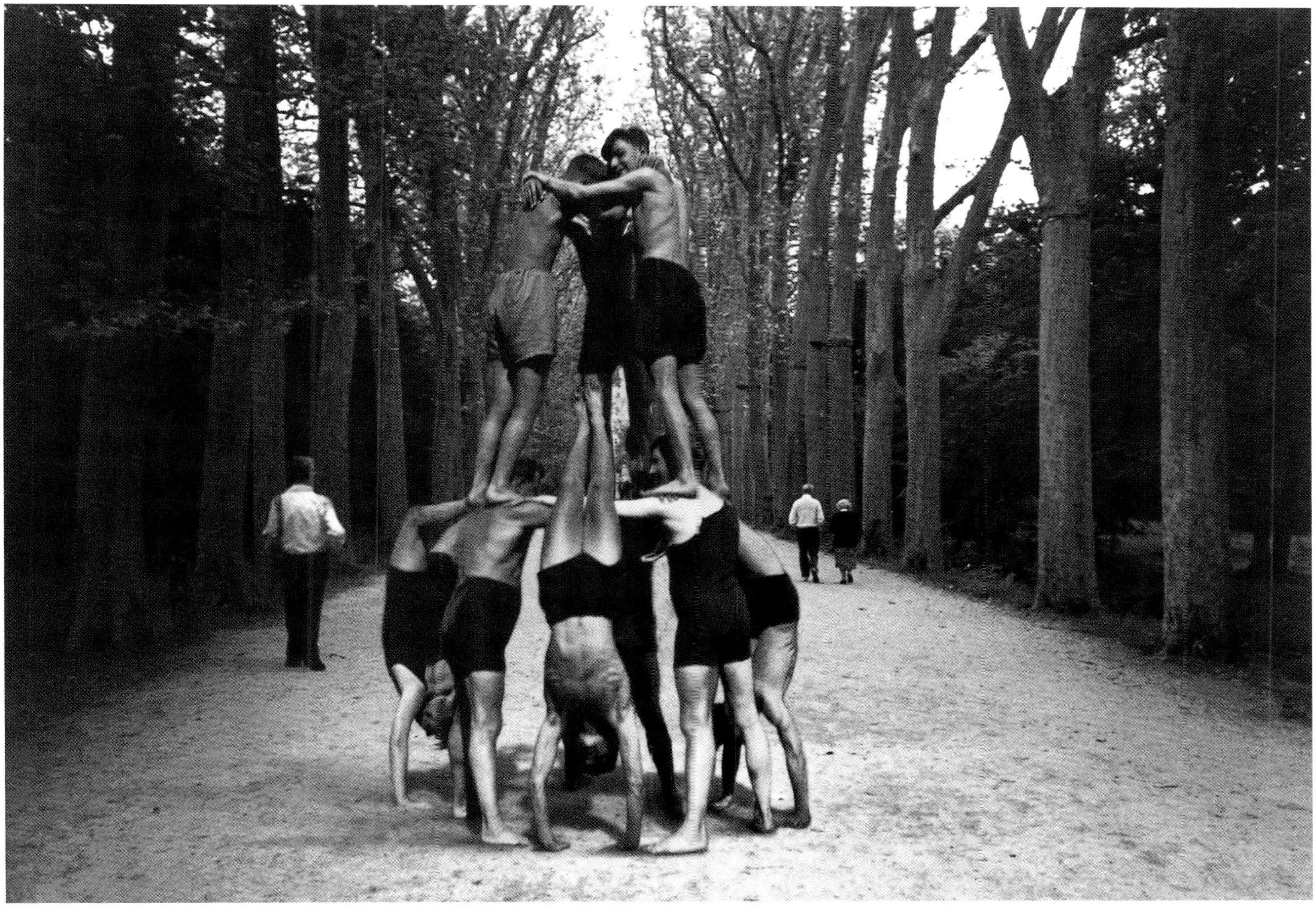

49 **OCTOBER FIRST (MOM'S BIRTHDAY), 2005**

Selenium-toned silver gelatin print, 14 x 11 inches, edition of 5

Courtesy of the artist and Galerie Lelong, New York

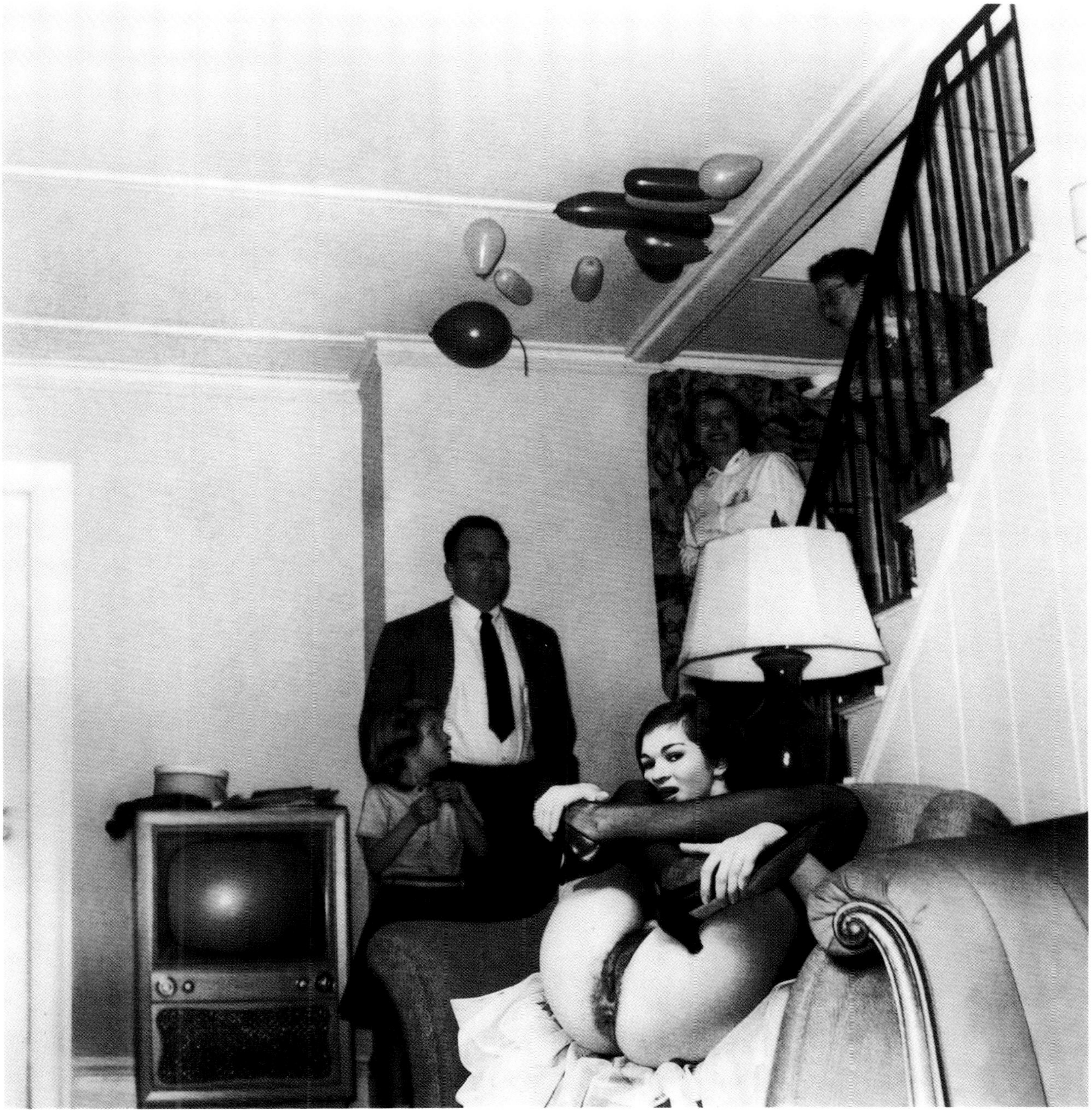

THE MAGIC MAGIC BOOK, 1995

50 Two-volume artist book by Ricky Jay and Vija Celmins, Jane Hammond (detail shown), Justen Ladda, Glenn Ligon, Philip Taaffe, and William Wegman; slipcover: stamped velvet; interior: wood engravings, hand-printed dye-transfers, linoleum cuts, woodcuts, and computer-generated offset lithographs; $10^{5}/_{8}$ x $8^{1}/_{2}$ x $1^{5}/_{8}$ inches, edition of 100, published by the Library Fellows, Whitney Museum of American Art

Collection of the artist

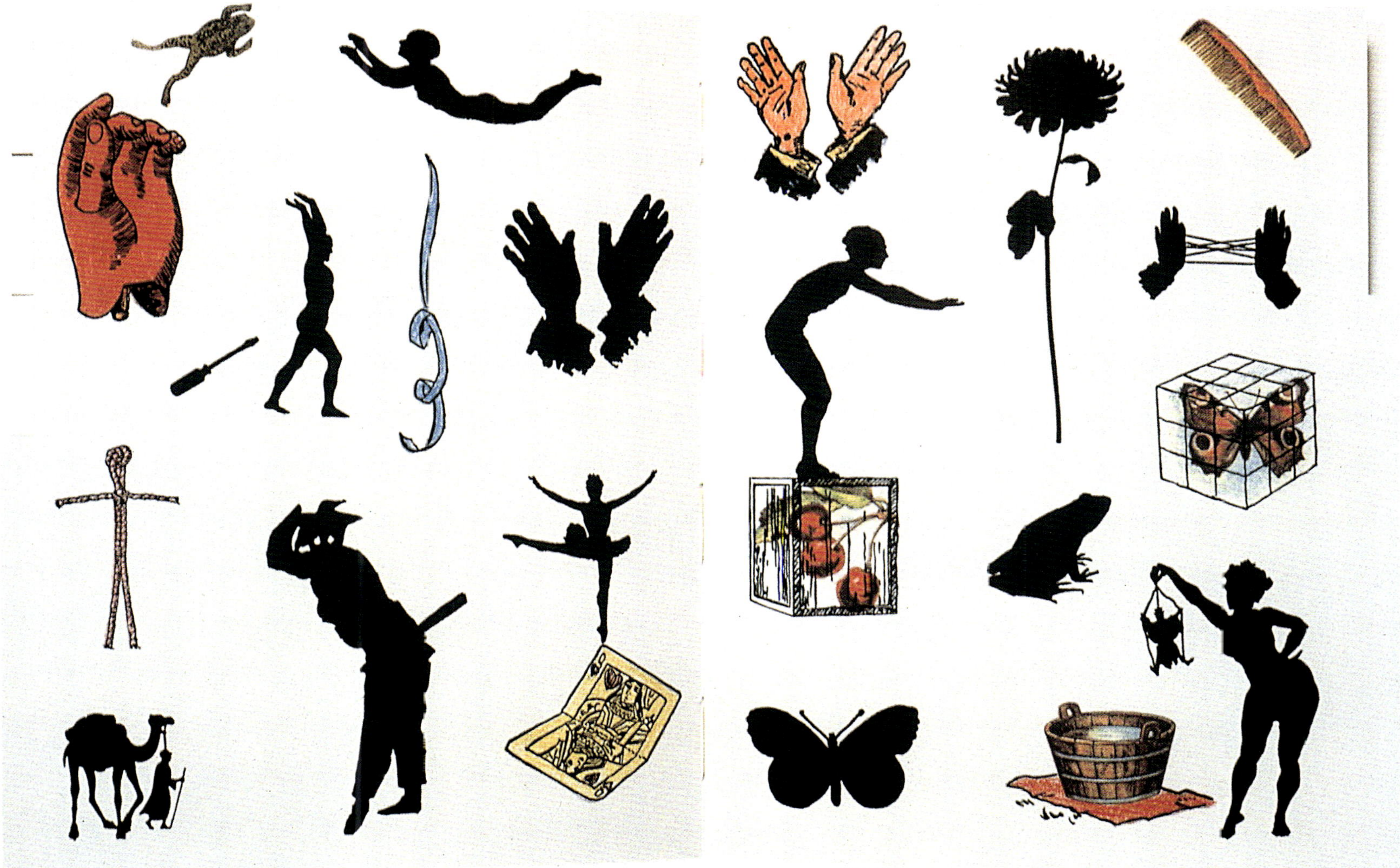

BE ZANY, POISED HARPISTS/BE BLUE, LITTLE SPARROWS, 2002

51 Artist book with poems by Raphael Rubinstein; slipcover: raw Indian silk; cover: cotton rag and abaca paper with Mylar, ink, thread, and fabric couched in between; interior: colored abaca papers with stencil cut-outs, digital prints on acetate, glassine, acetate silhouettes couched between Japanese rice paper with thread, archival digital prints with collage, hand-coloring, found postage stamps, and rubber stamps; $13\frac{1}{2}$ x 11 x 2 inches, edition of 30, published by Dieu Donné Papermill, Inc., in cooperation with Dieu Donné Press and Silicon Gallery Fine Art Prints

Courtesy of the artist and Dieu Donné Papermill, Inc., New York

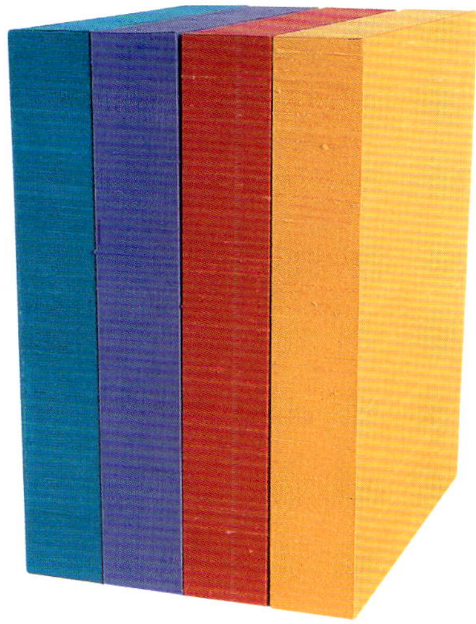

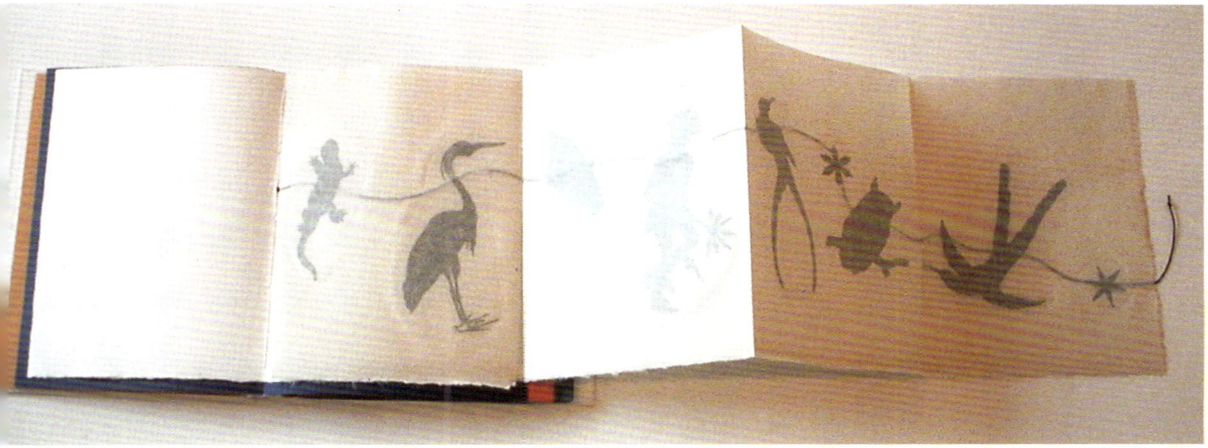

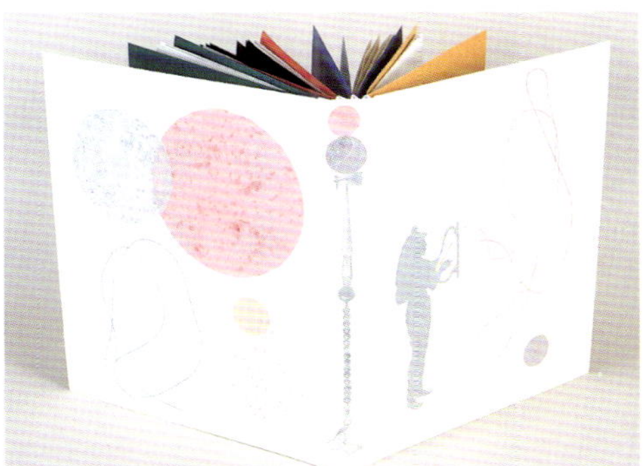

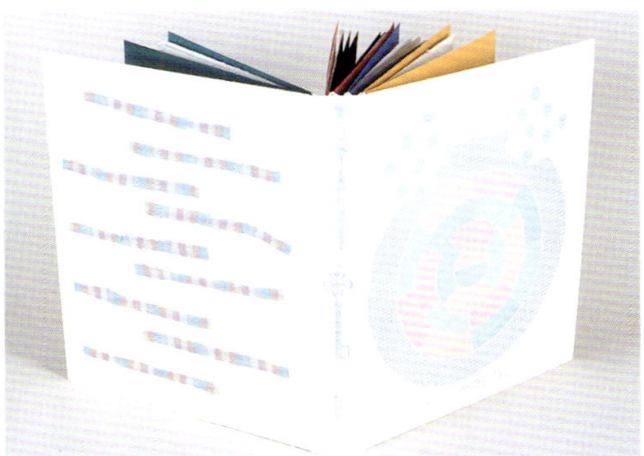

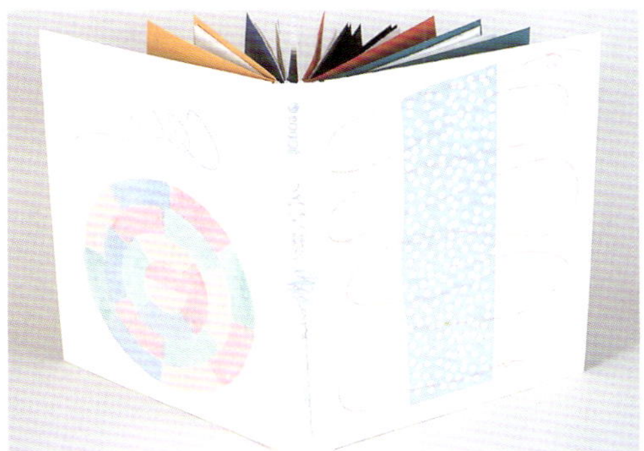

52 **STAMP BOOK, 2005**

Artist book consisting of 64 unique, hand-cut digital inkjet prints set into archival rag papers with silk book cloth, archival book board, Jade glue, cotton book thread, linen binding tape, and transfer adhesive, $12\frac{1}{4}$ x $10\frac{3}{4}$ x $4\frac{1}{4}$ inches, edition of 6, published by the artist

Courtesy of the artist and Galerie Lelong, New York

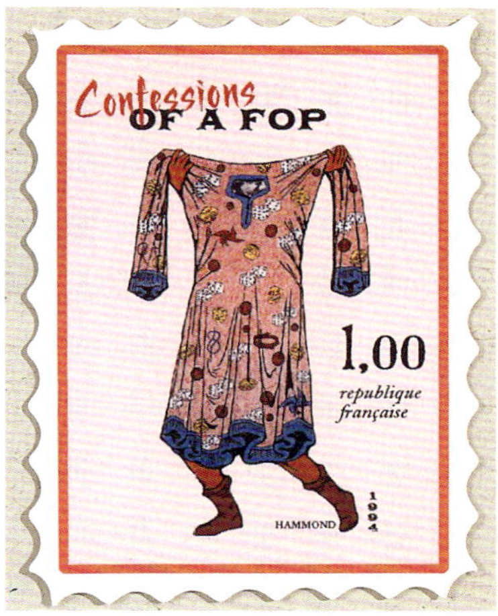
Confessions
OF A FOP
1,00
republique
française
HAMMOND
1994

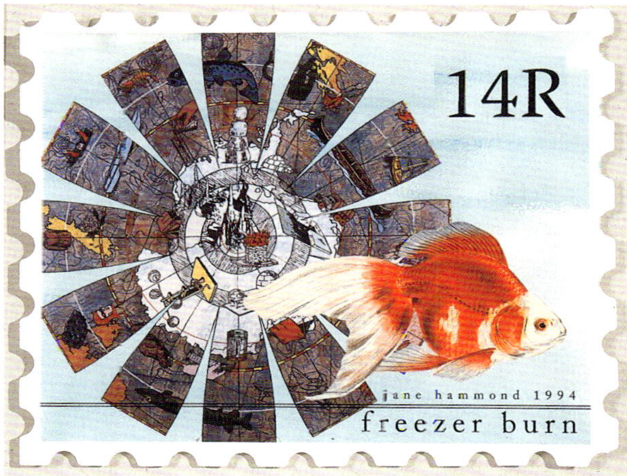
14R
jane hammond 1994
freezer burn

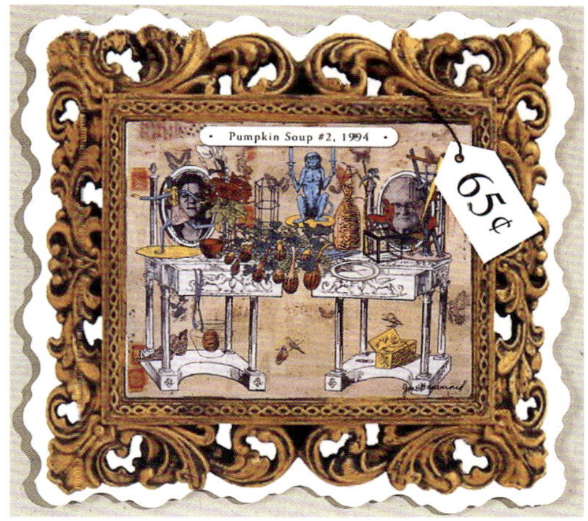
Pumpkin Soup #2, 1994
65¢

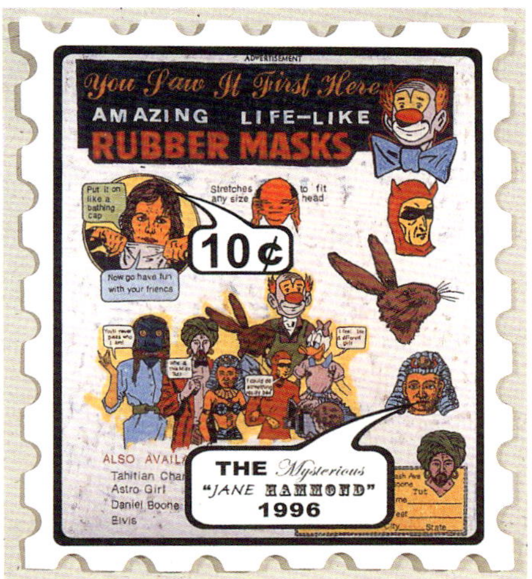
You Saw It First Here
AMAZING LIFE-LIKE
RUBBER MASKS
Stretches any size
to fit head
10¢
Now go have fun with your friends
ALSO AVAIL
Tahitian Cha
Astro Girl
Daniel Boone
Elvis
THE Mysterious
"JANE HAMMOND"
1996

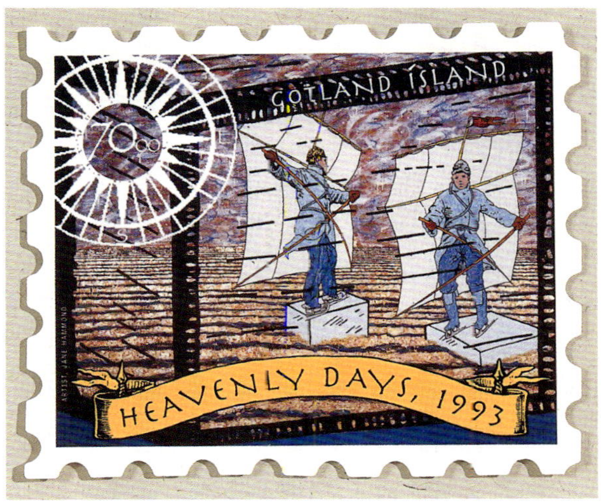
GOTLAND ISLAND
70
HEAVENLY DAYS, 1993

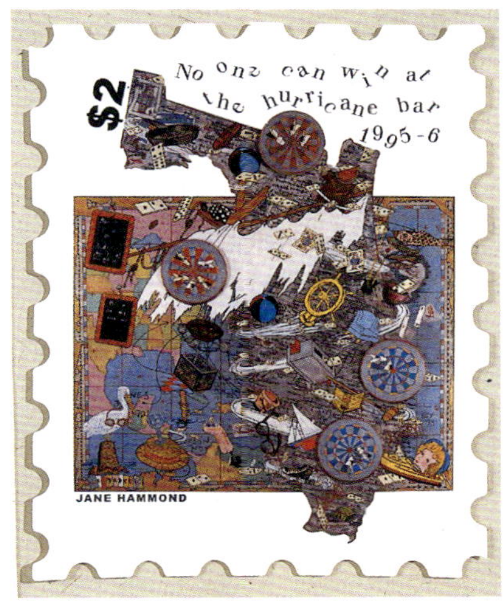
$2
No one can win at
the hurricane bar
1995-6
JANE HAMMOND

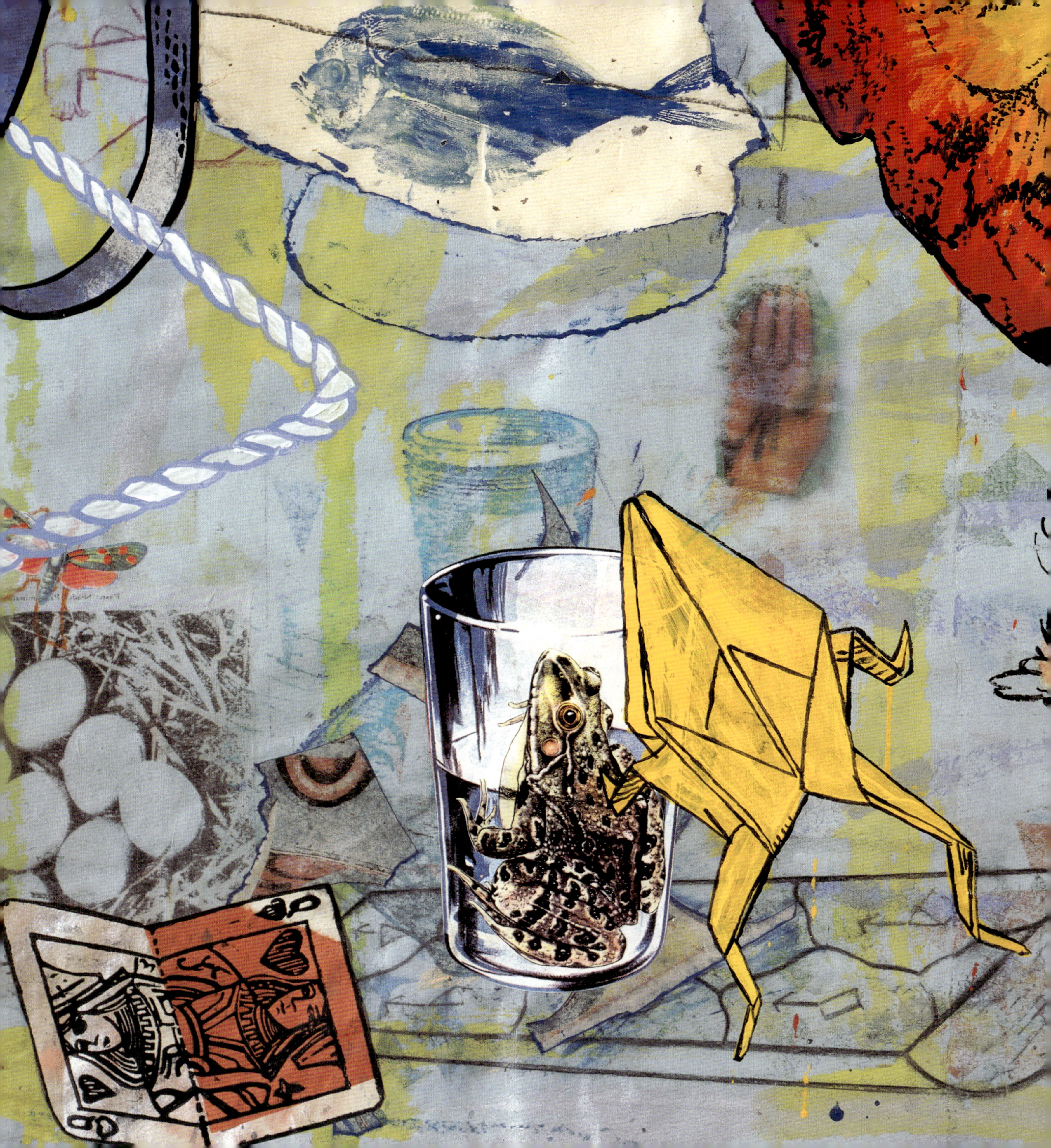

Selected Public Collections

Addison Gallery of American Art, Phillips Academy, Andover, Massachusetts

Albertina Museum, Vienna

Albright-Knox Art Gallery, Buffalo, New York

The Art Institute of Chicago, Chicago

The Baltimore Museum of Art, Baltimore

La Bibliotèque nationale de France, Paris

Brooklyn Museum, Brooklyn, New York

Chazen Museum of Art, University of Wisconsin, Madison

Cincinnati Art Museum, Cincinnati

The Colorado Collection, CU Art Museum, University of Colorado, Boulder

The Contemporary Museum, Honolulu

Davis Museum and Cultural Center, Wellesley College, Wellesley, Massachusetts

The Detroit Institute of Arts, Detroit

The Fogg Art Museum, Harvard University, Cambridge

Fort Wayne Museum of Art, Fort Wayne, Indiana

Grunwald Center for the Graphic Arts, Armand Hammer Museum of Art and Cultural Center, University of California, Los Angeles

Herbert F. Johnson Museum of Art, Cornell University, Ithaca, New York

Honolulu Academy of Arts, Honolulu

Hood Museum of Art, Dartmouth College, Hanover, New Hampshire

Maryland Institute College of Art, Baltimore

El Museo de Arte Contemporáneo, Mexico City

The Metropolitan Museum of Art, New York

Milwaukee Art Museum, Milwaukee

Mount Holyoke College Art Museum, South Hadley, Massachusetts

Museum of Contemporary Art, Chicago

Museum of Fine Arts, Boston

The Museum of Modern Art, New York

National Museum of Women in the Arts, Washington, D.C.

The New York Public Library, New York

Orlando Museum of Art, Orlando, Florida

Portland Art Museum, Portland, Oregon

Saint Louis Art Museum, Saint Louis

San Francisco Museum of Modern Art, San Francisco

San Jose Museum of Art, San Jose, California

Toledo Museum of Art, Toledo, Ohio

Tucson Museum of Art and Historic Block, Tucson, Arizona

Walker Art Center, Minneapolis

Weatherspoon Art Museum, The University of North Carolina, Greensboro

Whitney Museum of American Art, New York

Yale University Art Gallery, New Haven

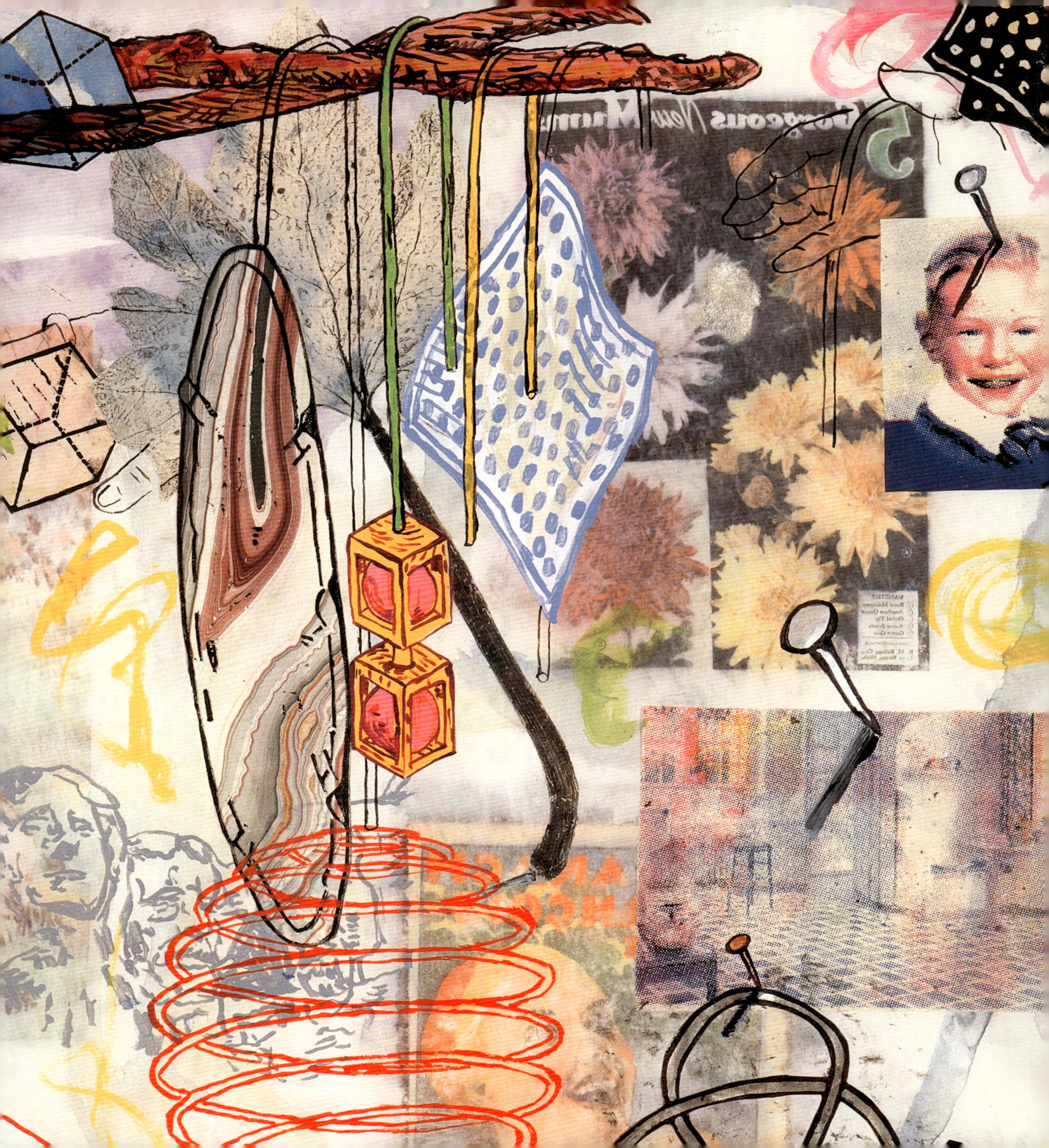

Selected Exhibitions

solo exhibitions

2005

Galerie Lelong, New York

Wetterling Gallery, Stockholm

Byron Cohen Gallery, Kansas City, Missouri

Galería Senda, Barcelona

2004

Greg Kucera Gallery, Seattle

2003

Jane Hammond, Falk Visiting Artist, Weatherspoon Art Museum, The University of North Carolina, Greensboro

Be Zany, Poised Harpists / Be Blue, Little Sparrows, Marjorie G. and Carl W. Stern Book Arts and Special Collections Center, San Francisco Public Library, San Francisco

John Berggruen Gallery, San Francisco

Vanguardia Gallery, Bilbao, Spain

Lemberg Gallery, Ferndale, Michigan

David Floria Gallery, Aspen, Colorado

2002

Whitney Museum of American Art at Philip Morris, New York

Be Zany, Poised Harpists / Be Blue, Little Sparrows, The Gallery at Dieu Donné Papermill, New York

Galería Senda, Barcelona

2001

Galerie Lelong, New York

Jane Hammond: The John Ashbery Collaboration, 1993–2001, Museum of Contemporary Art Cleveland, and travel to The Contemporary Museum, Honolulu; Madison Museum of Contemporary Art, Madison, Wisconsin; Blaffer Gallery, The Art Museum of the University of Houston

Lemberg Gallery, Ferndale, Michigan

2000

Greg Kucera Gallery, Seattle

1999

Lemberg Gallery, Ferndale, Michigan

Galería Senda, Barcelona

Jane Hammond and Judy Pfaff, Byron Cohen Gallery, Kansas City, Missouri

1998

David Beitzel Gallery, New York

Zolla/Lieberman Gallery, Chicago

David Floria Gallery, Aspen, Colorado

Galerie Barbara Farber/Rob Jurka, Amsterdam

1997

Luhring Augustine, New York

Greg Kucera Gallery, Seattle

Mesaros Galleries, West Virginia University, Morgantown

1996

Lemberg Gallery, Ferndale, Michigan

Galerie Barbara Farber/Rob Jurka, Amsterdam

Jose Freire Fine Art, Inc., New York

1995

Zolla/Lieberman Gallery, Chicago

Ruth Bloom Gallery, Santa Monica, California

Jose Freire Fine Art, Inc., New York

1994

Orlando Museum of Art, Orlando, Florida, and travel to Freedman Gallery, Albright College, Reading, Pennsylvania

Jose Freire Fine Art, Inc., New York (collaboration with John Ashbery)

1993

Cincinnati Art Museum, Cincinnati

Greg Kucera Gallery, Seattle

Feigenson/Preston Gallery, Birmingham, Michigan

1992

Transepoca Gallery, Milan

Wetterling Gallery, Stockholm

1991

fiction/nonfiction Gallery, New York

Feigenson/Preston Gallery, Birmingham, Michigan

1990

Wetterling Gallery, Stockholm

Zolla/Lieberman Gallery, Chicago

Honolulu Academy of Arts, Honolulu

fiction/nonfiction Gallery, New York

1989

Exit Art, New York

1987

Nina Freudenheim Gallery, Buffalo, New York

GROUP EXHIBITIONS

2005

Points of View: Landscape and Photography, Galerie Lelong, New York

Summer Group Show, Lemberg Gallery, Ferndale, Michigan

Steven Scott Collects: Donations and Promised Gifts to the Permanent Collection, National Museum of Women in the Arts, Washington, D.C.

25 ans d'Art Contemporain, Le Tenniseum, Musée de Roland-Garros, Paris

Portraits on Paper, Larissa Goldston Gallery, New York

Five Presses: Selected Works, Arvada Center for the Arts and Humanities, Arvada, Colorado

2004

Toy/Box, John Berggruen Gallery, San Francisco

Livres d'artistes américains en Europe, 1960–2000, Musée d'Art Américain Giverny, Giverny, France

New Prints 2004/Summer, International Print Center, New York

What's That? Children's Museum of Manhattan, New York

The Exit Art Print Show, Exit Art, New York

The Flag Project, Rubin Museum of Art, New York

The Sporting Woman: The Female Athlete in American Culture, Mount Holyoke College Art Museum, South Hadley, Massachusetts

Four Decades of Printmaking, 1960–2000: Selections from the Maslow Collection, Everhart Museum of Natural History, Science and Art, Scranton, Pennsylvania

Constructing Realities, Part 2, Selby Gallery, Ringling School of Art and Design, Sarasota, Florida

Toys 'R' Art, Galería Senda, Barcelona

Ten, Byron Cohen Gallery, Kansas City, Missouri

The Buddha Project, Cleveland State University Art Gallery, Cleveland State University, Cleveland

Art, Artists, and the Addison, Addison Gallery of American Art, Phillips Academy, Andover, Massachusetts

ULAE: The Print Show, Oklahoma City Museum of Art, Oklahoma City

Arte Termita Contra Elefante Blanco, Museo Colecciones ICO, Madrid
Super-Sized: The Big Print Show, Greg Kucera Gallery, Seattle
Roberta Lieberman, A Sharp Eye: An Art Dealer's 40-Year Journey, Evanston Art Center, Evanston, Illinois
ULAE: New Editions, Works on Paper, Inc., Philadelphia

2003

Divergent, Galerie Lelong, New York
I Love New York, Mary Ryan Gallery, New York
Color, Form, Figure, John Berggruen Gallery, San Francisco
Splendid Pages: The Molly and Walter Bareiss Collection of Modern Illustrated Books, Toledo Museum of Art, Toledo, Ohio
A Way With Words, John Berggruen Gallery, San Francisco
Art a Century Apart: 1903 and 2003, Mississippi Museum of Art, Jackson
On Paper: Masterworks from the Addison Collection, Addison Gallery of American Art, Phillips Academy, Andover, Massachusetts
Contemporary Prints and Photographs from the Bruce Brown Collection, Colby College Museum of Art, Colby College, Waterville, Maine
ULAE: Recent Editions, David Floria Gallery, Aspen, Colorado
Word/Image, Westport Arts Center, Westport, Connecticut
ULAE: New Editions, Lemberg Gallery, Ferndale, Michigan

2002

177th Annual, National Academy Museum, New York
American Painting, Christian Dam Gallery, Oslo
Universal Limited Art Editions, Devin Borden Hiram Butler Gallery, Houston
New York, New Work, Now! Currier Museum of Art, Manchester, New Hampshire
Resisting Categories, Pierro Gallery of South Orange, South Orange, New Jersey
The Art of Healing II, Greg Kucera Gallery, Seattle
One Thousand Words: Storytelling Images from Cultures Around the World, John Michael Kohler Arts Center, Sheboygan, Wisconsin
Remarkable Women, Peltz Gallery, Milwaukee

2001

Digital Printmaking Now, Brooklyn Museum, Brooklyn, New York
Curator's Choice: A Personal Look at Prints, The Detroit Institute of Arts, Detroit
Summer in the City, John Berggruen Gallery, San Francisco
Bugs, Pace Prints, New York
Underfoot, Associação Alumni, São Paulo, Brazil
Kinds of Drawing, Herter Gallery, University of Massachusetts, Amherst
Summer Group Exhibition, David Beitzel Gallery, New York
High Art: Art of the Bank of America Tower, Bank of America Gallery, Seattle
Din Art 4, Museum für Kommunikation, Frankfurt
State of the Art 2001, International Biennial Watercolor Invitational, Parkland Art Gallery, Parkland College, Champaign, Illinois
Luck of the Drawn, Geoffrey Young Gallery, Great Barrington, Massachusetts
Celebrating Women's Art—Benefiting Women's Health: In Honor of the Lynne Cohen Foundation for Ovarian Cancer Research, Bobbie Greenfield Gallery, Santa Monica, California

2000

Picturing the Modern Amazon, New Museum of Contemporary Art, New York
1001 Nights, Oberösterreichische Landesmuseen, Linz, Austria
Mapping Cities, Boston University Art Gallery, Boston
Drawing and Photographs, Matthew Marks Gallery, New York
The Likeness of Being: Self-Portraits by Contemporary Women Artists, DC Moore Gallery, New York
The End: An Independent Vision of the History of Contemporary Art, Exit Art, New York
Reconstructions: The Imprint of Nature/The Impact of Science, The Sidney Mishkin Gallery, Baruch College, The City University of New York, New York
Selections from the Permanent Collection and Loans from Private Collections, Portland Art Museum, Portland, Oregon
UTEP Millennium Printmaking Invitational, Fox Fine Arts Center, The University of Texas, El Paso
New Prints, David Adamson Gallery, Washington, D.C.
Lasting Impressions, Portland Museum of Art, Portland, Maine

1999

The Broad Spectrum: Color on Paper, Past and Present, The Art Institute of Chicago, Chicago
Summer Group Exhibition, David Beitzel Gallery, New York
The Body as Question, The Speed Art Museum, Louisville, Kentucky
A Sense of Risk, Selections from the Shiffler Foundation, Miami University Art Museum, Miami University, Oxford, Ohio
Faster Than a Speeding Bullet: Superheroes in Contemporary Art, Museum of Contemporary Art Cleveland, Cleveland
Gallery Artists, Zolla/Lieberman Gallery, Chicago
Fabled Impressions, Georgia Museum of Art, Athens, Georgia
Women in Print, Jim Kempner Fine Art, New York

Elliot Green, Jane Hammond, David True, Trevor Winkfield, Tibor de Nagy Gallery, New York

Domestic Pleasures, Galerie Lelong, New York

Portraits, Jim Kempner Fine Art, New York

The New Museum Annual Benefit Exhibition, New Museum of Contemporary Art, New York

Calendar 2000 Project, The Center for Curatorial Studies, Bard College, Annandale-on-Hudson, New York

Die Kunst der Linie (*The Artistic Possibilities of the Line*), Landesgalerie Oberösterreich, Linz, Austria

Contemporary Narrative in American Prints, Whitney Museum of American Art at Champion, Stamford, Connecticut

1998

Secret Victorians, Firstsite/The Minories Art Gallery, Colchester, England, and travel to Arnolfini, Bristol, England; Ikon Gallery, Birmingham, England; Middlesbrough Art Gallery, Middlesbrough, England; Armand Hammer Museum of Art and Cultural Center, University of California, Los Angeles; The Fabric Workshop and Museum, Philadelphia

Prints in the '90's from ULAE, Marlborough Chelsea, New York, and travel to Fay Gold Gallery, Atlanta; City Arts Center, Oklahoma City; Locus Gallery, Saint Louis; James Kelly Contemporary, Santa Fe, New Mexico

Artists on Line for ACOR, Gagosian Gallery, New York

Preview, Byron Cohen Gallery, Kansas City, Missouri

Knowing Children, David Beitzel Gallery, New York

Preserving the Past, Securing the Future, National Museum of Women in the Arts, Washington, D.C.

Masters of the Masters, The Butler Institute of American Art, Youngstown, Ohio

Paper + Works on Dieu Donné Paper, The Gallery at Dieu Donné Papermill, New York

A Sustaining Passion: The Tsagaris/Hillberry Collection, Cedar Rapids Museum of Art, Cedar Rapids, Iowa, and travel to Dubuque Museum of Art, Dubuque, Iowa

1997

New Work by Gallery Artists, Lemberg Gallery, Ferndale, Michigan

Livres d'Artistes, Espace Culturel de Tigeaux, Tigeaux, France

Michael Banicki, Jane Hammond, Tim Rollins + KOS, Gahlberg Gallery, McAninch Arts Center, College of DuPage, Glen Ellyn, Illinois

ULAE: A Print Survey, Greg Kucera Gallery, Seattle

Proof Positive: 40 Years of Contemporary American Printmaking at ULAE, 1957–1997, The Corcoran Gallery of Art, Washington, D.C., and travel to CU Art Museum, University of Colorado, Boulder; Armand Hammer Museum of Art and Cultural Center, University of California, Los Angeles; Sezon Museum of Art, Tokyo

New York, Galleri F15, Oslo

Collector's Choice, Orlando Museum of Art, Orlando, Florida

1996

Making Time, Kittredge Gallery, University of Puget Sound, Tacoma, Washington

The Changing Image, Gian Ferrari Arte Contemporanea, Milan

Talk Back! A Forum for Critical Discourse, http://www.lehman.cuny.edu/gallery/talkback

100 Years of Collecting, Cornell Fine Arts Museum, Rollins College, Winter Park, Florida

Contemporary Floral, Steven Scott Gallery, Owings Mills, Maryland

1995

Recent Print Exhibitions, The Museum of Modern Art, New York

Insight. David Beitzel Gallery, New York
Summer Group Show. Luhring Augustine, New York
This End Up: Selections from the Robert J. Shiffler Collection. University of Wyoming Art Museum, University of Wyoming, Laramie and travel to South Dakota Art Museum, South Dakota State University, Brookings; Arvada Center for the Arts and Humanities, Arvada, Colorado; Museum of Contemporary Art Cleveland, Cleveland
Group Painting Show. Galleri K, Oslo
Playtime: Artists and Toys. Whitney Museum of American Art at Champion, Stamford, Connecticut
Ten Young American Artists. Wetterling Teo Gallery, Singapore
Anxiety and the Irrational: Selections from the Permanent Collection. Whitney Museum of American Art, New York
Prints to Benefit the Foundation for Contemporary Performance Arts. Brooke Alexander Editions, New York
The Magic Magic Book. Whitney Museum of American Art, New York
Reinventing the Emblem: Contemporary Artists Recreate a Renaissance Idea. Yale University Art Gallery, Yale University, New Haven
Large and Small: Prints from Universal Limited Art Editions. The Art Institute of Chicago, Chicago
Sex. Greg Kucera Gallery, Seattle

1994

Selections from the Collection: Recent Print Acquisitions. Whitney Museum of American Art, New York
A Garden. Barbara Krakow Gallery, Boston
Who Chooses Who. New Museum of Contemporary Art, New York
Not for the First Time. Richard F. Brush Art Gallery, St. Lawrence University, Canton, New York
Night Visions and Other Obsessions. Marguerite Oestreicher Fine Arts, New Orleans
Drawings for Lacanian Ink. Thread Waxing Space, New York

1993

ULAE: New Editions. Brooke Alexander Editions, New York, and travel to Bobbie Greenfield Gallery, Santa Monica, California
Living with Art: The Saul and Ellyn Dennison Collection. Morris Museum, Morristown, New Jersey
Scratching the Surface. The Picker Art Gallery, Colgate University, Hamilton, New York
New York Works on Paper. Geoffery Young Gallery, Great Barrington, Massachusetts
Regarding Masculinity. Arthur Roger Gallery, New Orleans
Figure as Fiction. Contemporary Arts Center, Cincinnati
Benefit for the Foundation for Contemporary Performance Art. Leo Castelli Gallery, New York
I, the Enunciator. Thread Waxing Space, New York
The Fine Art of Patronage. Cranbrook Art Museum, Cranbrook Academy of Art, Bloomfield Hills, Michigan
Hypnosis. Maryland Institute College of Art, Baltimore

1992

Fear of Painting. Arthur Roger Gallery, New York
Painting Culture. The University Art Gallery and Room Gallery, University of California, Irvine
Group Exhibition. John Berggruen Gallery, San Francisco
Landscape as Stage. Locks Gallery, Philadelphia
Hair. John Michael Kohler Arts Center, Sheboygan, Wisconsin
Collectif Génération, Le Peintre, l'écrivain et le livre, 1988–1992. Low Memorial Library, Columbia University, New York
Jane Hammond, Valerie Parks, Archie Rand. Feigenson/Preston Gallery, Birmingham, Michigan
Selections 1991: Recent Acquisitions of the Honolulu Advertiser Collection. The Contemporary Museum, Honolulu
Gallery Selections. Feigenson/Preston Gallery, Birmingham, Michigan
Painted Word/Written Image. Greg Kucera Gallery, Seattle
Four Painters. Galerie Nichido, Tokyo, and travel to Galerie Nichido, Nagoya, Japan
Drawn in the Nineties. Katonah Museum of Art, Katonah, New York, and travel to Indiana University Art Museum, Indiana University, Bloomington; Illingworth Kerr Gallery, Alberta College of Art and Design, Calgary, Alberta, Canada; Huntsville Museum of Art, Huntsville, Alabama

1991

43rd Annual Academy-Institute Purchase Exhibition. American Academy and Institute of Arts and Letters, New York
Painting Culture. fiction/nonfiction Gallery, New York
Livres d'Artistes of Collectif Génération. The Center for Book Arts Gallery, The Center for Book Arts and French Cultural Services, New York
Marking the Decades: 1960–1990. The Baltimore Museum of Art, Baltimore
Group Exhibition—Drawings. Charles Cowles Gallery, New York
New ULAE. Pence Gallery, Davis, California
Words & #s. University Art Galleries, Wright State University, Dayton, Ohio
Drawing Conclusions. Molica Guid'Arte, New York

Europa / America, Molica Guid'Arte, New York

Abstract Information: First Impressions, Last Resorts—Printmaking at the End of the Century, The Gallery of Contemporary Art, Sacred Heart University, Fairfield, Connecticut, and travel to The Center for Curatorial Studies, Bard College, Annandale-on-Hudson, New York

Gallery Artists, fiction/nonfiction Gallery, New York

Presswork: The Art of Women Printmakers, National Museum of Women in the Arts, Washington, D.C., and travel to Atlanta College of Art Gallery, Atlanta College of Art, Atlanta; Frederick R. Weisman Art Museum, University of Minnesota, Minneapolis; Chazen Museum of Art, University of Wisconsin, Madison; The Butler Institute of American Art, Youngstown, Ohio; Fine Arts Gallery, Federal Reserve Bank of Kansas City, Kansas City, Missouri; Ulrich Museum of Art, Wichita State University, Wichita, Kansas; Portsmouth Museums, Portsmouth Community Arts Center, Portsmouth, Virginia; George A. Spiva Center for the Arts, Joplin, Missouri

Benefit Exhibition: 14th Anniversary, New Museum of Contemporary Art, New York

The ICI 15th Anniversary Print Portfolio, Castelli Graphics, New York, and travel to Pace Gallery, New York; Brooke Alexander Editions, New York; Meyers/Bloom Gallery, Los Angeles

Eye for Art II, The Detroit Institute of Arts, Detroit

Cross Sections—Contemporary Art Collections in Detroit, Meadow Brook Art Gallery, Oakland University, Rochester, Michigan

Barrett, Hammond, Salo, Wesley, fiction/nonfiction Gallery, New York

Black and White, Nina Freudenheim Gallery, Buffalo, New York

Retakes—Prints and Drawings by 6 Canadian and 6 American Artists, Extension Gallery, Toronto, Ontario, Canada

Word as Image: American Art 1960–1990, Milwaukee Art Museum, Milwaukee, and travel to Oklahoma City Museum of Art, Oklahoma City; Contemporary Arts Museum Houston, Houston

1990

42nd Annual Academy-Institute Purchase Exhibition, American Academy and Institute of Arts and Letters, New York

The Unique Print, Museum of Fine Arts, Boston

11th British International Print Biennale, Bradford Museums, Galleries and Heritage, Bradford, England

La Bibliothèque Imaginée de Collectif Génération, Victoria and Albert Museum, London, and travel to Musée de Graveline, Graveline, France

Sixth Sense, Pence Gallery, Davis, California

Out of Abstraction, Islip Art Museum, East Islip, New York

Intimate Inventions/Gestural Abstractions, Madison Museum of Contemporary Art, Madison, Wisconsin

Waterworks, Universal Limited Art Editions, Inc., Bay Shore, New York

Gallery Selections, fiction/nonfiction Gallery, New York

Faces, Marc Richards Galleries, Los Angeles

Works on Paper, Shea and Beker Gallery, New York

Gallery Selections, Feigenson/Preston Gallery, Birmingham, Michigan

The Fifth Essence, Gracie Mansion Gallery, New York

A Selection of Selections, Parsons The New School for Design, New York

1989

Selections from The Laila and Thurston Twigg-Smith Collection, The Contemporary Museum, Honolulu

25th National Print Exhibition, Brooklyn Museum, Brooklyn, New York

Visions of the Volcano, East Hawaii Cultural Center, Hilo, and travel to The Contemporary Museum, Honolulu; Stones Gallery, Lihue, Kauai

New Work, Feigenson/Preston Gallery, Birmingham, Michigan

Ten Gallery Artists, Nina Freudenheim Gallery, Buffalo, New York

Summer Group Exhibition, Shea and Beker Gallery, New York

Invitational with Gallery Artists, fiction/nonfiction Gallery, New York

Summer Group Exhibition, Ledis-Flam Gallery, New York

Summer Group Exhibition, Dolan/Maxwell Gallery, Philadelphia

Invitational, Feigenson/Preston Gallery, Birmingham, Michigan

Works on Paper, Summer Invitational, Dolan/Maxwell Gallery, Philadelphia

Small Paintings, Nina Freudenheim Gallery, Buffalo, New York

Prints and Trial Proofs, Simon James Gallery, Berkeley, California

Earth Remembered, Hook Gallery, Brooklyn, New York

Drawing and Related Prints, Castelli Graphics, New York

100 Women's Drawings, Hillwood Art Museum, Long Island University, C.W. Post Campus, Brookville, New York, and travel to Blum Helman Gallery, New York

1988

The New Generation, Elaine Benson Gallery and Sculpture Garden, Bridgehampton, New York

Underknown in New York II, The Bertha and Karl Leubsdorf Art Gallery, Hunter College, The City University of New York, New York

1987

Painters Make Prints, Maryland Institute College of Art, Baltimore, and travel to The Community College of Baltimore County Essex, Essex; Hodson Gallery, Tatem Arts Center, Hood College, Frederick; Stephanie Ann Roper Gallery, Fine Arts Building, Frostburg State University, Frostburg, Maryland

Pastel Anthology II, Grace Borgenicht Gallery, New York

Invitational Exhibition, Stux Gallery, New York

Paper, Dalsheimer Gallery, Baltimore

1986

SmallScale Abstraction, Grace Borgenicht Gallery, New York

Inaugural Exhibition, Cavin-Morris Gallery, New York

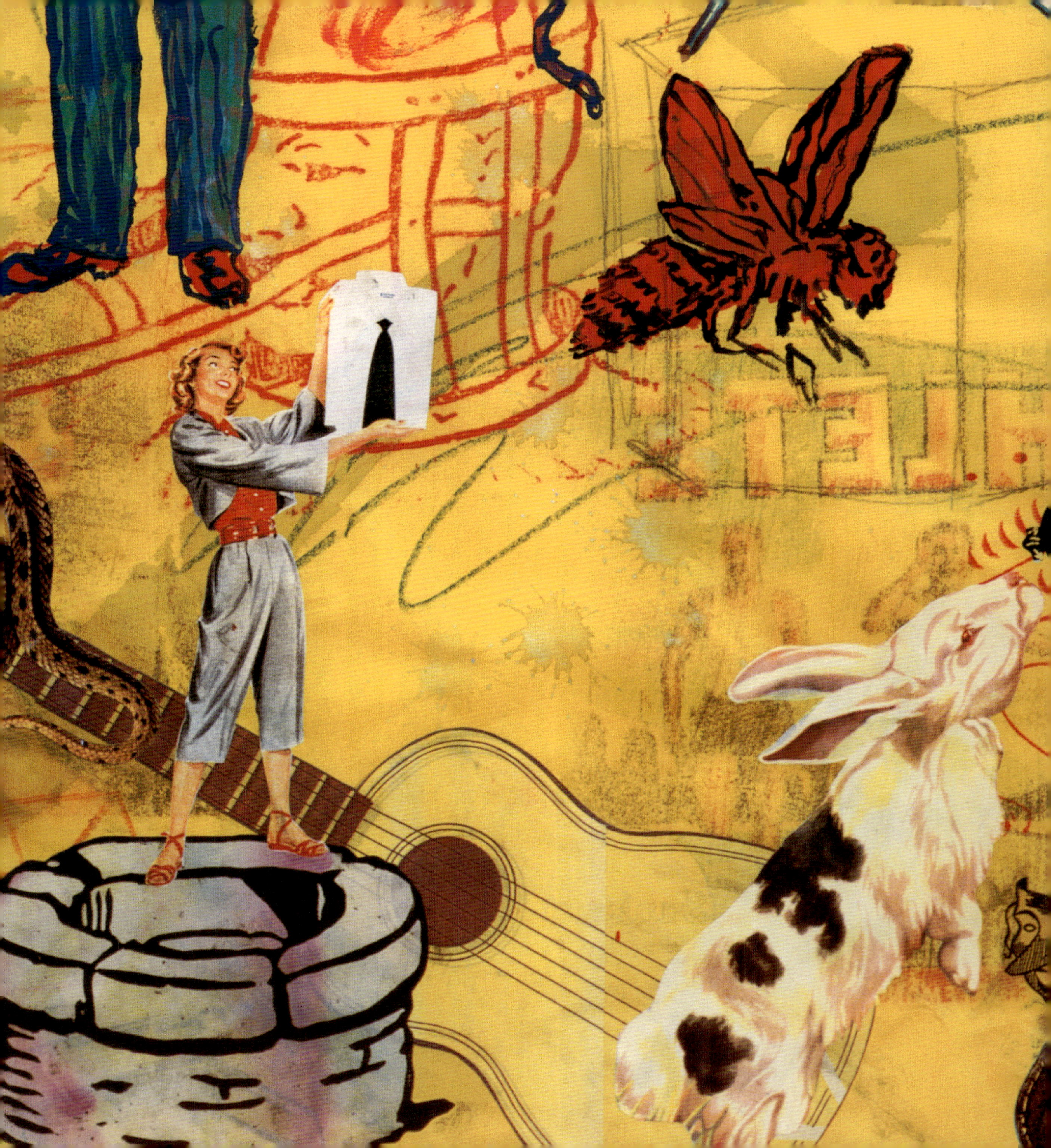

Selected Bibliography

Ackley, Clifford. *The Unique Print Today*. Boston: Museum of Fine Arts, 1990.

Ament, Doloris Tarzan. "New York Artist Makes Beautiful Impressions." *Seattle Times*, April 8, 1993.

"Art of the Butterfly: Body Language 2002 by Jane Hammond." *American Butterflies*, summer 2002, 42–43.

Ashbery, John. *Jane Hammond New Paintings*. Stockholm: Wetterling Gallery, 1990.

Atkins, Robert. *Arena* (Spain), June 1989, 109–10.

Barckett, Lynda. "Jane Hammond at the Zolla/Lieberman Gallery." *Reader*, November 23, 1990, 29.

Bass, Ruth. "Jane Hammond." *Arts*, May 1989, 171–72.

———. "New York, New York." *ART-TALK*, August–September 1987, 58.

Bee, Susan, and Mira Schor. "Jane Hammond." *New Observations* (New York), winter 1996, 8–9.

Bembnister, Theresa. "Jane Hammond." *Kansas City Star*, September 15, 2005, 31.

Betti, Claudia, and Teel Sale. *Drawing, A Contemporary Approach*. Belmont, California: Wadsworth, 2004, 286–87, 308, 318, 341.

Bradford Art Galleries and Museums. *11th British International Print Biennale*. Bradford Art Galleries and Museums, Bradford, England, 1990.

Brody, Jaqueline. *Paper*. New York: Dieu Donné Papermill, 1998.

Brooklyn Museum of Art. *Digital: Printmaking Now*. Brooklyn: Brooklyn Museum of Art, 2001.

Cameron, Dan. "Critical Edge: The Easel Way Out." *Art & Auction*, December 1994, 66–69.

———. "Critical Edge: What Goes Around. . . ." *Art & Auction*, October 1993, 81, 82.

———. "The Outlaw Academy." *Art & Auction*, April 1992, 96–98.

Campbell, Shane. "Jane Hammond." *New Art Examiner* (Chicago), September 1996, 47.

Carrier, David. "Jane Hammond at the Cleveland Center for Contemporary Art." *Artforum*, March 2002, 144.

Cembalest, Robin. "The Woman in the Mirror." *Elle*, January 2000, 34.

Christopher, Andre. "Art History." *Tennis Week*, May 6, 2003, 43.

Cirincone, Janine. "Review." *Cover Magazine*, April 1989, 14.

Cohen, Keri Guten. "Jane Hammond: Shanghai Costumes." *Detroit Free Press*, May 18, 2003.

———. "Jane Hammond at Lemberg." *Detroit Free Press*, February 25, 2001, 7G.

———. "Jane Hammond." *Detroit Free Press*, May 2, 1999, 2E.

Colby, Jay Hakanson. "Jane Hammond Puts Her Energy on Paper." *Detroit News*, March 2, 2001.

———. "Anything Goes . . . Together in Hammond's Art." *Detroit News*, April 4, 1996, 1E.

———. *Detroit News*, March 29, 1991, 1–2C.

"Collaboration/Collage." *Indiana Review*, summer 2005, 146–47.

Corbett, William. "Queen Jane Approximately." *Modern Painters*, summer 1998, 88–89.

———. "Highlights New York." *artsMEDIA*, June 1997, 35.

Cotter, Holland. "Jane Hammond." *New York Times*, April 23, 1993, C28.

Creeley, Robert. *Never Lose Your Paper*. Bay Shore, New York: Universal Limited Art Editions, Inc., 1990.

———. *Here*. New York: Exit Art, 1989.

Curtis, Cathy. "Women's Work: Rich, Shocking." *Los Angeles Times*, October 16, 1992.

Cyphers, Peggy. "New York in Review." *Arts Magazine*, September 1991, 7.

David Lehman. "Jane Hammond." *BOMB*, fall 2002, 28–35.

Devine, John. "What's in a Name." *Houston Press*, October 31, 2002, 58.

Dorsey, John. "Six Painters Try Their Heads at Printmaking." *Baltimore Sun*, June 4, 1987, E1, 6.

Drucker, Johanna. "Visual Pleasure: A Feminist Perspective." *Meaning*, no. 11, May 1992, 3–11.

Dubin, Zan. "Painting Themselves Out of a Corner." *Los Angeles Times*, October 10, 1992.

Enders, Alexandra. "Family Portraits." *Art & Antiques*, October 1990, 67.

Evans, Steven. "Review of Painting Culture." *New York Observer*, November 10, 1991, 34.

Fels, Sophie. "Jane Hammond, Galerie Lelong." *Time Out New York*, April 28–May 4, 2005, 74.

"Finite Universe." *New Yorker*, April 12, 1993, 14.

Flor, Harald. "Vold og Tyggis." *Dagbladet* (Norway), October 1, 1997.

Frueh, Joanna, Laurie Fierstein, and Judith Stein. *Picturing the Modern Amazon*. New York: Rizzoli and New Museum Books, 2000.

Fugate, Marty. "The Elephants in the Room." *Longboat Observer* (Sarasota, Florida), December 16, 2004, C5.

Genocchio, Benjamin. "To Understand These Pictures, You May Need a Dictionary." *New York Times*, December 21, 2003, Connecticut edition, 13.

Glueck, Grace. "Images of the Great Beyond, No Reality Check Required." *New York Times*, November 2005, B11.

———. "With Artists Among Alumni, A School Can Be a Collector." *New York Times*, July 26, 2004, E30.

Gonzalez, Allyson. "Space Crunch." *Weekly Planet* (Sarasota, Florida), November 17–23, 2004, 41.

Hackett, Regina. "Jane Hammond at the Greg Kucera Gallery." *Seattle Post-Intelligencer*, January 23, 2004.

———. "Hammond's Savvy Surrealism Makes Conscious Use of the Unconscious." *Seattle Post-Intelligencer*, November 21, 1997, 21.

Hammond, Jane. Interview in *Inside the Studio: Two Decades of Talks with Artists in New York*, ed. Judith Olch Richards. New York: Independent Curators International, 2004, 114–17.

———. "In Her Own Words: Wonderful You." *Women in the Arts*, fall 2002, 8–9.

———. Interview by Josephina Ayerza. *Lacanian Ink*, 1992, 68–75.

Handy, Ellen. *Abstract Information—First Impressions, Last Resorts: Printmaking at the End of the Century*. Fairfield, Connecticut: Sacred Heart University, 1991.

———. "The Pearls and the String: Jane Hammond's Associative Method." *Arts Magazine*, September 1990, 47–51.

Harrison, Helen A. "Updating and Adapting Traditions, of a Country or a Medium." *New York Times*, February 14, 1999, 23.

———. "Blurring Artistic Distinctions." *New York Times*, July 8, 1990, Long Island edition,12.

Heartney, Eleanor. "Jane Hammond at Galerie Lelong." *Art in America*, September 2005, 150–51.

Henry, Gerrit. "Reading Jane Hammond." *Print Collector's Newsletter*, September–October 1989, 128–29.

Hermanns, Ralph. "Pussellexicon för Konstnarer." *Dagens Industri* (Sweden), 1992, 43.

Hess, Elizabeth. "Death to the Masters." *Village Voice*, October 22, 1991.

———. "Fly on the Wall." *Village Voice*, February 27, 1990: 84.

Hirsch, Faye. "Working Proof: Jane Hammond and Raphael Rubinstein." *Art on Paper*, December 2002, 54–55.

———. "Paper Pulse: A Conversation with Jane Hammond." *Art On Paper*, March–April 2002, 64–69.

———. "Working Proof." *Art on Paper*, July–August 2001, 62.

———. "Working Proof." *Art on Paper*, March–April 2000, 64.

Hirsh, David. "Summer Thrills for Humid Heat." *The New York Native*, July 24, 1989, 30.

Hixson, Kathryn. "Chicago in Review." *Arts Magazine*, January 1991, 107.

Holg, Garrett. "Jane Hammond." *ARTnews*, February 1996, 141.

Huntington, Richard. "Hammond Paintings Present a Challenge." *Buffalo News*, December 9, 1987, 27.

Iannaci, Anthony. "Jane Hammond." *Artforum*, January 1993, 92–93.

Jensen, James. *Recent Paintings*. Honolulu: Honolulu Academy of Arts, May–June 1990.

Johnson, Ken. "Jane Hammond at Jose Freire." *Art in America*, October 1993, 126.

Johnson, Patricia C. "Play on Words." *Houston Chronicle*, September 28, 2002, D9–10.

Jortvei, Anne Karin. "Chanel, pistalskudd-og liuslinjer." *Klassekampen* (Norway), October 4, 1997, 33.

Kertess, Klauss. *See Jane Paint*. New York: Jose Freire Fine Art, 1993.

Kimmelman, Michael. "Painting Culture." *New York Times*, November 1, 1991, C16.

Kozik, K. K. "Jane Hammond, fiction/nonfiction." *Cover Magazine*, October 1991.

Lance, Tony. "Poster Girl." *Tennis Magazine*, June 2003, 44.

Lehody, Frank K. "Jane Hammond en Sept Questions." *La Tribune de Roland Garros*, April–May 2003, 1–2.

———. "The Model Daughter." *Roland Garros Magazine*, no. 27, 2003, 56–60.

Levin, Kim. "Jane Hammond." *Village Voice*, April 16–22, 1997, 12.

———. "Voice Choices: Jane Hammond at fiction/nonfiction." *Village Voice*, June 4, 1991, 115.

Liberio, Lydia. "What If Andy Warhol and Roy Lichtenstein Had Been Women?" *Irvine World News* (California), October 15, 1992, B17.

Liorca, Pablo. "The Termites and the Elephant." *In Arte Termita Contra Elefante Blanco*. Madrid: ICO Foundation, 2004, 200–205.

Lovelace, Carey. "Jane Hammond at Galerie Lelong." *Art in America*, April 2002, 152–53.

Lulaki, Susi, and Laura Berman. "The Rules of the Game." *Review* (Kansas City), April 2004, 44–47.

Lustfeldt, Heather. "Jane Hammond at Cohen." *Review* (Kansas City), December 1999, 21.

Lutticken, Sven. "De beeldbank van Hammond." *Het Parool* (Amsterdam), March 1, 1996, 27.

McCracken, David. "Hammond Leaves Pictorial Story to Viewer." *Chicago Tribune*, November 16, 1990.

McGovern, Adam. "Summer Group Show: Prints and Works on Paper." *Cover Magazine*, September 1990.

Mahoney, Robert. "New York Reviews." *Art & Antiques*, October 1991.

———. "Jane Hammond." *Arts*, Summer 1989, 96.

Mellby, Julie. *Splendid Pages. The Molly and Walter Bareiss Collection of Modern Illustrated Books*. New York: Hudson Hills Press; Toledo: Toledo Museum of Art, 2003.

Miro, Marcia. *Detroit Free Press*, March 31, 1991, 4C.

———. *Detroit Free Press*, August 13, 1989, 6G.

Morse, Marcia. "Archaeology of the Surreal." *Honolulu Weekly*, May 22–28, 2002, 9.

———. "Disparities the Eye Somehow Connects." *Sunday Star-Bulletin and Advertiser* (Honolulu), June 17, 1990, E10.

Myers, Terry R. *(jane hammond's) composition (notebooks) as (much more than) explanation*. Greensboro, N.C.: Weatherspoon Art Museum, 2003.

———. "Fear Strikes Out." *QW*, October 4, 1992, 33–39.

———. "New York Fax." *Art Issues*, May 1990, 34.

Myles, Eileen. "Jane Hammond at Exit Art." *Art in America*, October 1989, 217–18.

"New Prints Review." *Art on Paper*, November–December, 2004, 63.

Newhall, Edith. "Set Pieces." *New York Magazine*, January 21–28, 2002, 95.

Oksenhorn, Stewart. "Creating Art Out of Pandemonium." *Aspen Times Weekly*, June 27–28, 1998, 1B, 9B-10B.

Olofsson, Anders. "Jane Hammond." *Material*, no. 8, 1992, 43.

Olsen, Ragnhild. "Med (tyggis) under stolen." *Moss Avis* (Norway), September 12, 1997, 12–13.

Osman, Jana, Juliana Spahr, and Janet Zweig. "Different Languages." *Chain*, no. 5. Berkeley: Small Press Distribution, 1998, 96–98.

Pagel, David. "Entering a Psychic World of Stimulating Hyperactivity." *Los Angeles Times*, January 19, 1995, F8.

Papadakis, Andrea, ed. *New York, New Art*, no. 5 (England), 1989, 62–65.

Princenthal, Nancy. *Be Zany. Poised Harpists, Be Blue, Little Sparrows*. New York: Dieu Donné Papermill, 2002.

———. "Now You See It, You Don't: The Magic Magic Book." *Parkett* 47, 1996, 184–87.

Provenzano, Frank. "Layered Lyricism." *Metrotimes* (Detroit), May 15, 1996, 20.

Rizk Mysoon. "Jane Hammond at the Cleveland Center for Contemporary Art." *New Art Examiner* (Chicago), May–June 2002, 91.

Rosenberg, Barry A., and Carol Nathanson. *Words & #s*. Dayton, Ohio: Museum of Contemporary Art, Wright State University, 1991.

Rubenstein, Raphael. *En Quête de Miracle*. Montpellier, France: Editions Greges, 2004, 61–62.

———. "A Quiet Crisis." *Art in America*, March 2003, 39–45.

———. *Back Stage: Secrets of Scene Painting*. New York: Whitney Museum of American Art at Philip Morris, 2002.

———. "Ashbery in Dargerland." *Art in America*, February 2000, 37–39.

———. "Jane Hammond at Luhring Augustine." *Art in America*, September 1997, 106.

Sandberg, Lotte. "New York pa Jeloy." *Aften Posten* (Norway), October 12, 1997, 25.

Schaffner, Ingrid. "Hula Dancer, Meet Mahatma Gandhi." *Mount Holyoke Alumnae Quarterly* Spring 2004, 18–24.

Schmerler, Sarah. "Jane Hammond." *ARTnews*, September 1997, 130.

Shestak, Mel. "New York." *Contemporanea*, September 1989, 33.

Smith, Roberta. "A Neo-Surrealist Show with a Revisionist Agenda." *New York Times*, January 12, 1996, C23.

———. "Jane Hammond at Jose Freire." *New York Times*, November 4, 1994, C30.

Stein, Judith. "The Word Made Image." *Art in America*, May 1995, 98–101.

Streitfeld, L. P. "Creating New Cosmologies at Westport Art Center." *Advocate and Greenwich Time* (Stamford, Connecticut), December 14, 2003, D3–4.

Suto, Wilma. "Een oor met ogen en een open boek." *Volkskrant* (Netherlands), February 9, 1996.

Taylor, Fredrieke, "Alchemy." *New Observations* (New York), no. 84, 1991.

Thorson, Alice, "Cohen's 'Preview' United Abstract Talents." *Kansas City Star*, July 24, 1998, 11.

Uberquoi, M. C. "Jane Hammond." *El Cultural* (Barcelona), December 5–11, 2002.

Wagner, Van, and Judy K. Collischan. *Lines of Vision*. New York: Hudson Hills Press, 1989, 69.

Walker, Barry. *Projects and Portfolios*. Brooklyn: Brooklyn Museum, October 1989.

Wallach, Amei. "To a Painter, Words Are Worth a Thousand Pictures." *New York Times*, October 13, 2002, Arts and Leisure, 2, 35.

Whitney Museum of American Art. *American Visionaries: Selections from the Whitney Museum of Art*. New York: Whitney Museum of American Art, 2002.

Yovens, Rachel. "The Likeness of Being: Contemporary Self-Portraits by 60 Women." *New York Arts* 5, no. 1, 2000, 49–52.

Zimmer, William. "A Return to the Stories that Viewers May Have Been Missing." *New York Times*, January 16, 2000, Connecticut edition, 14, 18.

Zinnes, Harriet. "Jane Hammond." *Art Papers*, March and April 1995, 57.